MAP

of a part of the State of LOUISIANA exhibiting the route of the

-ORLEANS, OPELOUSAS & GREAT WESTERN RAIL ROAD.

BY *G. W. R. Bayley.*

ENGINEER

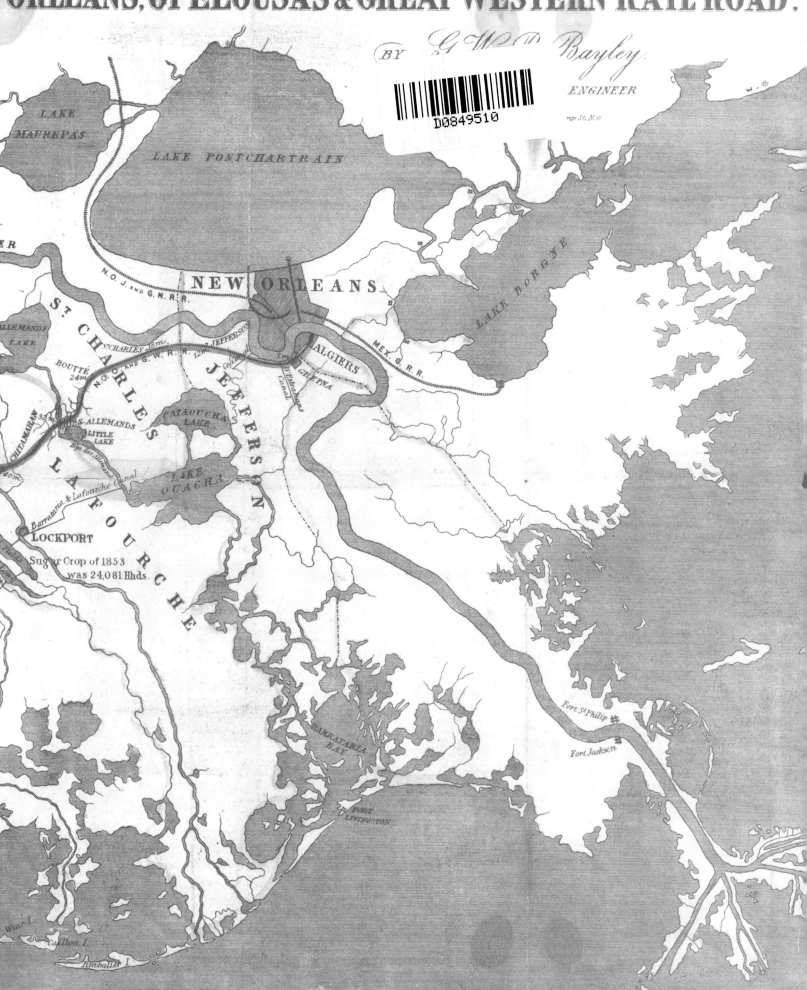

LAKE MAUREPAS

LAKE PONTCHARTRAIN

NEW ORLEANS

LAKE BORGNE

N. O. J. AND G. N. R. R.

ST CHARLES

ALLEMANDS LAKE

St Charles 18m.

JEFFERSON

JEFFERSON

ALGIERS

MEX. G. R. R.

BOUTTÉ 24m.

N. O. AND G. W. R. R. 12m

Col. Coal

GRETNA

D'Estrehan's Canal

CHITAMAHAN 32m

DES-ALLEMANDS

LITTLE LAKE

Bye des Allemands

CATAOUCHA LAKE

LAFOURCHE

40m

Barataria & Lafourche Canal

LAKE OUACHA

LOCKPORT

Sugar Crop of 1853 was 24,081 Hhds.

BARATARIA BAY

Fort St Philip

Fort Jackson

FORT LIVINGSTON

Wine I.

Caillou I.

Timbalier I.

EYES OF AN EAGLE

Jean-Pierre Cenac, Patriarch

AN ILLUSTRATED HISTORY OF EARLY HOUMA-TERREBONNE

By **Christopher Everette Cenac, Sr., M.D., F.A.C.S.**
with **Claire Domangue Joller**   *Foreword by* **Carl A. Brasseaux, Ph.D.**

EYES OF AN EAGLE

Jean-Pierre Cenac, Patriarch

AN ILLUSTRATED HISTORY OF EARLY HOUMA-TERREBONNE

By **Christopher Everette Cenac, Sr., M.D., F.A.C.S.**
with **Claire Domangue Joller**   *Foreword by* **Carl A. Brasseaux, Ph.D.**

EYES OF AN EAGLE: JEAN-PIERRE CENAC, PATRIARCH
An Illustrated History of Early Houma-Terrebonne
Christopher Everette Cenac, Sr. M.D., F.A.C.S.

Library of Congress Control Number: 2011928371

ISBN: 978-0-615-47702-2

Book and cover design: Scott Carroll, Scott Carroll Designs, Inc.

Dust Jacket: Sailing luggers docked at Houma Fish & Oyster Co.,
Ltd., Bayou Terrebonne, Houma, Louisiana c. 1902
Front End Sheet: New Orleans, Opelousas & Great Western
Railroad map by G.W.R. Bayley, 1860
Back End Sheet: The *Pan American*, once owned by the Cenac
family. The Biloxi schooner was built in the Mississippi port in
the 1920s along with identical Cenac vessels the *Ursula C.* and the
Perfection. The 74-footer had a long career as an excursion boat
ferrying passengers to barrier islands off the Biloxi coast, then
worked the waters of Terrebonne Parish in oystering. The vessel
was rebuilt as a pleasure yacht in the 1990s.

Moonlight and Magnolias by Mort Künstler
©1997 Mort Künstler, Inc.
www.mortkunstler.com

JPC, L.L.C.
3661 Bayou Black Drive
Houma, LA 70360

Allons enfants de la Patrie
Le jour de gloire est arrivé.

Arise children of the motherland
The day of glory has arrived.
Opening verses of
The French National Anthem
La Marseillaise

Although this is the story of one man's
life, these experiences and local settings
were echoed in the lives of thousands of
French immigrants in Louisiana. Their
descendants will recognize much that their
forebears held in common.

ACKNOWLEDGEMENTS

The authors thank the following for their valuable assistance with this project: Clifton Theriot of the Nicholls State University Archives for finding obscure resources, verification of innumerable dates and sources of images, and helping to establish the Cenac Collection; Jackie Jackson for her editing expertise; Emilie Pitre of the NSU Archives staff; Glen Pitre and Michelle Benoit for their advice and counsel; author Shane K. Bernard, Ph.D., historian and curator for the McIlhenny Company for sharing his knowledge and resources; Scott Carroll for his masterful graphic design and for his advice; Hope King for her design support; Michel Goitia-Nicolas for an introduction to Basque influence; Chris Pena for permission to use his Civil War book so extensively; Dr. Carl Brasseaux for his advice and permission to use his published material so extensively; Dr. Don Davis and Dr. Brasseaux for sharing their enormous store of knowledge and photo collections; Rosalie Authement Tipton for her French translations; the Cenac medical office staff—Faye Parker, Peggy Darsey, Mona Griffin, and the late Rosie Comeaux for their extraordinary work on this project over several years; French cousin Jean LaPorte, his wife Adrienne, and daughter Christine for their hospitality and help; Madeleine Cenac and Robert Smith for sharing their knowledge of French architecture and landscape design; the late Tommy Cobb for his encouragement; Terrebonne Clerk of Court Bobby Boudreaux and his staff, for allowing generous access to public records; the Terrebonne Parish Public Library staff, particularly Judy Soniat and Darryl Eschete of the reference department; the Historic New Orleans Collection's Mary Lou Eichhorn and Daniel Hammer; Charlette Poché of the Terrebonne Parish Council Clerk's Office; Kevin Allemand, Mary Duet, and Cecilia Richard at the Diocese of Houma-Thibodaux Archives; the Terrebonne Genealogical Society, particularly Jess Bergeron; Gary J. Whipple and the late Harry F. Hellier, Jr. for information on currencies; Warren A. Perrin of the Acadian Heritage and Culture Foundation; Whitney Broussard, Ph.D., of the University of Louisiana at Lafayette Institute for Coastal Ecology and Engineering; attorneys Matthew H. Hagen and Roy S. Bonner for research assistance; Charles M. Cook; Bobby Vice; Douglas J. Authement; Brian W. Larose; Mike Voisin; Thomas Becnel, Ph.D; R. Luke Bordelon, M.D.; Veranese E. Douglas, Dan Davis, Gerald Voisin and C.J. Christ; Arlen B. Cenac, Sr.; Arlen B. Cenac, Jr.; Enola A. Trahan and the late Maurice E. Trahan; Jessie P. Thibodaux and the late Oliver J. Thibodaux; Henry A. Adams, Alvin J. Benoit, and Carroll J. Cenac, all deceased; Bayou Writers members; Emil W. Joller; Louis Lewald Blum, Jr.; "Ted" L. Jones; Melvin Henry, James Brunet Sr. and Jr., Dan Comeaux, and Michael Hebert for restoring artifacts; Tim Hebert and Dale Robertson for assistance on church history and photographs; Vincent and Ying Kraemer for photographic reproduction and restoration; Donald J. Cenac for his many contributions to this book; Louise Violet Cenac Bourg for preserving official documents of Pierre for so many years; Tom Roddy, James R. Carrere and Arthur R. Cenac, Jr., the A.P. Cenac, Sr. family, Dorothy C. Oubre, Gail Wurzlow Ehrensing, M.D. and many other Cenac relatives who shared their family genealogical information, artifacts, photographs, and personal memories; others who had even a small part in our work on this book, whom we may inadvertently not have mentioned by name; the authors' immediate families who lived with stories of Pierre for these past years; and especially Cindy Trahan Cenac for her patience with the time and energies that her husband had to devote to realize completion of this book.

Dr. Philip Louis Cenac, Sr.

Dorothy Lee Stodghill Cenac

January 27, 1946

For my father, Dr. Philip Louis Cenac, Sr., and my mother,

Dorothy Lee Stodghill, whose maternal influence her children

will forever feel. My father loved his family and appreciated

his ancestors, their lives and their labors. He would have been

proud to have their story told.

C.E.C., Sr.

DÉPARTEMENT DES
HAUTES-PYRENEES

Acte n° 13

Naissance de
CENAC Pierre

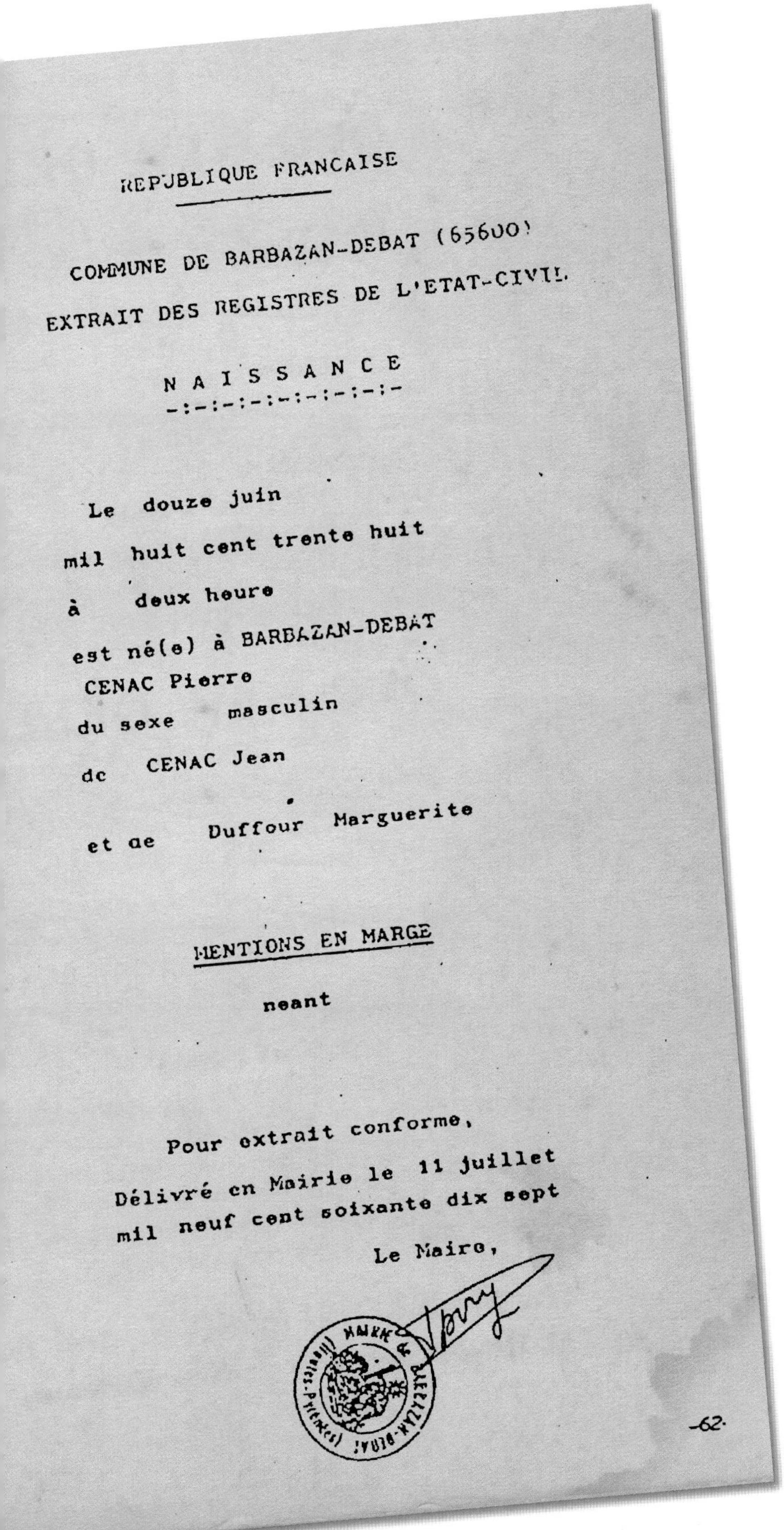

REPUBLIQUE FRANCAISE

COMMUNE DE BARBAZAN-DEBAT (65600)

EXTRAIT DES REGISTRES DE L'ETAT-CIVIL

NAISSANCE

Le douze juin
mil huit cent trente huit
à deux heure
est né(e) à BARBAZAN-DEBAT
CENAC Pierre
du sexe masculin
dc CENAC Jean
et ae Duffour Marguerite

MENTIONS EN MARGE

neant

Pour extrait conforme,
Délivré en Mairie le 11 juillet
mil neuf cent soixante dix sept

Le Maire,

-62-

Jean-Pierre Cenac

Born June 12, 1838

Barbazan-Debat
Canton of Tarbes
District of Lower Barbazan
Departement of Haute-Pyrénées
France

Died April 29, 1914

Terrebonne Parish
Houma, Louisiana
United States of America

ESTABLISHED 1891

HOUMA FISH & OYSTE

PACKERS & SHIPPERS

SALT WATER FISH

Houma Fish & Oyster Co., Ltd., present-day 8061 Main Street, Houma, c. 1930

CONTENTS

FOREWORD

During the decades immediately preceding the American Civil War, New Orleans was a boomtown and the Francophone civil parishes in the city's economic orbit were among the nation's most prosperous counties. This unbridled prosperity served as a magnet for Europe's "huddled masses yearning to breathe free." Indeed, for much of the antebellum period, the Crescent City was the nation's second-leading port of entry. As one would expect, Gallic immigrants—popularly known as the Foreign French to distinguish them from native French-speakers—constituted a large percentage of south Louisiana's swelling multitude of European transplants.

After initially gathering in the great port city's immigrant slums, many of the Foreign French dispersed in search of better opportunities and living conditions in the rural parishes. This migration followed a rather predictable pattern as anxious immigrants—often travelling alone—sought out friends, relations, and even acquaintances who had established the initial rural beachheads. Literate members of the Foreign French community generally tended to congregate in towns, where they constituted the backbone of the professional classes, while persons with farming backgrounds typically became yeomen in the countryside. Once afforded an opportunity to set down permanent roots, these economic refugees quietly, systematically, and resolutely set about the work of expanding and enhancing economic infrastructures in their respective host communities. The results have been dramatic throughout Louisiana's coastal plain, where the Cenacs, Burguières, Patouts, and a host of other families have played major roles in the region's diversification and modernization.

Louisianians in general, and south Louisianians in particular, nevertheless know little of their noteworthy modern contributions, in large part because of the families' propensity for avoiding the limelight. Still less is known about the critical early years of the immigrants' adaptation to their new homeland, particularly during the turbulent years of Civil War, Reconstruction, and Redemption, when Acadiana's economic development was literally rolled back a half-century. This enduring informational lacuna magnifies the significance of Eyes of an Eagle, the intriguing story of Pierre Cenac's migration to Louisiana on the eve of the Civil War, his subsequent professional odyssey as a baker-turned-entrepreneur, and, finally, his twilight years as the patriarch of a large and successful family. I'm sure that, like me, you'll find Pierre's triumphal saga as fascinating as it is informative.

Carl A. Brasseaux, Ph.D.

One of the world's leading authorities on French North America. Author, co-author, and/or editor of more than 40 books, and articles, academic papers, essays, poetry. Doctorate from the University of Paris. Former Distinguished Professor of History at the University of Louisiana at Lafayette, former director of the Center for Louisiana Studies and director for Cultural and Eco-Tourism at ULL. Recipient of a research fellowship at Yale University and numerous awards at the state and national levels.

PREFACE

Readers will want to be aware of a device the authors have used to give this book greater scope than it would have had otherwise.

At a point when much of the documentation was completed, the authors became aware (through the honesty of friends) that Pierre's story as written then was lacking one compelling dimension. We did not see and hear Pierre enough as it was then recorded. We needed more of Pierre the person instead of just Pierre the public record.

It was at that time that we settled upon the idea of alternating fictional and factual chapters, each building on one another, to make Pierre more alive.

The liberty we took in the fictional chapters was that of imagining Pierre and his family in situations in which they found themselves at various crucial time periods. That liberty, rather than being plucked from thin air, sprang in living color from the cold facts we had already gleaned from official records and from what we already knew about his life journey.

Therefore, we were able to give him a voice and an emotional life. With the foundation of our own personal ancestors' first-hand stories, coupled with the factual documentation, we conceptualized Pierre's thought processes, feelings, and vision.

Each odd-numbered chapter is fiction based on assumptions reasonably formed. Each even-numbered chapter gives documented information, carefully researched and cited. It was our intention that the fictional chapters give human dimension to the factual ones.

An additional intention was to document the manner in which the majority of men, women, and children in south Louisiana of the 1800s and early 1900s all bore their own respective responsibilities in order to survive. The delineated roles of both patriarch and matriarch were, by necessity, both demanding. Although this is an account of a family and their home place, readers can find in this volume life experiences representative of their own forebears' stories.

Seining on the lower Terrebonne coast. Sailing lugger on right, paddlewheeler on left; c. 1900

*Christopher E. Cenac at his
birthplace, Naval Air Station
Memphis, Millington, Tennessee,
c. 1957*

INTRODUCTION

Every summer during part of my childhood in the fifties, Uncle Bill Cenac took me out trawling on his lugger, the *Flossie*. Those vacation days began when I was nine or ten, and they are among my life's fondest memories. Those times also helped to form within me a profound sense of family.

We would leave from behind the oyster shop on the bayouside of Park Avenue across from his father's home at what is now 8039 Park Avenue in Houma, Louisiana. Then we would make our way just a little stretch upstream to East Park Grocery to buy whatever the men aboard did not grow or make themselves. That particular store was our first stop because it belonged to Cecile "Aunt Nan" Cenac and her husband "Uncle" Guy Guidry. Then we'd head farther up the bayou to Houma Ice Company at what is now the corner of Church and Park in downtown Houma. After loading 300-pound blocks of ice, the men turned the boat around and steered down Bayou Terrebonne until we reached Presque Isle, where Bayou Terrebonne veers left and Bayou Little Caillou begins on the right.

The men then made what was sometimes a spur-of-the-moment decision about our course. Wherever it took us, we trawled "inside" waters, and frequently we ended up at Timbalier Island or Isle Dernière (Last Island), where we

Above, walkway bridge over Bayou Terrebonne at Gabasse Street, c. 1950. Boats are the Flossie *(c. 1910), the* Donald C. *(c. 1941), and the* Phillip C. *(c. 1938). Below, the Houma Ice Company c. 1940. Bottom, boat on Bayou Terrebonne in downtown Houma, c. 1947*

Top, oyster camp of Jean Pierre Cenac, Jr. on Big Bayou Dularge, early 1900s. Above, coffeepot and below, ice tongs from the Flossie.

stayed at E.A. "Uncle Mannie" Cenac and Arthur "Uncle Tutty" Cenac's houseboat. Sometimes we lodged at Jean Pierre Cenac, Jr.'s camp—still being used by his sons Henry Pierre and Martin—on Bayou Dularge near King Lake, or the shrimp platform owned by Thaddeus Pellegrin at Sea Breeze, accessible via Bayou Terrebonne.

Trips were usually a week or so long, during which we trawled, fished, and did a lot of talking. Afterward, we most often headed back home, gave away the catch to family and friends, then repeated the process with other trips that combined both the semi-businesslike activity of trawling with an excursion-type atmosphere.

Aboard the boat most often were men who had a profound effect on my young life. Uncle Bill and three of his cousins, Henry "T-Pierre" Cenac, Jean Pierre Carrere, Jr., and Steve Fanguy, most often composed the adult contingent aboard the *Flossie*. At night the men would sleep inside the cabin, and I would bed down on a mattress atop the lower cabin roof under a *moustiquaire* (mosquito net). In the dark, French music from the large black radio lulled us asleep. I awakened every morning to the smell of strong coffee dripping into the small metal coffeepot, and to the sounds of the morning French radio programs broadcast from KJIN in Houma and KLEB in Golden Meadow.

From these men, I learned to cook, fish, trawl, harvest oysters, and to use and make dip nets, cast nets, and trawls. I credit them with teaching me French, because that was the language of the waters that we spoke together—a language that defined an entire culture. Although I had to work aboard the boat and at the fishing camps, I loved that life experience until high school and its activities, college and athletics, medical school, residency, and a surgical career commanded my time and interests.

Trawling still remains my favorite outdoor activity. I often think of that converted sailboat, the *Flossie*, which my grandfather William Jean Pierre Cenac commissioned to be built circa 1910, afterward owned by his son Bill, and later enjoyed by my father, brothers, cousins, and me for many years.

What developed during those early times, as well as through my physician father's stories about family lore, was my interest in and respect for my kinsmen's history, diverse livelihoods, and the deep-seated connections we all have with the local landscape.

In later years, this interest became a quest to collect information about the hundreds of people whose blood ties are close to my own. Ever since I was a teenager, I have compiled documents both official and otherwise, and have received information from many Cenac relatives, all of us descended from a single immigrant to the New World.

A momentous occasion for me was my initial trip to the town where my great-grandfather grew up in the *Hautes-Pyrénées* of France. I stood across the street from the site of his family's house, which dated back to the 1700s, and visited the homes of my French cousins who remain in that village. I walked the lanes

that my great-grandfather walked when he made what must have been a courageous decision to emigrate to a foreign country in 1860, knowing he would probably never see his own family again.

It is my pleasure to share with others now the story of the first Cenac to arrive in Terrebonne Parish, Louisiana, and of his many descendants.

These people, and those of subsequent generations, have lived in a symbiotic relationship with coastal Louisiana for 150 years. Land and waters provided fertile environments for individual opportunities, while the hard work and personal enterprise of many Cenacs and related families affected the course of Terrebonne Parish's progression to current times.

My intention has been to compile, as accurately as possible, a history for descendants of Pierre Cenac and for other readers beyond our kin who savor real stories about real people and real places. I trust that the factual chapters reflect the years of research it took to compile this book, and that the fictional chapters, based on reasonable assumptions, take you back in time to glimpse the living, breathing Pierre and his world.

This is the account of one "Good Earth" family whose history mirrors that of their home place.

Chris Cenac, June, 2011

Dr. Christopher E. Cenac, Sr. is one of the many great-grandchildren of the original French Cenac immigrant to Terrebonne Parish, Louisiana.

Mantel in the French home of Pierre Cenac's brother Jean, 1 Rue de Verdun, above left. Top photos, right, courtyard at the home of Louis Paul Laporte with house and barn forming the typical L shape. Middle top, dairy cattle in barn. Middle bottom, wine press in the barn. Bottom, entrance to Barbazan-Debat. All photos taken 2003

Village in the High Pyrenees c. 1880

CHAPTER 1
1858: Barbazan-Debat

"Where are you in that head of yours, Pierre? You sit at this table, drinking coffee with us. But your eyes always go to the window. And you haven't heard a word of what I've said for the last five minutes."

Pierre Cenac turned to his older brother Jean, and focused his eyes in the relative dimness of the rustic kitchen. "Sorry, Jean." Pierre tweaked the cheek of the infant that Jean's wife Magdeleine was swaying in her arms. "She's thriving finally, eh?"

Jean looked over and made a cooing sound toward his baby. While his brother's attention was diverted, Pierre shifted and sat up taller in his wooden chair. He took a deep breath. The smell of their Sunday potato-onion *tarte salée* lunch still lingered in the small room.

Pierre began slowly. "Jean, I'm already 20 years old, and my job as apprentice *boulanger* pays next to nothing. Your farm feeds you and your family...but you've been feeding me too many times since Papa and Maman died. I can't live with you or in the little room over the *boulangerie* forever. Besides...."

"*Oui?*"

"Ever since the pilgrims going to Lourdes began passing through here, I've begun to wonder what it would be like to leave this village. Go somewhere that I can work and get ahead a little."

Pierre Cenac as a young man

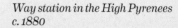

Way station in the High Pyrenees c. 1880

Lake Gaube near Lourdes, France, late 1800s

"But Pierre, where would you go? It's bad enough that Dominique and young Brother Jean are God-knows-where with the army. Are we going to lose you, too?"

Those words rang in Pierre's ears as he took a stroll down the main street of Barbazan-Debat. No children played in the street in these afternoon hours. The only sounds Pierre heard were muffled voices from the old stone street-side houses, and, somewhere in the distance, a lone oxcart lumbering on an unseen byway.

*Oxen cart in the High Pyrenees.
Below, the railway station at
Bordeaux c. 1880s*

He saw no small clusters of young men who used to chat on street corners when he was growing up. His own boyhood friends were in the army, had moved outside town to work on the surviving farms, or had left for larger cities.

The only person he encountered was *Père* Millet, his black robes jostled by the priest's hurried stride down the center of the main street. He greeted Pierre by name, but mumbled that he had to hurry to "*Madame* Labat. Near death, you know."

Pierre looked after the priest. *More deaths here than births for many years. So many funeral cortèges down this street the past year alone. I wonder. Not enough to eat? Not enough to live for? Or both?*

The young man's dark eyebrows nearly met as he frowned and shook his head. *Next Sunday, I'll use this day off to walk the 10 miles to Lourdes. At least there are different faces, a lot of them, since the spring was found.*

As he walked beside one house in the village's center, he heard from an open window a child's whining plea, "But Maman, why won't you let me go swimming in the lake? The water's not as cold as you think it still is. It's May, Maman. Please...."

Pierre smiled. *Poor fellow. You can't go, but there is nobody to stop me. Might clear my head.* He turned on his heel, and headed out of town in the shade of ancient sweet oak trees lining the lane that meandered upward to the mountain lake. The only interruption to his solitary thoughts was a pack of puppy *Chiens de Montagne des Pyrénées* yelping at their breeder's commands as they passed by on their way to the high meadows.

Four different days during the following week, travelers from the east and north of Barbazan stopped at the bakery as they made their way to Lourdes. One came all the way from a village near Milan.

When the owner of the *boulangerie* headed out back toward the stone oven, the friendly Italian chatted with Pierre from across the counter in broken French. He wasn't going home after Lourdes. "Too much war, too long, at home. America. That's where I go. My cousin goes to New Orleans, United States, two years ago. Jobs for everybody, he writes to me. So I follow him."

Pierre kept his promise to himself the next Sunday and walked to Lourdes in the early-morning hours, the lanes becoming increasingly crowded the closer he got. Pierre was as impressed by the diversity in the throng as he was by what was going on there. Old, young, and children speaking in different dialects he had never heard before.

Tired after his long walk, Pierre sat on a rock beside another man who looked near his own age. Edouard Freneau was from near Bordeaux on the coast and had come to see the miracle, he told Pierre. But he seemed determined to tout his home place.

"I tell you, my friend, there is nothing more beautiful than my city," Edouard told Pierre as they worked their way toward the spring site. "The large buildings, the straight streets. What I love most are the ships, when they glide down the broad river in full sail. A sight to behold."

"And where do they go?" Pierre asked.

"All over. Some to the United States. Some to South America. Some to Africa." Edouard glanced down at his chest and brushed what Pierre recognized as pastry crumbs off his shirt. As he continued flicking fingers over his expansive abdomen, Edouard continued, "You should see the men our age applying for passage to America. I work near the riverfront, and make it a point to ask questions."

Pierre asked him, "Do they tell you why they are leaving?"

"A lot of people, with a lot of different reasons. From here in the *Pyrénées,* most say they can't find work, can't support their families. The ones from this *département* all look skinny. Like you, Pierre."

Pierre looked down at his loose pants. As he raised his head, Pierre's jaw took on an attitude of resolve.

I have to leave Barbazan. Sounds like a lot of people need bread in Bordeaux. I can at least go where the prospects are better...and where I can fill out these pants.

Family with a litter of Great Pyrenean (known as Great Pyrenees in America) Mountain Dogs, above. Below, Pyrenean shepherd with his flock

Below, Le Grande Théâtre in Bordeaux. Bottom, L'Eglise St. Croix, Bordeaux, both c. 1880s

BORDEAUX. 15.

Port of Bordeaux, 1860. Opposite, stone bridge over the Garonne River

CHAPTER 2
Descending the Mountains

Jean-Pierre Cenac left his ancestral French village of Barbazan-Debat in the *pays Basque* (Basque country) of the High Pyrenees sometime before February 1860, and made his way to the port city of Bordeaux. In this southwestern French metropolis wrapped around a crescent section of the Garonne River, he had his first taste of life in a large city.

In Bordeaux, he was surrounded by a planned classical cityscape. There he saw the first stone bridge built over the Garonne, completed in 1822. He also encountered cultures other than the rural French Basque who lived in his native mountainous region near the French-Spanish border. Because of the bustling *Port de la Lune* (*the port of the moon*, from the crescent-shaped river bend dominating the city), he had to meet not only urban dwellers, but also those of other European and African citizenship. Bordeaux was a major point of sea departure for many nationalities besides Jean-Pierre's fellow Frenchmen.

In Bordeaux Pierre lived at 95 *Rue Montaigne*. It was there that he made the final decision to leave his country for America. As he worked in a bakery and walked the city's crowded streets, Pierre was no doubt weighing familiarity against the unknown. Economic survival, better prospects and perhaps wanderlust were considerations, but this had to be balanced against his family roots, which ran deep. Pierre could trace by name four generations of Cenacs who had lived in Barbazan-Debat; there had been Cenacs in Barbazan before 1723, when his great-grandfather was born. Pierre had grown up in the same village, in a household of parents and seven children.

The Cenac name is derived from the ancient Basque surname De L[a] Atzena'ko, from the word *Atzena*, according to Basque scholar Michel Antoine Goitia-Nicolas in a 2010 interview.[1]

In the Romance languages, the terms *de, de la,* and *du* frequently connote nobility, meaning *of the noble house or place of* preceding a family name. In this case the *de la* is dropped because of the connecting *A* in *Atzena'ko*. Most Basque names were geographically-referenced, and the ancient form of Cenac, *Atzenac,* means "at the rear of town," possibly indicating the high ground away from a town's waterfront.[1]

The family names Abadie, Carrere, Cenac, Labat, Lemoine, and Marmande are found in the region of Spanish Navarra,

St. Bernadette (Marie Bernarde) Soubirous and the Maison Cenac in Lourdes c. 1904, above

Above and right, country peasants in the Hautes Pyrénées

French Basse-Navarre, and Soulé. These particular familiar south Louisiana names are registered as noble names in Basque nomentary records.[2]

In the 1941 novel *The Song of Bernadette* by Franz Werfel, mention is made that the visionary Bernadette Soubirous, during her interrogations by civil authorities, was taken into the "elegant" house of the Cénac family, "who, like the Lafittes, Millets, Lacrampes, and Baups, belonged to the patrician group of Lourdes."

With the Celts of more northerly regions, the Basque population was the oldest race, civilization and culture of Europe, predating the arrival of the Romans and later, the Indo-Europeans from countries of southern Eurasia. Romans found the 1,000-year-old Basque civilization already ensconced in the Pyrenees, and bestowed universal nobility upon the entire Basque people.[3] This subsequently enabled Basques to apply for positions—regardless of their economic status—which would have been denied them otherwise because of their previous "peasant" status; this became especially important in the feudal system which dominated Medieval Europe, when moving above one's "caste" level was all but impossible.

OURDES. — Types du Pays. — LL.

Although all Basque names are in the Registry of Noble Names in France and Spain, the people themselves came to occupy all strata of society, including the peasantry. The Basque character could be described as predominantly hard working isolationists who often became prosperous because of their determination. Typical physical features of Basques were "anvil" faces wider at the eyes, narrower at the jawline, heavy eyebrows and often large ears.[3]

Although they are commonly thought of as Spanish, Basques were original to France, with those in Spain being "spillovers" from what are now the boundaries of France. People where Pierre grew up would have spoken Basque and the dialectical French of the region.[3] In 1860, as many as 65 percent of Napoleon III's Second Empire spoke the separate languages of the peripheral provinces, not "Parisian" French. Most Basques would have spoken the Napoleon-imposed French language, or Spanish, as well as Basque (the common dialect, Gascon, is a Latinized form of Basque).[3]

Pierre's home town sat at an elevation of 1,540 feet in the *Hautes-Pyrénées* (High Pyrenees) mountain chain. Some mountains around Barbazan stretched far above the village, their snow-capped peaks shining white in the winter, the green meadows grazing sheep, and mountain lakes sparkling in the spring. This village, these mountains, and the dense sweet oak forests in the countryside had been Pierre's comfort zone all his life. When he left Barbazan-Debat for Bordeaux, he had to travel downhill all the way, leaving a completely mountainous region to reach the sea level of the port city on the Garonne River, which flows into the Atlantic.

Pierre grew up in a house on the corner of *Rue de 8 Mai* and *Rue du 14 Juillet* in Barbazan, very near the second church to be built in the town, *Notre Dame de l'Assomption* (on the corner of *Rue de l'Égalité* and *Rue de Glaieuls*). As a child he attended classes in a two-story stone schoolhouse on *Rue des Pyrénées*.

Farming and wine production were practiced in Barbazan-Debat environs since time immemorial. The village itself had its origins before the 1300s. Around 1344, a farming family named Barbazan from Ancille in the French Basque state of Soulé settled there.[3] The name is derived from the Basque expression *Rivera de Gran Bosque*, which means "a great forest on the coast of a river." The other part of the town's name, *Debat,* derived from *de* and *ate*, which together means "river passage"[3] (perhaps a reference to *Canal de L'Alaric* which courses through the center of town). One of its most famous native sons, Arnaud Guilhem de Barbazan—known as "The Knight Without Reproach"—was born there in 1360. *Notre Dame de Pietat,* the village's oldest church, dates from 1593. The old town which predated *that* edifice was secure in its permanence, where countless generations lived in its L-shaped clay-and-stone masonry houses with family quarters above and animal shelters below. By 1860, the village had a long history but had a population of only 689, where agriculture was still the subsistence livelihood.

When not walking, local inhabitants used oxcarts for transporting themselves and the work of their hands. Barbazan-Debat was served only by water wells and the *Canal de l'Alaric*.

Church of Notre Dame de Pietat, Barbazan-Debat

Notre Dame de l'Assomption Church and graveyard, Barbazan-Debat, above.

Left, a Basque country village, c. late 1800s

Girondin Memorial, Bordeaux, late 1800s

The entire region of the *Hautes-Pyrénées* was in a serious economic decline by the time Jean-Pierre grew to manhood. Farmers owned their own land, but most holdings consisted of fewer than seven and a half acres, or three *hectares* [one hectare equaling 2.47 acres]. Land was scarce in the mid-1800s in the Pyrenees, one of the poorest parts of France. The country was overpopulated, and when wheat crops in the High Pyrenees failed, the people survived on the corn they were able to grow.[4] Civil and family documents indicate that Pierre's father, grandfather, and his only paternal uncle were all farmers.

Wine production became the only means of earning income after the crops' failure, but from 1852 to 1856, a powdery mildew grapevine disease, *oidium*, destroyed all vintages in that area of the High Pyrenees. The rural regions south of Bordeaux became very poor because there was no industry for the manpower freed by crop failures. Younger Frenchmen, especially, began to emigrate because of the scant economic prospects in the place of their birth.

One researcher from the High Pyrenees isolated the 1850s, and later 1866 to 1872, as the peak years of emigration from that area. The emigrants are described as being "usually very young, under 20," many of them "craftsmen (carpenters, tailors, blacksmiths, bakers....)"[4]

If not in Barbazan-Debat, then surely in Bordeaux, Jean-Pierre witnessed other young men saying goodbye to their families and leaving for Atlantic crossings which would take them to the Americas. The southeast section of the province (called a *département*) favored emigration to Louisiana, while others made their way to other sections of the United States, and many to Argentina.[4]

As he walked along the neat cobblestone levees of Bordeaux, backed by classic brick and stone buildings along tree-lined streets, Jean-Pierre had a lot of pondering to do when he arrived there before February 1860. Could he leave everything he knew for a place that was an unknown? Would he be welcomed in a new country, or ostracized? The largest of the ships with their sails billowing as they left port had to be an impressive sight to a highlander. But when he stood on the cobbled Bordeaux *quai* where sailing vessels took on goods and passengers, he must have questioned the safety of those ships against often treacherous waters. He had also heard stories about conditions aboard ships, and about passengers who never made it to the New World.

The siren call of something new, stories of abundant expanses of land in America, not locked into generations of the same families or to enforced limitations, had to tickle the young man's ears. Since others from his *département* had been emigrating beginning the previous decade, Jean-Pierre was sure to have heard stories from Pyrenees emigrants' families about their relatives' new homes, some of them in *la Nouvelle Orleans à la Louisiane*. Louisiana was historically the major port of entry for Basques.

Inducement for Europeans to make New Orleans their destination by the mid-1800s is summarized by another source, who wrote, "Louisiana drew so many people from around the world for one simple reason: it was a place where you could get rich quick. 'A person need do no more than hang up his sign,' wrote German cabinetmaker Joseph Eder in a letter to the folks back in the Old Country."[5]

Palace Gate, Bordeaux, late 1800s

Quay at Port St. Jean, Bordeaux 1860

Pierre took a first step by obtaining a character reference, then called a certificate, from the mayor of Barbazan-Debat. Its translation reads:

We, Jean-Marie Bruno, Mayor of the town of Lower Barbazan, Canton of (Southern) Tarbes, Département of Hautes-Pyrénées, do certify that the said Pierre Cenac, born in Lower Barbazan on June 12, 1838, is now residing in Bordeaux, is of good health, and of good habits, and that his conduct has been irreproachable during all the time in which he has resided in Lower Barbazan.

In faith whereof we have delivered unto him this present certificate. Done in our Court House of Lower Barbazan this Feb. 4, 1860.[6]

To the document is affixed a stamp reading "Timbre Imperial" and two other illegible seals, one of which lies beside the signature, "The Mayor Bruno."

This one document authenticates several points. One is that he was known then and thereafter not by his full official first name, Jean-Pierre, but as Pierre. Another is that, since this documents Pierre as "now residing in Bordeaux" on February 4, 1860, he had been living in the city for some time before that date. A third is that Pierre was not trying to escape any type of personal unpleasantries in his home place, since the mayor attested to his "good habits" and "irreproachable" conduct.

Taking the final steps to emigrate did not come until eight months later. After all, Pierre would have to leave behind his older brother Jean, a farmer, and his wife; his soldier brothers Dominique and Jean; another married brother, Jean-Marie, who was a servant and gardener; and Jean-Marie's twin sister Jacquette, a novice of the cloistered Discalced (barefoot) Carmelites of Lisieux. He was leaving in the cemetery of *Notre Dame de l'Assomption* the gravesite of his brother Jean-Puis Jacques, who died at the age of two.[7]

Another practical reason for his extended months of residence in Bordeaux prior to boarding a ship was the necessity to earn money for his passage. While there, he applied for (from G. Bardon at 12 Dauphine Place) and carried with him a booklet (*Livret d'Ouvrier*) serving as a worker's in-country authorization to travel, based on his occupation. Since there was at the time no substantial means of income for an unestablished young baker in Barbazan-Debat, he worked in the larger city before his plans became full-blown.

French inheritance laws were applicable to Pierre's situation. Unlike some other countries in which the oldest son inherited the family properties, French law made it compulsory for parents' estates to be divided into equal parts, "although the [eldest son's] share could be legally augmented by a quarter of the whole estate in exchange or in return for taking care" of the parents in their old age, one source wrote. This source continued, "...the younger ones who wanted to emigrate were not utterly destitute. They could borrow money for the crossing (the cost of the crossing was equal to the value of one-third hectare, that is to say about 0.80 acre), they could borrow from fellow countrymen in America to start a

Mayor's office, Barbazan-Debat, 2003

Opposite, Pierre's character reference certificate from Mayor Bruno, dated February 4, 1860

Nous, Jean-Marie Bruno,
maire de la commune de Barbazan-Débat,
canton de Tarbes(sud), département des Hautes-
Pyrénées, certifions que le nommé Pierre Cenac,
né à Barbazan-Débat le 12 juin 1838, et actuelle-
ment demeurant à Bordeaux, est de bonne vie et
de bonnes mœurs, et que sa conduite a été irréprochable
pendant tout le temps qu'il a habité Barbazan-
Débat.

En foi de quoi nous lui avons délivré
le présent certificat.

Fait en notre mairie de Barbazan-Débat,
le 4 8bre 1860.—

Le Maire,

Bruno

Le Maire de la Commune de
Barbazan debat, Canton de Tarbes (Sud),
arrondissement dudit Tarbes, département des
Hautes Pyrénées.

Certifie, que le nommé Cénac (Pierre),
profession de Boulanger, né et domicilié à
Barbazan, Canton, arrondissement et département
précité, est dans l'intention de se rendre à la
Nouvelle-Orléans (E. U. d'amérique), et
qu'il n'existe aucun empêchement à ce qu'il lui soit
délivré un passeport pour cette destination.

Certifie en outre, que Cénac (Pierre), a
concouru au tirage au sort dans son Canton,
(classe 1858), qu'il y a obtenu le N° 67, &
qu'il a été exempt, comme frère d'un militaire
en activité de service.

En Mairie de Barbazan debat le
Vingt octobre mil huit cent soixante.

pour le maire absent
Vinquery adjt

business because of their right to inherit."[4] Since Pierre seemed to have worked a considerable time in Bordeaux, it is unlikely that he negotiated such a loan with anyone already in America.

Official French documents confirm that it was no easy process for Pierre to sever all official ties to Lower Barbazan. Mayor Bruno's February character reference certificate was followed toward the end of October by yet another stamped document which provides more specific information about Pierre, his intentions, and his eligibility to receive a passport.

After the initial paragraph that reads much the same as the first certificate, this second document continues:

Does certify that the said Cenac (Pierre), a Baker by profession, born and domiciliated at Barbazan, in the hereinabove named canton, district and département, has the intention of going to New Orleans (U.S. of America) and that there exists no objection to his being furnished with a passport to that destination.

Does moreover certify, that Cenac (Pierre), participated in the drawing of lots in his said Canton (Class of 1858), that he drew No. 67, & that he was exempt, as a brother of a military man in active service.

The document bears a seal, the date October 20, 1860, and the closing, *Acting for the mayor in abstentia* (signed) *Virguery* _____ [name illegible].[6]

From the more local government, Pierre's next step was to apply to the higher authority of the "Prefect of Hautes-Pyrénées" whose statement of October 22, 1860, records briefly:

...having seen the herein-above certificate, the accuracy whereof having been verified, does declare that there is no objection to a passport to a foreign country being furnished to Mr. Cenac.

It is sealed and signed *For the Prefect* by *A. Cazabonne*.[6]

From these official records we know that Pierre was not dodging military service in the armies of Napoleon III's Second Empire (1852-1870), nor was he avoiding a legal or domestic problem. It may reasonably be assumed that Pierre was seeking a more economically friendly setting, fueled by favorable reports from other emigrants who had gone before him, as well as the appeal of adventure and the quest for land.

Opposite, document asserting Pierre's eligibility to receive a passport, dated October 20, 1860

Napoleon III

NOTES

1. Founding president of the Louisiana Basque-American Society and Cultural Organization, LA BASCO

2. Jean-Baptiste Orpustan. *Les Noms des Maisons Médiévales en Labourd, Basse-Navarre et Soulé*, 2000

3. Michel Antoine Goitia-Nicolas, LA BASCO president

4. From historical research conducted at the request of a Cenac family member by Frenchwoman Jeanette Legendre, an academic and genealogist from the Hautes-Pyrénées region

5. C.E. Richard. *Louisiana: An Illustrated History*, Foundation for Excellence in Louisiana Public Broadcasting, 2003

6. Official documents are part of the Cenac Collection in the Nicholls State University Archives in Thibodaux, Louisiana.

7. From genealogical information provided in 2005 by researcher, writer, and historian Thierry Cenac, a Parisian and distant relative to Terrebonne Parish Cenac family members

LIVRET D'OUVRIER.

❖

Loi du 22 Juin 1854.

NAPOLÉON, par la grâce de Dieu et la volonté nationale, EMPEREUR DES FRANÇAIS, à tous présents et à venir, salut.

AVONS SANCTIONNÉ ET SANCTIONNONS, PROMULGUÉ et PROMULGUONS ce qui suit :

ART. 1 . Les ouvriers de l'un et de l'autre sexe attachés aux manufactures, fabriques, usines, mines, minières, carrières, chantiers, ateliers et autres établissements industriels ou travaillant chez eux pour un ou plusieurs ~~tenus de se munir~~ ...

DÉPARTEMENT DE LA GIRONDE.

ARRONDISSEMENT DE BORDEAUX.

PRÉFECTURE DE LA GIRONDE.

SÉRIE. Nº 16

Profession : *Boulanger*

Bordeaux, le 16 *8bre* 1860

Le Nº *Cénac*

Pierre

SIGNALEMENT :

Age : *24* ans

Taille : 1 m. *66* c.

Cheveux *Bruns*

Sourcils *Bruns*

Front *rond*

Yeux *Clairs*

Nez *large*

Bouche *moy.*

Barbe *naiss.*

Menton *rond*

Visage *oval*

Teint *Brun*

Signes particuliers :

Né à *Barbazan Debat*

Département d *Hautes Pyr.*

Demeurant à *Bordeaux*

rue *Séjant*

nº *24* ayant justifié de son identité et de sa position, a obtenu le présent livret contenant quatorze feuillets, cotés et para-

---

phés par premier et dernier, sur (1)

à la charge par *lui* de se conformer aux lois et règlements concernant les ouvriers.

Le porteur (2) *est* occupé en qualité d'ouvrier (3)

Signature de l'ouvrier,

Pour le Préfet de Gironde :

Le Secrétaire-Général délégué,

(1) Indiquer, s'il y a lieu, les pièces produites.

(2) Est *ou* a été.

(3) Attaché à un seul établissement, chez le sieur.............. demeurant à......, rue....., n......., ou travaillant pour plusieurs patrons.

CHAPTER 3
November 1860:
Determination

Clinging to his carpetbag satchel, Pierre hunkered down in a corner of the deck where he could brace himself against the jostling caused by high seas, wind, and rain. Only a few weeks out, and he had already learned that anyplace was better than the passenger hold below deck during a storm. Frightened women would be crying there, and children always took their cue from them. Even here above deck he could hear the children below screaming every time the barque slammed down into a violent wave. Most of the men tried to remain stoic, but he had seen the fear on their faces, too, and he didn't want to feel worse than he already did.

I'm glad I passed up my supper portion. The storm clouds were already on the horizon when the crew doled out our miserable meal, and I'd just be losing it now, anyway.

Maybe I shouldn't have tried so hard to board this particular barque at the last minute. But I was so tired of waiting. When the captain sent word down on the quai *that he could accommodate one more, I ran so fast I practically fell off the gangway. Passenger Number 88, Pierre Cenac. I couldn't stop grinning.*

Pierre smiled a wry grimace as salt spray smacked his face. *Number 88, huddled in the corner. Number 88, pants getting looser every day. Number 88, who'll never sail on the ocean again, if he ever reaches land.*

He tried to concentrate on what had sustained him for more than a month. *Remember how excited you were. Remember the high hopes and the feeling of adventure. Remember all the hard work to get to that gangway. One month of misery past, one more month to go.*

Pierre forced thoughts of his first days on the placid sea. He was fascinated by the large sea birds that followed the ship. With their wide wingspans and their long beaks, they were so different from the warblers and even the big crows in the fields and woods of the mountains.

When the crew up in the rigging had yelled that they sighted whales one sunny day, he was one of the first passengers to reach the rail. The big creatures' lumbering dives and surfacing had made him stop breathing for a moment. Pierre also loved the moonlit nights when he stood near the bow as its waves stirred up ocean phosphorescence and made the water glow.

The barque Sigyn, *sister ship of the* Texas

Opposite, Pierre's workman's travel visa dated February 16, 1860

Service de l'Émigration

Port de Bordeaux   Navire "Texas"

Destination : Nouvelle Orléans

Liste des Émigrants

Numéro d'ordre	Noms et Prénoms	Age	Profession	Lieu de Naissance		Sexe			Compie ou Agence	Observations Prix de Transport
				Commune	Département	Hom.	Fem.	Enfants		
81	Tarrou Jean Bertrand		Cultivateur	Saverdun	Hte Garonne	1	.	.	Nayens	160 f
82	Fenorbec Jn Bte St Pascal	18	menzi	Montanguey	.	1	.	.		163 f
83	Lazelle Jn Guillaume	17	Cuisinier	.	.	1	.	.		150 f
84	Soula Armand	28	Cuisinier	Frezigny	Hte Pyren	1	.	.		120 f
85	Toutite Michel	24	Cultivateur	Corrizols	.	1	.	.		180 f
86	Toutite Pierre	23	Paveshates	.	.	1	.	.		180 f
87	Tissegue Jn Marie	23	boucher	Lamarque	Hte .	1	.	.		180 f
88	Cenat Pierre	12	boulanger	Barbazan d'hors		1	.	.		170 embarqué à Paris au ...
					Totaux	7?	11	.		
					Total gal.		88			

Arrêté par nous Commissaire de Police délégué pour le Service de l'Émigration, la présente liste d'émigrants, embarqués sous le régime, sur le navire américain "Texas" allant à la Nouvelle Orléans expédié par M. Nayens, agent d'émigration, à la quantité de quatre vingt sept.

Certifié, 1° que les émigrants sont porteurs d'engagement signé par M. Nayens stipulant les droits qu'ils ont ... car de réclamation. Ils devront présenter ... engagement au Consul Français et le Capitaine devra ... à ... faute à la ... autorité.

2° Que les émigrants ont été visités par M. Dubreuil, médecin de la Commission d'émigration même qui a ...

Bordeaux le 11 Octobre 1860

L'agent d'émigration   Le ... de Police
Nayens

Le Capitaine

Oui, think of those things. That'll get you through tonight's storm.

But it was hard to sustain the good moments and much too easy to dwell on the misery he had felt on too many days. Fear of unpredictable sea conditions had subsided somewhat, several days after the ship emerged from the mouth of the Garonne River at Bordeaux. But sickness had broken out among the passengers, and many lay so enfeebled in their little berths that he was afraid that they would never reach New Orleans. Everybody got seasick, and Pierre was beginning to think he would never stop retching, even when he reached dry land.

As for company, there was a lot of it, but it was at too-close quarters. Not that there wasn't a lot to observe if he could position himself just right so that no one would see him watching and think him impolite. Fourteen-year-old Pablo had taken a liking to the blonde *fraulein* his own age, but no matter how many false starts he made in her direction, he never managed to achieve actual talking distance or a conversation. Pierre watched Pablo's daily battle with his awkwardness and felt compassion for the young man. Unobserved, Pierre could not help but hear the high-pitched voice of an old Parisian woman who made fun of the more provincial passengers and gossiped about the "scandalous" behavior of some of the crew.

Pierre often thought it would be nice if he could sit beside pretty Mademoiselle Suchet and exchange a few words, but her Maman guarded her like a tiger. He had thought about offering them part of the *baguette* he had been protecting for a month as an opening gesture, but decided Maman would turn up her nose at the stale, hard bread, no matter how hungry she and her daughter were. He couldn't talk to the Spaniards, and although a few of *les Allemands* spoke broken French, it was hard to understand.

Pierre adjusted his position a bit, and felt through the carpetbag fabric for his wine glasses etched with the family's coat of arms. He gripped the one stem he could feel to protect the glass from hitting the deck or the wall behind him. As he held on tight, he imagined a grand formal table set with fine china he had seen in Bordeaux shop windows, with these stemmed glasses taking pride of place. His eyelids began to droop, despite the constant heaving of the ship.

Stay awake. You can sleep tomorrow. You'll be one day closer then.

Cenac

The Cenac Family coat of arms

Opposite, Pierre's name, number 88 at the end of the passenger manifest, dated October 24, 1860, for his voyage on the Texas

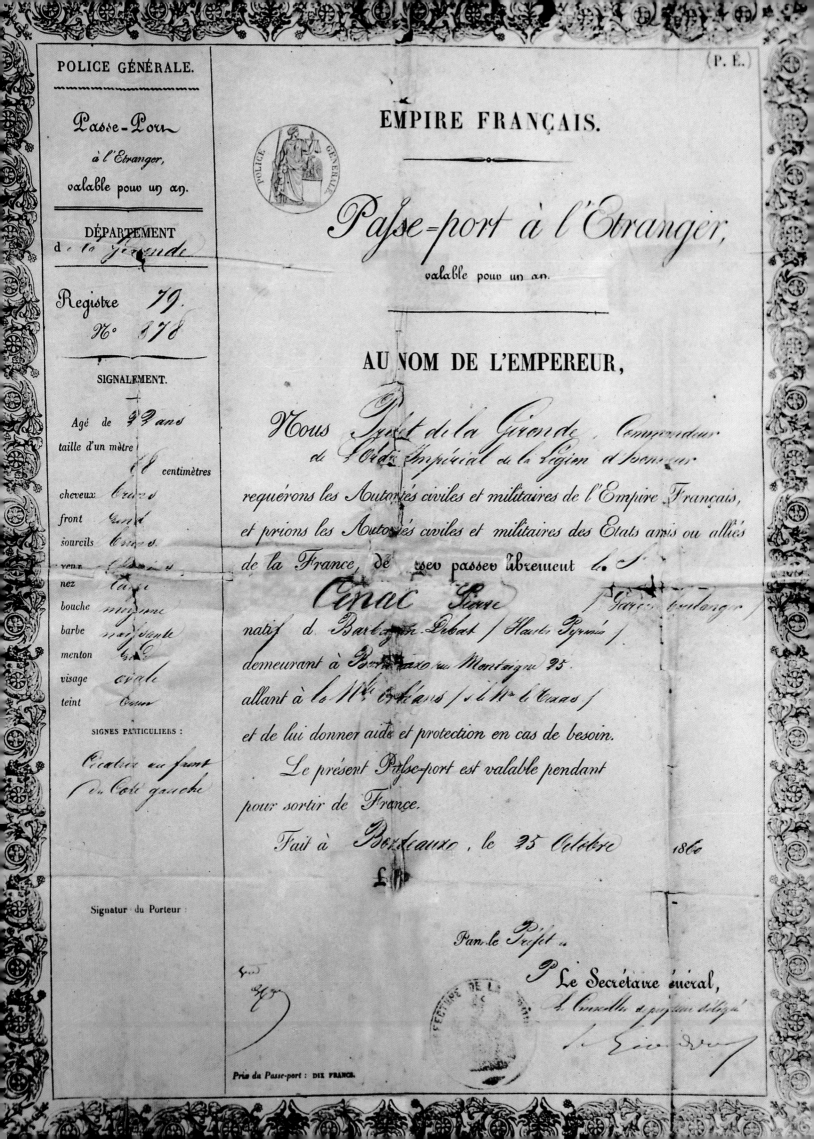

POLICE GÉNÉRALE.

Passe-Port
à l'Etranger,
valable pour un an.

DÉPARTEMENT
de la Gironde

Registre 79.
N° 878

SIGNALEMENT.

Âgé de 22 ans
taille d'un mètre
68 centimètres
cheveux bruns
front grand
sourcils bruns
yeux bruns
nez gros
bouche moyenne
barbe naissante
menton rond
visage ovale
teint brun

SIGNES PARTICULIERS :

Cicatrice au front
du côté gauche

Signatur du Porteur :

(P. É.)

EMPIRE FRANÇAIS.

POLICE GÉNÉRALE

Passe-port à l'Étranger,

valable pour un an.

AU NOM DE L'EMPEREUR,

Nous Préfet de la Gironde, Commandeur
de l'Ordre Impérial de la Légion d'honneur,
requérons les Autorités civiles et militaires de l'Empire Français,
et prions les Autorités civiles et militaires des États amis ou alliés
de la France, de laisser passer librement le S.
Cénac Pierre (Garçon boulanger)
natif de Barbazan-Debat (Hautes-Pyrénées)
demeurant à Bordeaux rue Montaigne 25.
allant à la Nlle Orléans (s.t Mle le Texas)
et de lui donner aide et protection en cas de besoin.

Le présent Passe-port est valable pendant
pour sortir de France.

Fait à Bordeaux, le 25 Octobre 1860

Par le Préfet

P. Le Secrétaire général,

Prix du Passe-port : DIX FRANCS.

CHAPTER 4
The Crossing

When Pierre left Bordeaux aboard the ship *Texas* on October 30, 1860, his passport's physical description gave a picture of the 22-year-old man as "one meter 68 centimeters" tall (5 feet 6.14 inches), with brown hair and eyebrows, round forehead, auburn eyes, large nose, medium mouth, nascent beard, round chin, oval face, and dark complexion. One "particular mark" was a scar on the left side of his forehead.[1]

The passport was issued on October 25 *au nom de l'empereur*—in the name of the emperor—Napoleon III, and cost Pierre ten francs (about two U.S. dollars). The document was valid for one year.

By far his greatest expense was fare for the journey, listed as 170 francs (approximately 35 U.S. dollars) on the ship's passenger record. This was no doubt paid out of his earnings as a baker for the better part of a year in Bordeaux.[1]

Listed as passenger number 88 on the ship's manifest, his name appears last, even though it was alphabetized up to the last several entries. This indicates that the captain, after taking on whatever goods he was commissioned to transport, saw that he could accommodate more passengers and allowed several more to board. Pierre was the last of these unguaranteed passengers.

The *Texas* embarked on what was expected to be a two-month crossing of the Atlantic. The ship was more accurately termed a *barque* or bark. It was a three-masted vessel with the fore and main masts square rigged, and mizzen or after mast rigged fore and aft. The ship's official papers indicate its owner was one

CARTERET FERRY CORPORATION
SHIP BUILDERS

BUILDERS OF WOODEN SCHOONERS AND WOODEN VESSELS OF ALL TYPES
NEW YORK CITY

Left, shipyard, New York City c. 1860
Opposite, Pierre's French passport, dated October 25, 1860

William Wakeman. Its *enrolment* (official detailed identification) was dated August 24, 1848, at the Port of New York, so it had been in service for a number of years already (and continued in service until at least 1864).

Its dimensions were 118 feet long, 30½ feet wide and 15 feet deep. Other particulars were that the barque consisted of one deck, three masts, a square stern, no galleries, and a billet head.[1]

Once the ship set sail, the land-bound nature of his upbringing must have confronted Pierre full-force as he stood at the rail of the ship on which he was to spend eight long weeks on the open sea.

By 1860 the crossing was less arduous than for earlier European émigrés, but was still not a pleasure cruise. On the high seas, passengers often experienced rough waters for days on end, inducing not only near-universal seasickness but also, in some cases, fear for their very lives.

Being lodged in small quarters with strangers, especially where parents habitually yelled at their children, or children were especially boisterous, was one irritation to which transatlantic travelers were subjected for weeks on end. Travel journals of the time record gossip among passengers, shipboard flirtations, as well as personal discomforts that occupied travelers' minds.

Official enrolment—*identification document—of the* Texas, *dated August 24, 1848*

Although making the crossing with people of different nationalities may have been fascinating for the open-minded and gregarious, more reserved passengers may have been less embracing of differences in languages, attitudes and even table manners. One travel diary of the period speaks of American, German, French, Spanish and English all aboard the same vessel. At table, some used forks to transport food to their mouths; some used knives; some, their hands.[2]

Besides cramped quarters and unsanitary conditions, food allowances were another hardship. The mortality rate among passengers was so high during the period 1820-1855 that the U.S. government passed a "final piece of antebellum legislation, that of March 3, 1855" governing minimal food provisions aboard ships crossing the Atlantic with passengers. A researcher wrote that "...under the best conditions, an immigrant on an eight week voyage to New Orleans, if he consumed equal proportions of everything he received each week, had a daily diet of four and one-half ounces of bread, three and a third ounces each of rice, oatmeal, peas and beans; two and a quarter ounces each of flour, salt pork, and beef; four and one-half ounces of potatoes, and less than a quarter of an ounce of vinegar. If a captain made legal substitutions, under this act he fed his passengers a little over a pound of bread, two and a quarter ounces of salted pork and beef, a quarter ounce of vinegar, and three quarts of water every day."[3]

No accounts of Pierre's voyage remain to document his thoughts and encounters during his Atlantic crossing. However, marine records in New Orleans newspapers do give detailed particulars of his arrival in America.

During the waning days of 1860, on Wednesday, December 19, the *Texas*, under command of Captain Jefferson Pendleton, anchored off the mouth of the Mississippi River. It was met by the towboat *Anglo American* with Captain Martin at the helm on Friday, December 21. Pierre's first taste of Louisiana weather before he reached port was favorable, according to the *New Orleans Daily Crescent* newspaper. In the issue of that same Friday, the paper reported, "The weather yesterday [Thursday] continued delightfully mild, clear and pleasant, with a light southerly breeze blowing." This was in sharp contrast to the weather of only a month before, when a hurricane had battered Louisiana's coast.

The *Texas*, the ship *Shatemuc* from Liverpool, England, and the barque *Young America* from New York were towed upriver through the Head of Passes toward the Port of New Orleans.

The *Anglo American* took the *Shatemuc* to dock at Baxter, Lovell & Company at New Orleans' First District. The *Texas* and the *Young America* arrived at Algiers Point across the Mississippi on Saturday, December 22. The *Texas* docked at Creevy & Farwell, and the *Young America* at George A. Fosdick & Company. The *Texas* was under contract to George W. Hynson & Co., shipping agents, located at 82 Camp Street in New Orleans proper.

Advertisement card for the ship Young America

Pilot's station at the mouth of the Mississippi River, drawing by Henry Lewis c. 1854-1857

Port of New Orleans c. 1860

THE ORDINANCE OF SECESSION.

Our South Carolina friends have at length made notable progress towards their assumption of independence. They have reached the literary point in the serious affair of declaring themselves a separate and independent people from the other states of this Union, and we cannot now doubt their determination to follow up by acts that which we are assured has been verbally consummated. To suppose that they will halt in their new career, that they will be revolutionary only in name, is to mistake the character of the people, for whether the politicians among them are serious or shamming, they certainly are thoroughly in earnest. This we have constantly impressed upon the minds of our readers since the Charleston bolt, when the enemies of the confederation constantly and falsely asserted, in opposition to our well-considered charge, that the disruption of the democratic party was not a part of the disunion programme, was not intended to so result, and ought not in truth to be so construed.—

When the *Texas*, under tow, approached the bend of the Mississippi River at New Orleans, Pierre saw a Crescent City situated in much the same configuration as the one he had left at Bordeaux. Cityscape and levee construction may have differed, but he went from one urbane city to another that was amazingly similar, in the Garonne's and the Mississippi's "crescent moon-shaped" ports. On Monday, Christmas Eve, December 24, 1860, Pierre was once again firmly tethered to land, and walked off the ship into a new world.

He had departed a country that had long been at war under the Second Empire of Napoleon III. One enduring result of these wars was that Swiss native Jean-Henri Dunant witnessed the suffering of wounded soldiers left on the battlefield at Solferino—which led Dunant to set into motion a process from which emerged the Geneva Conventions and the International Red Cross.

Although there must have been talk among sailors and passengers aboard the *Texas* of U.S. political unrest between northern and southern regions, Pierre thought he was to arrive in a peaceful United States of America. He must have been astonished to discover from New Orleans newspaper headlines of the very day he disembarked that the state of South Carolina had seceded from the Union on December 20, 1860.

When Pierre stepped onto Louisiana soil, the state already had a nearly two-century history with his native France. New Orleans still retained a European ambience, and was "predominantly Roman Catholic and foreign born in a nation that was Protestant and native born. It was urban in a region that was almost totally rural, and though located in the deep South many of its commercial and political leaders were Yankees."[4] By 1860 the city had the highest percentage of foreign-born white persons of any urban area in America, and was the fifth largest city in America. The Crescent City was one of the busiest ports in all the Americas. After New York, New Orleans before 1860 was the second busiest immigrant port of debarkation in the States.

Previous influxes of Francophone (French-speaking) immigrants attracted newcomers expecting to find, by the mid-1800s, kindred countrymen and culture. Dr. Carl Brasseaux, former director of the Center for Louisiana Studies at the University of Louisiana at Lafayette, enumerates 18 distinct groups of French-speaking immigrants beginning with the region's establishment as a French colony in 1699, through modern times.[5] Brasseaux's categories show that Pierre was part of the tenth such group, consisting of "successive waves of nineteenth-century French (known within Louisiana's Francophone community as *les français étrangers*)"—the so-called Foreign French.

In chronological order, the earlier subgroups were "the 1699 Canadian settlers; voluntary immigrants of the John Law era; forced immigrants of the early eighteenth century; French military personnel (many of whom opted to remain in the colony); Alsatian religious exiles; Acadian exiles; Saint-Domingue refugees; refugees from the French revolution; Bonapartist exiles." The period of Pierre's arrival in 1860 recorded the largest number—14,938—of French natives living in Louisiana during the time frame 1850-1990.[5]

The French culture Pierre encountered in New Orleans was a combination of the influence of these diverse groups of French, all having different histories, different socioeconomic and political experiences, different religions, and different points of native Continental or Caribbean origin. The state's and the city's French culture by 1860 had been affected to greater or lesser degrees by all of the groups Brasseaux names.

One major impact on the New Orleans in which Pierre arrived was the Saint-Domingue (Haiti) immigrants who had doubled the city's population when more than 10,000 refugees began to arrive in great numbers in 1809-1810. They had fled the Caribbean island in 1803 when black slaves staged a successful Haitian Revolution, the only successful such revolt in the Americas. Paul Lachance of the University of Ottawa, describing the Saint-Domingue refugees in a 1988 *Louisiana History Journal* article, recorded this group as "whites, free persons of color, and slaves... about equally represented in the refugee movement of 1809." A third of the white islanders had been killed, and those who immigrated to New Orleans via Cuba brought with them their own kind of French culture, which included a caste system.

In the three-tiered Creole caste system were whites of European ancestries born in the New World; *gens de couleur libres* defined as "free people of color—mixed in racial ancestry, Catholic in faith, and proudly French in culture"; and blacks.[6]

Top, Toussaint l'Ouverture, who led the Saint-Domingue slave revolt, c. 1800; Bottom, St. Pierre port on Martinique, c. 1900

Hill & Smith del.

New York, Published by

New Orleans from the lower cotton press 1852 by David William Moody

hers & C° 225 Fulton St.

Drawn on stone by D.W. M...

LEANS

TON PRESS 1852.

Above, scenes of Haiti c. 1890
Below, a New Orleans mulatto and child,
Civil War era

"Negro Indians" in Dulac, Louisiana c. 1930

Free people of color had been able to buy their liberty from slave owners. Other *gens de couleur libres* had been granted release by their owners, for various reasons. Both marital and extramarital alliances between whites of European ancestry and people of color began the resulting degrees of persons having "mixed blood" such as mulattos, quadroons, octoroons, and *passe blanc* (pass for white). "Mixed offspring" of white and Indian were known in French as *metis* and in Spanish as *mestizos*; those of Indians and blacks or mulattos were known in French as *griffes* or in Spanish as *zambos*. The practice of *plaçage* in Louisiana saw light-skinned women of mixed race "kept" in second households by rich white men, especially in New Orleans. Entire families resulted from these unmarried unions, often openly acknowledged in society. Through the process of manumission, many mistresses and their children were given their freedom.

Antillean Creoles had been the planter class in their home island. When they migrated to Louisiana, they disdained the pursuit of commerce. Instead, these highly educated people, preoccupied with social status, went into "noble professions" of government, legal and medical professions, education, journalism, and followed leisure-time pursuits of theatrical and operatic arts patronage. "...Creoles permitted the Anglo-American and Europeans of the nineteenth century to move into, and quickly dominate, the city's thriving commercial sector."[5]

The caste system was not limited to New Orleans, where Pierre first became acquainted with Creoles. The term *Creole* has always been subject to a complex and contested set of identifying characteristics. In Saint-Domingue, "*Creole* meant native-born 'without reference to color...In early Louisiana, the term meant the descendants of pioneers—French, Spanish, German, Irish, Italian, sometimes even English, and African— who were born in the region prior to the Louisiana Purchase."[5] *Creole* subsequently underwent a period of derogatory use towards native whites by newly-arrived European colonists who "considered themselves inherently superior to their American-born neighbors, whose brains, they believed, were addled by the tropical sun."[5] Eventually, earlier and later white colonists' families intermarried, and adopted the term *Creole* as a synonym for *aristocrat*, often more an affectation than a reality.

"Much to the horror of the white Creole community," descendants of manumitted slaves, *gens de couleur libres*, identified themselves as Creoles, as well.[5] The *Academia Real Espanola* holds that the word was coined by early Spanish colonials in the West Indies 'to refer to persons born of European parents in the islands as well as to locally born blacks.' Creole would come to describe those of Old World parents born upon New World soils, with no first-hand knowledge of the mother country."[6] Saint-Domingue usage of the term also prevailed in colonial Louisiana where native-born black slaves were consistently identified as *Creoles* to distinguish them from less-valuable imported slaves.

In the New Orleans of 1860, Pierre was introduced to all these nuances of Creole-ism, one in which even among blacks, the lighter-skinned looked down upon the darker-skinned.

Geographic divisions occurred along cultural lines in New Orleans as Creoles made their homes predominantly on the French Quarter side of Canal Street and Anglo-Americans in what is now Uptown and the Garden District. Politically, the two were often on opposing sides. After Germans, Irishmen began to arrive in great numbers, bolstering the Anglo-American ranks. Creoles saw for the first time in their history a decline in their political domination of the Crescent City.

By the time the Civil War started, "more than half the white population of the city had been born in another country. It proved to be too many too fast. Whether they were immigrants from overseas or from the eastern United States, the rapid influx of outsiders into New Orleans made for a volatile clash of cultures. Competition for jobs and political power was fierce, and ethnic scuffles became more and more common, ultimately fragmenting the entire community.

"Tensions between the Americans and the Creoles led to the division of New Orleans into three separate municipalities with independent governments, though operating under the leadership of a single mayor. The Uptown municipality was dominated by Anglo-American Whigs, while the French Quarter and the third city-within-the-city (bounded by Esplanade Avenue and St. Bernard Parish) were generally led by Creole Democrats. New Orleans remained politically balkanized in this fashion for sixteen years. When the three municipalities were once again united into a single city in 1852, the Anglo-American population was firmly in control, and the French Creole influence began its long, slow decline. New Orleans was now, indisputably, an *American* city,"[7] although the remaining European influence gave it a decidedly Continental flair.

Steamship Princess *at the port of New Orleans, between 1858 and 1861*

French Quarter of the period, depicted in Frank Leslie's Illustrated Newspaper *of March 19, 1883*

53

NORMAN'S PLAN
OF
NEW ORLEANS & ENVIRONS,
1845
BY
HENRY MOELLHAUSEN
Civil Engineer.
B. M. NORMAN, PUBLISHER.

Engd. by Shields & Hammond. 2 Camp St. N.O.

MISSISSIPPI

HOTELS & EXCHANGES	BANKS	CHURCHES	PUBLIC SCHOOLS	MARKETS

HOTELS & EXCHANGES
Exchange Hotel, St. Charles & Common Sts.
City Exchange St. Louis & Royal
Verandah Hotel, St. Charles & Common
Howlett's Exchange Common & Camp
Bank's Arcade Magazine & Gravier
Orleans Hotel Chartres near Toulouse
Merchant's Exchange Royal near Customhouse
Post Office in Merchants Exchange

BANKS
8 City Bank, Camp near Canal
9 Mechanic's & Traders Bank, Canal near Camp
10 Louisiana State Bank, Royal & Conti
11 Bank of Louisiana do. do.
12 Canal Bank, Magazine & Gravier
13 Commercial Bank, do. S. Natchez

CHURCHES
14 Cathedral Chartres & Orleans
15 St. Patricks Church, Camp near Girod
16 Obituary Church Rampart & Conti
17 Ursulines do. Ursuline near Condé
18 St. Augustine do. St. Claude & Bayou Road
19 Episcopal do. Canal & Bourbon
20 St. Pauls do. Camp near Bartholemew
21 Clapp's de. St. Charles & Gravier
22 Presbyterian de. S. side Lafayette Square
23 German de Clio near Nayades
24 Methodist de. Poydras & Carondelet
25 do de (colored) Gravier below Carondelet
26 Catholic de. Josephine near Laurel
27 Presbyterian Church Bellegarde near Josephine
28 Methodist de. St. Mary near Bellegarde
29 Presbyterian de. Calliope & Prytane

PUBLIC SCHOOLS
50 Louisiana Med. College Common & Phillippa
51 Washington Free School, Magazine near Basin
52 Franklin do. St. Charles near Julia
53 Lafayette da Laurel near Phillip

THEATRES
34 Orleans Theatre, Orleans near Royal
35 American do Poydras near Camp
56 Amphitheatre, Barenne & Poydras

HOSPITALS
57 Charity Hospital, Common opp. Villere
58 Maison de Santé, Canal & Claiborne
59 Circus St. Infirmary Circus below Poydras
40 Franklin da Elysian fields & Genius

41 Vegetable Market, Old Levee & St. Philip
42 Meat do. Old Levee opp. Madison
43 St. Mary's de. Tchapitoulas near Delord
44 Poydras de. Poydras & Circus

MARKETS
45 Market House Orl.
46 do. da Julia
47 do. da Bay.
48 do de Jack
49 do de Clai

50 Union Cotton Press
51 Orleans do
52 Mississippi do
53 Louisiana do
54 McNair's da

EXPLANATIONS
Municipality boundary lin...
Ward...
Fire Limits...
Elevation of the City above th...
¼ Mile distance Circles virgin...

Pierre Cenac was one of 7,500 French natives who came to the United States between 1851 and 1860. Basques in North America predated both the country's and the state's founding, providing further familiarity for French Basque newcomers to Louisiana.[8] Europeans fleeing war at the time Pierre immigrated, and even those with other motives (like Pierre), must have expected to encounter more peaceful conditions in the United States.

However, a month before Pierre arrived in Louisiana, results of the Presidential election on November 6, 1860, pointed to the state's divisions in loyalties. In New Orleans, a Unionist candidate, John Bell of Tennessee, won citywide, defeating Democrat John C. Breckinridge of Kentucky who was on the ballot in place of Senator Stephen A. Douglas, the official Democratic convention candidate. Although Bell carried New Orleans, Breckinridge carried the state. National Republican candidate Abraham Lincoln's name was not even listed on the Louisiana ballot.

After a brief period of only moderate reaction to a "Black Republican" president, mid-November saw New Orleans newspapers reflecting more hostility toward the North, and the city began to witness accelerated pro-secessionist rhetoric and the formation of quasi-military organizations.

Pierre's first days on American soil were, as a result, fraught with political upheaval. However, the young man was probably focused on maneuvering in his new physical surroundings, observing all he encountered in Louisiana—despite the controversy swirling around him. This had to begin on New Orleans' riverfront, which was a cacophony of sounds and a carnival of sights.

One description gives a good picture of what Pierre saw upon his arrival: "There is a rush upon the fifty-feet high pile of bales on the capacious lower deck of a Greenville and Vicksburgh, a Red River, or a Ouachita packet, and the monument to the industry of a dozen planters vanishes as if by magic...as the blacks wheeling the cotton pass the 'tally-man,' who stands near the steamer's gangways he notes the mark on each bale, and in a loud voice sings out to him wheeling it the name of the sign...under which it is to rest until sold to be removed. It is a broad-chested, ebony-breasted, tough-fisted, bullet-headed, toiling, awkward mass, this collection of roustabouts on the levee; but it does wonders in work."[9]

Pierre must have heard the "sharp voices of the skippers, the harsh orders of the masters of gangs, and the cheery and mirth-provoking responses of the help, mingled with the sibilations of escaping steam, the ringing of countless bells and the moving and rumbling of drays and carts and steam-cars...the jocund notes of the negro's song."[9]

Pierre might have stopped to purchase food from one of the many small merchants. The author lists some as "the old apple and cake woman, Irish and fifty," the orange-selling "smart young Sicilian woman, with a gay handkerchief pinned over her jet

Cotton on the levee at the Port of New Orleans, c. 1861-1865.

locks," "the coffee-and-sausage man," and others who sold various wares to workers and arrivals.[9] Native Americans sold their *filée* and Africans sold okra, a crop they introduced in the New World as *gombo*.

Vessels that Pierre may have seen were "Up river—ships and ships and ships! Down river—steamers and steamers and steamers! Sharp cut American, solid seagoing English, queer Spanish—eccentric vessels from every European port— flying almost every important ensign—lying at the levees, and discharging their cargoes into the bonded warehouses, or the drays drawn by the patient mules. The broad muddy current slips swiftly past the vessels' bows, bearing rafts and great ships away toward the passes."[9]

The port was strictly seasonal in nature, with maximum activity from fall through March, and a seasonal lull that followed during the rest of spring and summer (in part related to the threat of yellow fever during warmer months). Pierre arrived at the height of the port's seasonal commerce. By 1860 "the Crescent City had almost seven miles of shipping in front of it, and immigrants and any other individuals who disembarked along the levee could look up or down it and see no end to the maritime activities that transpired there."[9]

This Mississippi River and riverfront activity was compounded within the city itself by the tense political atmosphere of the times, with opponents to immediate secession ("co-operationists") and secessionists at noisy odds in the city streets.

But the day Pierre arrived was Christmas Eve, and the young man undoubtedly was full of expectations, even though the holiday had to prompt nostalgic thoughts of his family celebrating *Noël* without him. With finding room and board a necessity, his first Christmas in America was probably a meager one.

The *New Orleans Daily Crescent*'s weather report on December 25 read, "Yesterday was a rather doubtful sort of day; sunny

The steamer Magnolia *at the Port of New Orleans, c. 1858-1861*

and cloudy, chilly and warm, calm and gusty, by turns; a very miscellaneous sort of day. Though it threatened bad weather for to-day, we indulge the hope that the clear sunshine and sweet warm breezes will be permitted to brighten and regale the town to-day. Christmas is only half Christmas when the weather is bad; when the weather is bright and beautiful, Christmas is doubly Christmas."

During his first days in the city, Pierre could have consulted newspapers of the time, which carried what they entitled a "Strangers Guide." These features listed information for banks, exchange dealers, insurance companies, fire departments, relief committees, cotton presses, physicians and apothecaries, and railroads (including the New Orleans, Opelousas and Great Western Railroad).

Another resource from that time period was *Gardner's New Orleans Directory*, a precursor to current-day city directories. In 1861 the directory listed the names of two Cenacs, neither of whom was related to Pierre.

While Pierre was making his first forays into the Crescent City, the *Texas* had its cargo unloaded, including assorted merchandise, brandies, liquors, and wines. Newspapers document that these were delivered to Piaggio and Viosca, E. Rochereau, Lanata Frères, and others in the city. The barque took on common exports of the day—cotton, tobacco, cigars, molasses, staves, and other commodities. Any passengers would have had to apply to the captain on board for passage to France. The number of passengers allowed would have been determined by the weight of the cargo already loaded. The *Texas* was cleared and departed Algiers Point, bound for Bordeaux, on December 31, New Year's Eve. The ship had been in port only eight days since its arrival in New Orleans.

Did the imminence of war on this new soil make Pierre second-guess his decision to immigrate and quell his optimism? Did New Orleans' particular types of bustle and chaos fascinate and excite Pierre, or did they instead make him yearn for the quiet and tranquility of Barbazan-Debat? Did he stand on the levee and watch the departure of the *Texas*—knowing it was heading back to his home country—with a lump in his throat?

Steamers at the New Orleans levee and across at Algiers Point, 1858-1861

French Market and levee, c. 1861-1865

Stereoview card photo of sugar hogsheads at the port of New Orleans c. 1860

NOTES

1. In the Cenac Collection of the Nicholls State University Archives

2. A. Rugbean. *Transatlantic Rambles: A Record of Twelve Months' Travel in the United States, Cuba, & the Brazils*, George Bell and G. and T. Brooke, 1861

3. Fredrick Marcel Spletstoser. 1979 dissertation, *Back Door to the Land of Plenty: New Orleans as an Immigrant Port, 1820-1860*

4. Robert Reinders. *End of an Era: New Orleans, 1850-1860*, Pelican Publishing Company, 1964

5. Dr. Carl A. Brasseaux. *French, Cajun, Creole, Houma: A Primer on Francophone Louisiana*, Louisiana State University Press, 2005

6. Richard Campanella. *Bienville's Dilemma: A Historical Geography of New Orleans*, Center for Louisiana Studies, University of Louisiana at Lafayette, 2008

7. C.E. Richard

8. Michel Goitia-Nicolas, LA BASCO president, in 2010 interviews

9. Edward King. *Louisiana 100 Years Ago: Volume II*, Sun Publishing Company, 1976

The second St. Charles Hotel, New Orleans, c. 1858-1861.

CHAPTER 5
March 21, 1861:
The Decision

Dim gaslight lanterns on the narrow street helped Pierre to pick his steps over the curbside's reeking open gutter. He was headed toward the sound of commotion he estimated to be a few streets over. From that direction a brass band's loud oompahs mingled with loud voices and hurrahs. The fireworks that had first caught his attention from his boarding room window repeated themselves every now and then, pointing him in the right direction.

He knew that the Confederate constitution had been up for debate, and this celebration probably meant something, one way or the other. He was curious to find out what would happen now. Even though others were making their way on the uneven sidewalks in the same direction, he was able to maneuver past them. Pierre found it easy to make fast progress on these flat city streets after negotiating the hilly terrain in Barbazan and Bordeaux. Since December, he had become more confident in his knowledge of street layouts, and what areas to avoid.

Pierre breathed in the sweet scent of gardenias and jasmine. He strode more slowly past the courtyard he knew was its source. *I wonder if every spring comes this early, this warm. At home, Jean and Magdeleine won't see flowers in their little garden for at least two months. But then, most things are different here.*

He picked up his pace again and made a short detour to walk past a favorite place to feast his eyes on, the St. Charles Hotel, with all its bright lights and fine draperies. He watched well-dressed couples walking up the steps, the ladies delicately holding their dresses in practiced fingertips. He had often wished that he had the nerve to follow them through the grand doors to see the opulence he knew was inside those walls. Pierre laughed softly at the thought, and turned again.

What a changeable place this has turned out to be. First, I arrive in Les États-Unis. *But in the streets I see everywhere men wearing a pelican button with two streamers. Mrs. Ducos at the boarding house tells me it's called "the blue cockade," and it means those people do not want to be in the United States anymore. Every day in the newspapers I see advertisements for fireworks "suitable for political clubs." Every night I see the torchlight parades with banners, bands, and some fireworks, but not as grand as tonight's.*

"Creole Night at the French Opera House" image in Harper's Weekly, *1861*

Interior of St. Charles Hotel, from Frank Leslie's Illustrated Newspaper *of December 2, 1876*

Pierre rounded another corner and nearly ploughed into two men practically holding each other up. They looked sick to him, not drunk as he thought at first glance. He crossed to the other side of the street as fast as he could. He knew the stories about yellow fever here, and did not want to take chances.

His first day in *la Nouvelle Orleans,* he had learned about taking chances the hard way when he was commandeered by a silver-tongued brigand who took him to "a bargain of a boarding house." Pierre considered himself lucky to get away from that place with his money stash intact after the "friendly lady" on the stoop tried to get him to step all the way inside the dingy front door that did not dim the raucous shrieks from within. The spires of St. Louis Cathedral were among the first sights he had seen from the *Texas* when it docked. After that boarding house episode, he made his way toward those spires to get there in time for Christmas Eve's midnight mass. There during the familiar ritual Pierre resolved to stay away from trouble. He had crossed an ocean. He could take care of himself.

St. Louis Cathedral and Jackson Square, New Orleans, c. 1861-1865

Looking back at the two men staggering away down the street, Pierre let out his breath. *This place has so much sickness. Everyone says the water is bad. Maybe if the streets weren't so dirty. Now, what was I thinking? Ah,* oui. *So, after only a short time here, I learn this is no longer* la Louisiane *the state, but* la Louisiane *the nation. I see the new flag flying, I hear about a new army and government. I wonder what we'll be next. This noise has to mean another change.*

Pierre put his hands into his pockets, and felt his entire store of money sewn into a seam. *What money will we have to use now? In December I change my francs for bank notes. Two months go by, and I hear talk that money of all kinds is scarce, that the quais are not as busy as usual.*

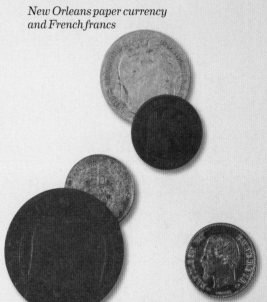

New Orleans paper currency and French francs

Dix Note

The fifth largest city in the nation, New Orleans was by far the largest city in the South—and for many people its very name was synonymous with the region as a whole. Local legend ascribes the origins of the term "Dixie" to a New Orleans-issued banknote. The Citizens' Bank, located in the French Quarter, printed its notes in both English and French. On the reverse of the $10 bill was the word dix—French for ten. Before long the bilingual banknotes, dubbed "Dixies" by visitors, had generated a new nickname for New Orleans. By the late 1850s, "Dixie" or "Dixieland" had come to refer to the entire South.

From The Historic New Orleans Collection's **A Closer Look, The Antebellum Photographs of Jay Dearborn Edwards, 1858-1861.** Curated by John H. Lawrence, John T. Magill and Pamela D. Arceneaux. Edited by Jessica Dorman and Erin Greenwald.

He stopped to take off his jacket, and tucked it into the crook of his elbow. *Well, business or not, the rich people here certainly have not stopped their night life. For three months I've seen wealthy planters and aristocratic Creoles and their wives getting into carriages in ball gowns and evening clothes. Their daughters, too. I hear about the tableaux, the quadroon balls, the opera house that opened just last year, and the soprano Adelina Patti performing now.*

But something is going to happen soon. Everybody says so. When I go to work at the bakery early every morning, I see the men in fine uniforms drilling in the streets. They march, but they look not too sérieux.

Pierre saw torches lighting the night ahead and caught his first sight of a large crowd. The people on the fringe seemed charged with a tangible excitement. One man he didn't even know slapped his back like an old friend. As he inched forward into the milling mass, he heard above the crowd's rumble the shouts echoing from several directions, "Long Live the Confederacy!"

Pierre examined the faces in the crowd and listened to the speaker who seemed to have most of their attention. He absorbed the speech for a while, then turned away. Before he was out of earshot, he heard the crowd take up the rousing chorus of "I Wish I Was in Dixie."

Slowly, slowly, he retraced his route the way he had come. When he climbed the steps to Madame Ducos' house, he had come to the decision he had been mulling over since he had arrived. *I have to leave this city. I know where I have to go.*

Opera House in New Orleans (corner Bourbon and Toulouse streets,1859-1919), by Adrien Persac c. 1859-1873

H. E. is earnestly requested to WRITE immediately to his deep anxious mother.

M. E.—I have RECEIVED both the LETTERS that you sent, for which I am very much obliged.

IF this should MEET the EYE of EDWARD MA-VEIOU, an American commercial traveller, who left London on the 5th of August last, for Manchester, E. C. is anxious to see him before his return to Australia. Address to the post-office, Little Sussex-place, Hyde-park, W., London, to be left till called for.

M. D. W.—I wish I could say I am much better, but I am remaining quiet, and my general health is very good. I wish to see you, as we have much to settle. I should hope (if all our duties are over and I get right) whether our business cannot be concluded early in July. Let me know your wishes, my dear sister,—Rome, Feb. 9.

LOST, a BUNCH of KEYS. FIVE SHILLINGS REWARD.—M. W., 53, Aldermanbury, E.C.

LOST, a DOCK WARRANT for J M, with O S and P under, and 2, one butt of Sherry, ex Leila, Orfeur, from Cadiz, entered by Evans, April, 1852. Apply to R. T., Messrs. Pottle and Son's, Royal Exchange, who will REWARD.

LOST, on Sunday last, in the neighbourhood of Westbourne-park, a LIGHT BROWN SKYE TERRIER. Answers to his name "Bob." Whoever will bring the same to 45, Westbourne-park-road, shall receive TEN SHILLINGS REWARD.

LOST, in the neighbourhood of Highbury, a BLACK SPANIEL DOG, very fat, with tan-coloured feet; answers to the name "Dash." Whoever will bring the same to Sissons', post-office, Highbury-grove, shall get FIVE SHILLINGS REWARD.

LOST, in Regent-street, on Friday, the 25th ult., a small TERRIER BITCH, with a tan spot over each eye, and tan-coloured feet. The ears and tail have been cut. Whoever will bring the same to St. Mary's Hospital, Paddington, shall receive ONE GUINEA REWARD. No further reward will be offered.

LOST, on Friday last, a TORTOISESHELL BACK COOMB, on the South-Western Railway, between Vauxhall and Barnes Stations; either left in the carriage, or in the waiting room at Barnes. Whoever will bring it, or inform Messrs. Rastall and Son, Stationers, Eccleston-street, S.W., where it may be had, shall receive TEN SHILLINGS REWARD.

FIVE SHILLINGS REWARD.—LEFT in a CAB, on Saturday night, the 9th inst., at half-past 10 o'clock, between Upper Wimpole-street and 31, Nottingham-place, a BLACK HAND BONNET-BOX, containing a bonnet trimmed with black riband, &c.

ONE POUND REWARD.—DOG LOST—a white and roan large Skye terrier. Whoever will bring the same to No. 55, Tavistock-square, shall receive the above reward. The dog answers to the name of "Ragg."

DOG LOST.—Feb. 7th, in the vicinity of Brompton—a small Black and Tan Terrier. Answers to the name of "Minnie." Had on black velvet collar, with pearl buttons. Whoever will bring the same to the Fulham-bridge Tavern, Brompton-road, will receive ONE POUND REWARD.

FIVE POUNDS REWARD.—To Photographers, Dealers in old Books and Prints.—LOST, from a carrier's cart, in the Mile-end-road, on the evening of Saturday, 26th of January, a PARCEL, containing a thick folio volume of photographs of Roman buildings, and other books. Whoever may have found the same will receive the above reward. Apply at District Surveyor's-office, 1, Stepney-green. No further reward will be offered.

BUNCH of GOLD CHARMS LOST, supposed to have been dropped in a cab, on Saturday afternoon, Feb. 9, which took up a gentleman, in the City-road, dressed in the uniform of the Hon. Artillery Company, and who was driven to the Bank. The articles lost are as follows:—a folding locket, with an inscription inside "Good Friday, 1860," a seal, gold key, locket with blue enamel on one side, and a gold dollar. Whoever has found the same, and will bring them to 336, City-road, Islington, shall be handsomely REWARDED.

FOUND, a BRINDLED CARRIAGE BITCH. If not owned it will be SOLD to pay expenses. Apply at 40, Elizabeth-street, S.W.

FOUND, on the 4th of February, 1860, in the Vestibule of the Conservative Club, St. James's-street, £15 in BANK of ENGLAND NOTES, which, if not claimed will be APPROPRIATED by the Committee. Application on the subject to be made to the Secretary. By order, E. C. HAMPTON, Sec., Feb. 11, 1861.

MR. DIPSAY or KOWASCH, from Marosvásárhely, in Sielenbürgen, who was employed as a clerk in a city house about three years back, or anyone who can give any information regarding the same, is requested to COMMUNICATE his ADDRESS by letter to A. B., Mr. R. Gravatt's, 11, King-street, Cheapside, as an important communication has to be made to him.

TO BANKERS, Brokers, &c.—Any banker, broker, or other person, who can give INFORMATION as to the PAPERS or PROPERTY of the late HUGH GIRVAN, surgeon on board H.M. ship Camilla, which went down recently on the coast of China, is anxiously requested to COMMUNICATE with Ivie H. Mackae, Esq., stockbroker, 10, Tokenhouse-yard, London, E.C.; or David Brown, Esq., solicitor, Maybole, Ayrshire.

TO CLERGYMEN and PARISH CLERKS.—TEN POUNDS REWARD will be given for DISCOVERY of the REGISTER of MARRIAGE of MARTHA HAWKINS with one STRONG, supposed between 1760 and 1780. Baptisms of their children also wanted. Send information to Messrs. Brittan and Son, No. 3, Mitre-court, Fleet-street, London.

BANK of ENGLAND.—Unclaimed Stock.—Application having been made to the Governors of the Bank of England to direct the re-transfer from the Commissioners for the Reduction of the National Debt of the sum of £31 13s. 10d. Reduced Three per Cent. Annuities, heretofore standing in the names of WILLIAM TAYLOR, of Church-street, Spitalfields, gentleman; THOMAS JOHNSON, of Crispin-street, Spitalfields, labourer; and WILLIAM JENNINGS, of Old Broad-street, gentleman, and which was transferred to the said Commissioners, in consequence of the dividends thereon not having been received since the 5th April, 1850; notice is hereby given that, on the expiration of three months from this date, the said Stock will be Transferred, and the Dividends thereon Paid, to William Jennings, the survivor, unless some other claimant shall sooner appear and make out the same, unless some other claimant shall sooner appear and make out his claim thereto.

LUNACY.—Conviction for Receiving an Uncertified Lunatic Patient.—At the Central Criminal Court, on the 29th of January, 1861, Dr. H. E. KELLY, of Pinner, was indicted, by direction of the Commissioners in Lunacy, for having, in violation of the 90th section of the 8th and 9th Victoria, cap. 100, re-

---

ROYAL SOCIETY of MUSICIANS.—The ANNIVERSARY FESTIVAL will take place on Thursday, March 14, at the Freemasons'-hall, on the usual extensive scale. President of the Day—The Hon. F. HENRY F. BERKELEY, M.P. Tickets one guinea each. STANLEY LUCAS, Sec., 210, Regent-street, W.

SACRED HARMONIC SOCIETY, Exeter-hall: Conductor, Mr. COSTA.—On Friday, February 22, will be repeated HAYDN's ORATORIO, the CREATION. Principal vocalists—Madame Lemmens-Sherrington, Mr. Sims Reeves, Mr. Montem Smith, and Mr. Weiss, with orchestra of nearly 700 performers. Tickets, 3s., 5s., and 10s. 6d. each, at the Society's office, No. 6, in Exeter-hall.

ST. JAMES'S-HALL.—NEW PHILHARMONIC CONCERTS: conductor, Dr. WYLDE.—The Tenth Season will commence on Monday evening, March 11, and comprise six grand evening performances, and five grand public rehearsals, on Saturday afternoons. On June 3, a grand performance of Mendelssohn's Antigone Music; the Poem recited by an eminent tragedian. Subscription tickets—Sofa stalls, £2 2s.; first row, balcony, 1½ guinea; second row, balcony, 1 guinea: all tickets are transferable. The celebrated orchestra of these concerts will perform Beethoven's Pastoral and Choral Symphonies, Spohr's "Power of Sound," Schubert's Symphony in C, Mozart's "Jupiter," and Mendelssohn's two Symphonies. The following artistes have been engaged at these concerts, many of whom, with others, will appear during the season:—Mesdames Louisa Pyne, Borghi-Mamo, Lemmens-Sherrington, C. Hayes, Castellan, Parepa, Anna Bishop, Rudersdorff, Sainton-Dolby, MM. Sims Reeves, Formes, Reichardt, Pischek, Belletti. Pianistes:—Madame A. Goddard, Schuman, Pleyel, Clauss, MM. C. Hallé, J. F. Barnett, Lubeck, Rubenstein. Violinists:—Joachim, Wienowski, Sivori, Ernst, Becker, Vieuxtemps. Subscribers' names received at Cramer and Co.'s, No. 201, Regent-street; Keith, Prowse, and Co.'s No. 48, Cheapside; Austin's ticket-office, St. James's-hall; and by the Hon. Sec., W. Graef Nicholls, Esq., 33, Argyll-street, W.

CRYSTAL PALACE.—THIS DAY.— ...at 10... Orchestra...
...Vil-...
5. I. Mow...Mr...
la B...
2. Owls...
3. W...
Balfe...te.
6. Tw...
D'vving
Festi... Pictur'rs
under...
P...fla...fee of...
March than fage
Addiso...
P...H...nd
fere
March 4...
Membery...
and 16th Hollier, ro...
H...fir-
day, 23d. of Rifle Cor...
A...ir-...of
and Mme...alone be...me
G...RA...to Brix...
fessor, Mr...aid
play, in p...
M...issic
brie...
Edinburgh...
Warrington...fic
ark Villas...
M...ENI...MON
sequence of on-
on Monday...
Ries, Carroc Vi-
may be secur...of
N...ATIO...
direction...rn
informed that...ide
rules of the...
on Ash Wedn...eas
the Messiah,...
repeated. An...to
spectacles at th...
F...ATHE...00
COMPAN...
with their new...rn
of 100 years go
TO-NIGHT, an...
ances, Wednes...
area, 2s.; galler...
P...OLYTEC...CAL ENTH,
BALLADS, eve...,
by splendid Dia...re
past 2. All the...he
The laboratory is op...
Institution is op...
on payment of 6d...la,
schools and familie...
on the most liberal...ty
M...R. CHASre...
the Monday...
evening next, Feb...of
op. 53, dedicated to
MM. Vieuxtemps,...ew
violin, viola, and vi...
Ottet and play Bacl...
5s.; balcony, 3s.;...u a
Bond-street; Cram...
Prowse, and Co., 48,...the
TO-NIGHT...rch
CERTS. St...

NOTICE to MARINERS.—WRECK in SEA REACH, River Thames.—Trinity-house, London, 8th February 1861.—Notice is hereby given, that a GREEN BUOY, marked with the word "Wreck," has been laid 10 fathoms to the northward of a vessel sunk off Yantlet.
The buoy lies in 4½ fathoms at low water spring tides, with the following mark and compass bearings, viz.:—
Pitsey Mill in line with a large Barn, open
  west of the Chapman Lighthouse .. .. .. N.N.W.
Yantlet Buoy .. .. S.S.E. ¾ E.
      (Distant ¾ cables' length)
By order, P. H. BERTHON, Sec.

STEAM to DUNKIRK, Lille, and Paris.—The SCREW STEAM SHIPPING COMPANY's VESSELS will leave Irongate-wharf, as under:—

From London.	From Dunkirk.
Thursday, Feb. 14, 3 morn.	Thursday, Feb. 14, 3 morn.
Sunday, Feb. 17, 4 morn.	Sunday, Feb. 7, 4 morn.

Fares to and from Dunkirk:—Saloon, 10s.; fore cabin, 7s. Lille:—Saloon and first-class rail, 13s.; saloon and second-class rail, 11s.; for cabin and third-class rail, 9s. Paris:—Saloon and first-class rail, 31s.; saloon and second-class rail, 23s.; fore cabin and third-class rail, 17s. 6d. Passengers booked by W. H. Carey and Son, 34, Mark-lane, or at the Universal-office, Regent-street.

BOMBAY direct, will shortly be despatched, the new Swedish clipper CARL XV., 3-3ds=A 1, E. G. OSTERBERG, Commander; in Victoria Docks. Apply to G. Higgin and Co., No. 30; or to Toulmin, Livingston, and Co., 31, Great St. Helen's, E.C.

BOMBAY direct, the first-class regular trader ALIPORE, 3-3ds, A 1, 811 tons register, ALFRED HELLYER, Commander; loading in the London Docks. Has very superior poop accommodation for passengers, and has just delivered her cargo from Bombay without...

...year...
...will...
...vess...
...sen...
...has Geo...

R...load...
this and Syd...ship Bro...

C...sail...
are ship Cair stro...
sligh pass...

D...to...
WA Son...
East acco...
airy diat...
freig Lin...

L...of f...
splen...
M. P. beer... of p...
tern...
Mes No...

S...for BOMBAY.—The ...will leave Gravesend in a few days... or eight cabin passengers. For freight... Osterberg, on board the vessel... Messrs. Uncuius and Paton, ...trad...desp...403... Thi...
For...

M...ons...
burg Messrs. Green's ship... prote...tons, Captain GEORGE... on the 1st of March, and fore Messrs. Grindlay and Co., velopa and Co. 72, Cornhill, E.C. bound and W. SMITH will... they... ing A 1 ships at the under-...nt accommodation for pas-...much... artic...
J...

...AM, Commander; to sail March 14. squar... Parliament-street, S.W.; or per tog...
J...sail... of c...
ing 2 despatch, the clipper... costi...ons register, G. O. LANE, width... Apply to Toulmin, Living-...
P...spa...1860 Feb...

A Ma... for G gist T... For the...
handi... clipper CLYDE, this... loading in the East India convey... freight or passage apply to shoul...d-street.
cent.
—The British-built and A pri...100 tons, loading in the... ons passengers and light pay a...et, E.C. A 113 years, will follow.

same, fast-sailing, well-... is the...rs, 910 tons register, J. Jour...n the East India Docks. by th...rs, and carries an ex-... in pr... Railway and Co., 55, Par-... from Royal Exchange-build-...
J...
time as a large portion regar...despatched), the Liver-...530 tons register, seced... Katharine's Docks. "sen...in, Livingston, and
Holla S' LINE of their UR, A 19 years, 458 State...s. Apply to David for the foreig...t, passengers, than class VESSELS will "will" Feb. 25.
Mar 15.
S D sple... SMI two seco... Low No... from tot...

oppor...Smith's fine men...646 tons register, tion use Dock, Liver-... that for passengers, and the...change-buildings, the la...
after... first-class ship PARSONS, Com-... store...of her cargo from... ched... full poop, under oug...y to W. S.

CHAPTER 6
The Call of the Good Earth

When Louisiana seceded from the Union on January 26, 1861, the state became for two months an independent nation with its own flag, army, and government. Louisiana joined the Confederacy on March 21, almost exactly three months after Pierre Cenac stepped off the ship in New Orleans. It was the sixth state to secede and subsequently join the Confederacy.

When Confederate and Union sides began saber rattling, Pierre already had good reason to consider leaving the city proper. New Orleans' status as the Confederacy's largest port and, indeed, its largest city, made it a prime target for Union attack. Pierre's departure from New Orleans was no doubt heavily influenced by assumption of this eventuality, and was probably timed soon after his arrival in the city.

Why did Pierre choose New Orleans in the first place?

One practical reason that French émigrés chose Louisiana, especially south Louisiana, was that of language. This may seem contradictory, because Louisiana's early eighteenth century French immigrants came from a country of "highly distinctive subregions whose linguistic, cultural, legal, and social conditions were often incompatible. Parisians...did not speak the same language as natives of Languedoc or Provence, and Bretons typically could not communicate with these groups. Nor could the French Basques, German-speaking Alsatians and Lorrainers....In the isolation of Louisiana, however, French frontiersmen needed effective communication skills to survive,"[1] and a synthesis ensued in which the language that originated in Paris' Île-de-France region became what was called "colonial French" in Louisiana—but "is, in fact, standard French."[1]

French-associated immigrants following the colonial period introduced even more dialects. As a result, a linguistic process took place in Louisiana in which "a *pidgin*, a greatly simplified, hybrid version of the dominant language, intermingled with words and phrases from the other, subordinate tongue. A pidgin enables each group to communicate with the other while continuing to use its own speech."[1]

Some form of French, then, was spoken by many Creole and other residents of New Orleans during the mid-nineteenth century. Additionally, the ancient dialects of Basques and French Acadians thrived throughout all south Louisiana, so that

TEN FLAGS

HAVE FLOWN OVER LOUISIANA

1542 - *Spanish flag flown by explorer Hernando de Soto*

1763 - *British flag flown over territory east of the Mississippi and north of New Orleans when Spain ceded territory to Great Britain*

1682 - *French flag flown by explorer Sieur de La Salle, who named Louisiana for his king, Louis XIV*

1769 - *Spanish Governor Alejandro O'Reilly established 12 administrative districts called posts and 22 ecclesiastical parishes. The system of posts died with the end of Spanish rule, but parishes ultimately persisted as the primary county-level administrative unit under territorial and state governments.*

1800 - *Flag of Louisiana when Spain returned Louisiana west of the Mississippi to France*

1861 - *Flag of Louisiana as an independent nation after the state's secession from the Union for two months*

1803 - *U.S. flag's use followed the Louisiana Purchase of 1803*

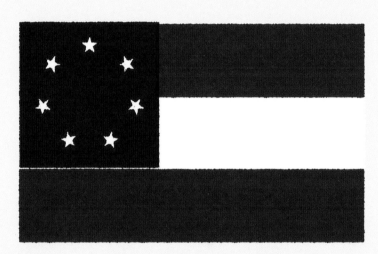

1861 - *Confederate States of America flag flown after Louisiana joined the Confederacy*

1810 - *Flag of the Florida Parishes after Americans took control of the area away from Spain*

1912 - *Official Louisiana state flag adopted by the state legislature in 1912, still in use today*

new French arrivals need only plug their own dialects into the linguistic processes at work in order to overcome communication difficulties. Some newspapers of the day even published in both English and French, side by side, well into the twentieth century.

Another reason immigrants from the same area clustered together was the "network of relations woven abroad between members of neighboring villages."[2]

This would explain Pierre's eventual destination. Just more than halfway to Lourdes from Barbazan-Debat was the town of Benac (1861 population 806), which is a little past five miles southwest of Pierre's birthplace. Benac would have been easily accessible on foot, since people of Pierre's time did not shy away from walking considerable distances. The fact that Pierre could have known at least one former Benac resident in a small southeast Louisiana town becomes important in considering possible inducements for his choice of relocation from New Orleans.

Top, clipping from a Thibodaux Minerva of 1855; articles in French and English. Above, "Excited Populace of New Orleans" sketch in Harper's Weekly at the time of Louisiana's secession from the Union

Top, clipping from a Thibodaux Minerva *of 1855; articles in French and English. Above, "Excited Populace of New Orleans" sketch in* Harper's Weekly *at the time of Louisiana's secession from the Union*

Numerous conditions in the city of 1861 could have prompted a young, independent man such as Pierre to seek a home elsewhere. New Orleans crime was no doubt repellant to immigrants who had left their own countries with high hopes for this new land. Although Irish and German immigrants had systems in place to help their immigrant countrymen in the city, other nationalities were not as organized. The newcomer from most other countries, left to negotiate on his own in New Orleans—whether he intended the city as a way station or as permanent destination—might find himself the hapless victim of petty thieves, con men and ruffians who frequented the port's levees and city streets in anticipation of the naïve or the weak. A professional criminal class of foreign and U.S. eastern origin arrived annually during winter months, and they were "sustained by a sizeable homegrown product as well."[3]

In addition to expatriate-network and crime explanations, yet another possible reason for Pierre's departure from New Orleans is that he was escaping diseases which were more quickly spread in populous areas than in towns and country settings having smaller populations.

An astounding 41,000 New Orleanians died from *fièvre jaune* (yellow fever) epidemics between 1817 and 1905.[4] Contributing factors to these New Orleans outbreaks were undoubtedly its many unsanitary conditions, lack of clean drinking water, and the nearby soggy breeding grounds for the yellow fever mosquito.

Besides yellow fever, other epidemics of influenza, (especially deadly in a worldwide outbreak 1857-59), smallpox, cholera, malaria, typhoid and dysentery produced huge mortality rates, both localized and sometimes nationwide. *The Daily Delta* newspaper of December 26, 1860, reported 150 deaths (from a variety of causes) in the city the very week before Pierre Cenac disembarked there.

Regardless of the city's cosmopolitan attractions, its vulnerability to attack, disease, and crime were probably a significant cause of driving away Pierre and many like him who had been reared in a slow-paced, fresh-air country village.

At some point, probably following Louisiana's joining the Confederacy in 1861, Pierre set his course for Terrebonne Parish southwest of New Orleans.

A logical explanation for this choice is that he knew of French families from his same region (but not his same village) who already lived in Terrebonne Parish. Some names of émigrés who either had their origins in the south of France near the Pyrenees, or who left from Bordeaux, are Abadie, Benoit, Bourgeois,

Clippings from the Thibodaux Minerva *newspaper, all from 1855*

Algiers Station of the New Orleans, Opelousas & Great Western Railroad, c. 1855-1860

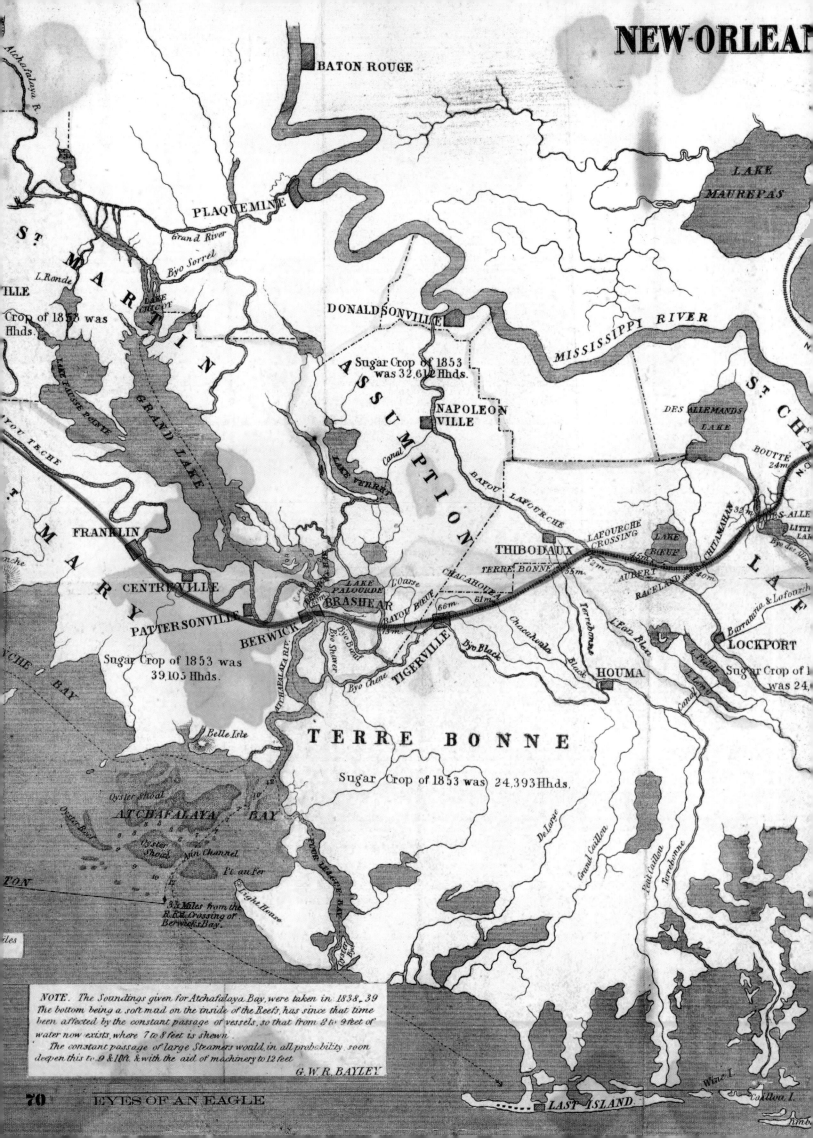

NEW-ORLEA

BATON ROUGE

Atchafalaya R.

PLAQUEMINE

Grand River

Byo Sorrel

ST. MARTIN

L. Ronde

Crop of 1853 was
Hhds.

DONALDSONVILLE

ASSUMPTION

Sugar Crop of 1853
was 32,612 Hhds.

NAPOLEON
VILLE

MISSISSIPPI RIVER

LAKE
MAUREPAS

ST.

DES ALLEMANDS
LAKE

BOUTTE
24m.

ST. CHA

Canal

LAKE VERRET

BAYOU LAFOURCHE

GRAND LAKE

LAKE
CHICOT

BAYOU TECHE

LAKE FAUSSE POINTE

FRANKLIN

ST. MARY

CENTREVILLE

PATTERSONVILLE

Sugar Crop of 1853 was
39,105 Hhds.

BERWICK

BRASHEAR

LAKE
PALOURDE

L'Oarse

BAYOU BOEUF

CHACAHOULA

THIBODAUX

TERRE BONNE

52m.

55m.

LAFOURCHE
CROSSING

45m.

AUBERT

RACELAND

40m.

CHITAMAHAN 32m.

LAKE
FIELDS

DES-ALLE

LITTLE
LAKE

Byo Des

Barrataria & Lofourch

61m.

66m.

Byo Beuf

Byo Shaver

13m.

Byo Chene

TIGERVILLE

Byo Black

Chacahoula

Black

Terrebonne

L'Pan Bleu

LOCKPORT

Sugar Crop of 1
was 24,

HOUMA

Canal

Belle Isle

TERRE BONNE

Sugar Crop of 1853 was 24,393 Hhds.

De Large

Grand Caillou

Petit Caillou

Terrebonne

Oyster Shoal

Oyster Bed

ATCHAFALAYA BAY

Oyster
Shoal

Min Channel

Pt. au Fer

PUNT LEAGUE BAY

Light House

12
10

8 7 8 9

9

10

8

3½ Miles from the
R.R. Crossing of
Berwick's Bay.

Oyster
Bed

LAST ISLAND.

Wine I.

Caillou I.

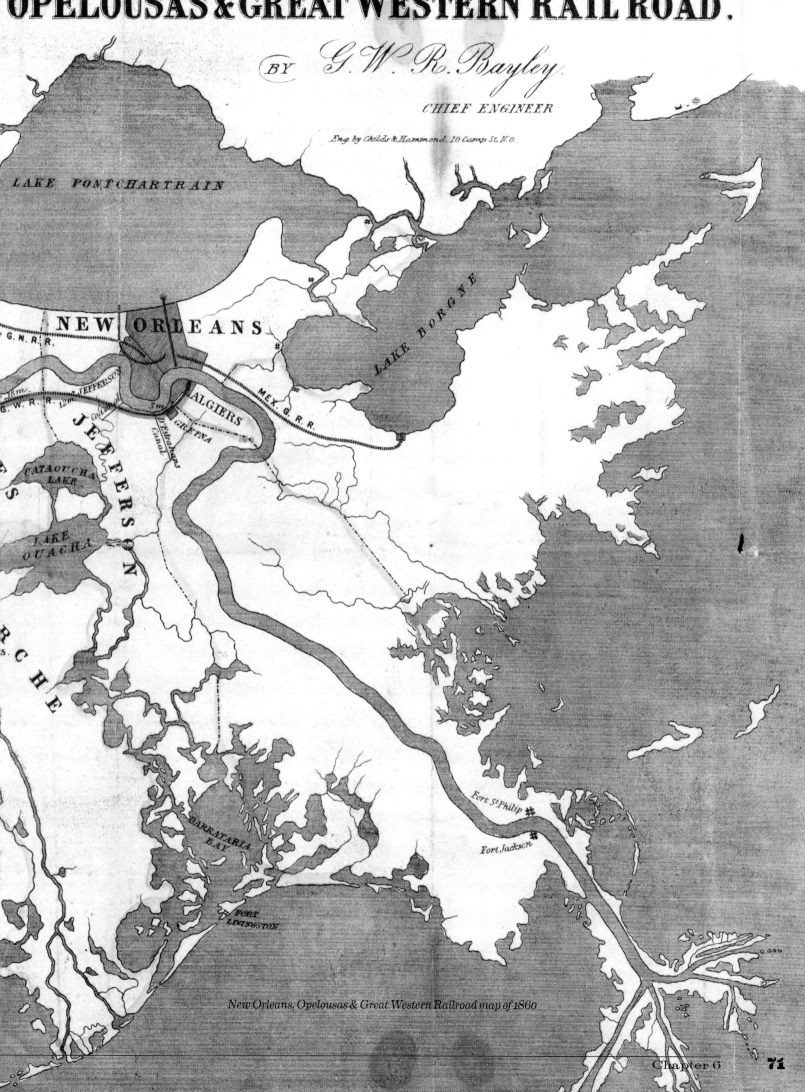

OPELOUSAS & GREAT WESTERN RAIL ROAD.

BY *G. W. R. Bayley.*

CHIEF ENGINEER

Eng. by Childs & Hammond, 10 Camp St. N.O.

New Orleans, Opelousas & Great Western Railroad map of 1860

*Opelousas Railroad Ferry, Jackson Square,
New Orleans, c. 1860, image by E.H. Newton*

From the Houma Ceres *edition
of December 25, 1858*

*Jean Pierre Viguerie (left), and Francois
Viguerie*

Carrere, Champagne, Dupont, Fournier, Labat, Marmande, Martin, Prevost, Richard, St. Martin.[5] Others arrived in different "waves" of French immigration. Some of them are the Menvilles from Encausse, the Anés from Maitres, the Bazets from Lassere, the Silvestres, Burguiereses, and Buquets from Paris, the Voisins from Libourne, the Pierrons and Richauds from Bordeaux, the Delcourt family from Belgium, and the Daspit, Angers, de la Bretonne, and Bonvillain families. Bourg forebears have lived in America since 1785 when three brothers emigrated from Alsace-Lorraine aboard the ship *La Ville d'Arcangel*. Many of these French expatriate families, designated as "the Foreign French" (*les Français étrangers*), became residents of Terrebonne Parish and naturalized citizens. Some of their descendants continue to reside in the area where many of Pierre's descendants remain.

Evidence of the homeland relational "network" is that Pierre Cenac's first job in Terrebonne Parish's governmental seat, Houma, was working with Jean-Marie Dupont in his bakery. Jean-Marie Dupont was also a French Pyrenean, specifically from the village of Benac. Therefore, the two men could easily have known each other in France. (This is given further credence by the fact that years later, Dupont was named godfather to Pierre's second son, Albert.) Jean-Marie's arrival in Terrebonne predated Pierre's by four years. Other Terrebonne Parish Frenchmen (from Heches, Canton de la Barthe, in the *Hautes*-Pyrénées) were Francois and Jean Pierre Viguerie, who arrived in New Orleans on August 15, 1849, aboard the ship *Victoria* from Bordeaux. The brothers subsequently settled in Terrebonne, eventually becoming substantial land and business owners.

When he decided to leave the Crescent City, Pierre could have reached Terrebonne Parish either by rail or by boat.

The most likely of his means of travel was by railroad. The New Orleans, Opelousas, and Great Western Railroad service had first reached northwestern Terrebonne Parish in 1855 at Terrebonne Station, current-day Schriever. It is probable that Pierre first placed foot on Terrebonne Parish soil from the step of a train there. If this was the case, he first bought a ferry ticket at the New Orleans railroad office, located opposite Jackson Square at the corner of St. Peter and Old Levee streets. Cost at the time was ten cents to cross the Mississippi River from the Crescent City to Algiers Station, where passengers boarded the train. An ad for the railroad in the *Houma Ceres* newspaper in December 1858 read in part, "The Ferry Boat, connecting with the Passenger Trains, will leave the landing, opposite Jackson Square, at 7½ o'clock, A.M." One Algiers history documented that in 1856, trains traveled to Tigerville (Gibson) daily, a distance of 66 miles. The train left the Algiers depot every day at 8:30 a.m., and arrived at Tigerville at 12:10 p.m. Fare each way was $2.50.[6]

If the railroad was indeed his choice, Pierre would have seen from the window of the train "... Bayou des Allemands, and a land filled with small still pools of deep black water"; "reed-grown and water-saturated expanse of the 'Trembling Prairie,' [*prairie tremblant*, or floating marsh] dotted with live oaks and stretches of cypress timber"; "Raceland, with its moist black fields and wide-extended sugar and rice plantations"; "LaFourche Bayou, on which lies the pretty, Frenchy, cultured town of Thibodaux" and Terrebonne Station before the train reached the "Indian mounds" of "Tigerville," now Gibson.[7]

He would have completed his journey by stagecoach or another horse-drawn express vehicle, since it was not until January 1872 that Houma was totally connected to New Orleans by rail with completion of the Houma Branch Railroad from Terrebonne Station.

Three express businesses that operated at that time were Houma's Price Hine & Co. and John Berger, and Thibodaux's Holden. The Berger line charged one dollar per individual for the trip from Terrebonne Station in Schriever to Houma. Whatever line Pierre chose, the conveyance would have taken him southeast from Thibodauxville along the Terrebonne Road following Bayou Terrebonne to the intersection of Main Street with Barataria Canal at Houma's western boundary. If he traveled during the rainy season, this more direct land route's dirt roads would have been impassable.

Other than the railroad, the other alternative for travel was by water—inland or by sea. If he chose the inland route, he would have used the services of the New Orleans and Lafourche Transportation Company's fast steam-powered passenger packets

Steamboat Lafourche *at Labadieville c. 1890, with St. Philomena Catholic Church in the background. Inset, freight bill for the* Lafourche *dated 1892*

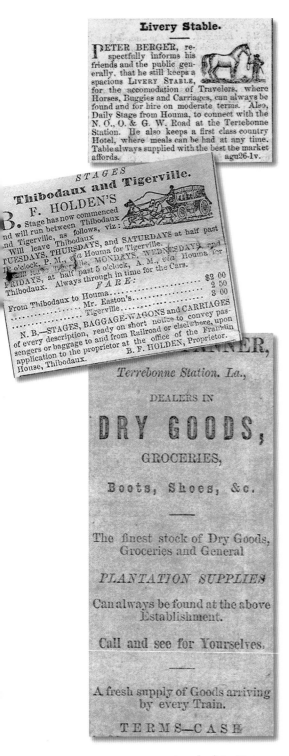

Music or *Lafourche*, or the Bayou Sara Mail Line Company's boats *Acadia* or *W.A. Andrew*. Using this means of transportation, Pierre would first have traveled the Mississippi River to Donaldsonville. On this route, Pierre would have glimpsed from the boat's deck the "castles along the river": San Francisco, Tezcuco, Ormond, Oak Alley, Houmas, Destrehan, and Laura plantation homes. The second leg of his journey beyond Donaldsonville would have taken him on to Thibodauxville via Bayou Lafourche, ending at Lockport.

If he disembarked at Thibodauxville, and continued to Houma by boat on Bayou Terrebonne (the original connecting waterway system to Houma) it could only have been done in high water situations, typically during spring and summer. On the other hand, if he traveled on to Lockport, he could have then boarded a smaller paddlewheel vessel and traveled through the Company Canal to Bayou Terrebonne to Houma.

A second potential inland water route available to Pierre was through a system of connecting waterways. If he used this method, Pierre would have left New Orleans by ferry to reach Westwego in order to begin a journey which followed the route of the Barataria and Lafourche Canal, *La Canal de la Companie*, now known as the Company Canal.[8] This project followed natural waterways as much as possible, with canals dug in areas where no interconnecting navigable waters naturally existed to facilitate boat travel from the New Orleans area to Terrebonne and Lafourche.

On this course, he would have traveled Bayou Segnette to Lake Salvador. Once across the lake, the boat would have navigated the Company Canal to reach Bayou Lafourche at Lockport. Through the locks there, the canal would have taken Pierre through Lake Fields and to Bayou Terrebonne at Canal Belanger, present-day Bourg. From Bourg, the final leg of his journey would have been northerly via Bayou Terrebonne, with Pierre's ultimate disembarkation in Houma from the vessel that had traveled up the small town's water main street.

Along this route, he would have encountered for the first time several sights unique to bayou lands. If he made the trip during wintertime, he would have seen lakes blanketed with *poules d'eau* and an abundance of other migratory duck, geese, whooping and sandhill cranes. Pierre would have spotted resident semi-tropical birds such as egrets and herons, as well as perhaps a glimpse of deer which were then abundant along the waterways' banks.

Alligators, muskrats and other swampy-land wildlife would have appeared along this water route as well during spring or summer.

Records show that vessels unloaded cargo at various docks along Houma's water main street (Bayou Terrebonne), including the old City Market founded in 1857 on the northwest corner of Main and Goode streets, across from the Courthouse Square. Smaller boats turned around at a cove excavated on the Main Street side of the bayou next to the Old Market. Steamboats and larger boats had to turn around at the junction of the Barataria Canal and Bayou Terrebonne, or back down Bayou Terrebonne. Barataria Canal, which had been dug in 1840 to connect Bayou Terrebonne with Bayou Black, was filled in during the 1930s and is now the narrow strip of land between Barataria and Canal streets.

The Barataria Canal-Main Street location in Houma was also the place of embarkation/debarkation of the express lines. So whether Pierre's journey was over land or through the interconnecting waterways between New Orleans and Terrebonne, he would have stepped into Houma at roughly the same area along the western edge of the small town.

Pierre's only other alternative to reach Terrebonne would have been by water via the Mississippi to the Gulf of Mexico, and through the mouth of one of Terrebonne's bayous. The most likely bayou would have been Bayou Grand Caillou, which had the deepest access to the sea. The Dulac community, situated at the confluence of Bayou Grand Caillou and Bayou Dulac, and also located north of bayous Grassy and Salé, was at the time one of the largest communities in the civil parish. Records show that Dulac was actually larger in population than was Houma when Pierre Cenac arrived.

Pierre's timing was perfect if he left the Crescent City in 1861. By May 26 that year, the Union steam war sloop *Brooklyn* anchored off Pass à L'Outre. Captain Charles Poor sent a dispatch to inform the Confederate commander of Fort Jackson, Major John Duncan, that New Orleans was blockaded from the sea. "Though it would be another year before the Bluecoats landed in the city...[New Orleans'] very *raison d'être* was terminated."[3]

Locks on the Company Canal at Lockport, Louisiana

Canal Belanger. The community of Canal Belanger, founded as Newport in the early 1800s, is present-day Bourg

NOTES

1. Dr. Carl A. Brasseaux. *French, Cajun, Creole, Houma: A Primer on Francophone Louisiana*, Louisiana State University Press, 2005

2. Jeanette Legendre

3. Robert Reinders

4. George Augustin. *History of Yellow Fever*, published 1909

5. Dr. Carl A. Brasseaux. *The Foreign French, Nineteenth-Century French Immigration into Louisiana*, *Volume III*, Center for Louisiana Studies, University of Southwestern Louisiana, 1993

6. William H. Seymour, *The Story of Algiers 1718-1896*, Algiers Democrat Publishing Co., Ltd., 1896

7. Edward King

8. Thomas A. Becnel, Ph.D., *The Barrow Family and the Barataria and Lafourche Canal: The Transportation Revolution in Louisiana, 1829-1925*, Louisiana State University Press, 1989

St. Bridgitte, home of Henry Schuyler Thibodaux, by Adrien Persac 1861; at approximate current site of St. Bridget Catholic Church, Schriever

CHAPTER 7
1862: First Encounter

Jacques Benoit and several other young men stood in a conversational huddle on the wooden *banquette* outside, on the corner of Main and Barrow. Jacques caught sight of Pierre using his wooden paddle to remove golden mounds of bread from the open-air oven behind Jean-Marie Dupont's bakery shop.

Pierre wiped the sweat from his forehead with his handkerchief, smiled, and called out to Jacques and the others, "War talk again, or *les femmes*?" They all chuckled because those two topics had indeed been the subjects of their short talk. Soon they had to rush off to their own jobs in the stores and markets along Main Street.

It had not even been a month since news came of New Orleans being occupied by Union forces. Soon after that, Baton Rouge and other places Pierre had started to learn about began to fall to federal troops. For months the war had been the focus of town talk, but Pierre was relieved not to hear of any major threat to Houma and Terrebonne...so far.

Later, after the early morning rush, Pierre stood beside the front door of the shop and looked up the street beyond the Courthouse Square. He could just see the point where he had first stepped foot in Houma, where the Bergers' express line ended at Barataria Canal. His eyes swept in both directions of Main Street, as far as he could see.

I thought Barbazan was small, but this place is even smaller. That suits me fine, after the still air and tight buildings in New Orleans. After all, it's what surrounds Houma that I'm interested in. All that beautiful black soil, a lot of it unclaimed. The flat land has taken some getting used to, but I even like it flat now. Easy to cultivate. No stones to clear, no rocks. Just trees and land. And beaucoup de l'eau. I've never seen so much rain, and I've never seen so many waterways. Perfect for transportation and irrigation.

An outdoor mud oven c. 1890

Portrait of Henry S. Thibodaux, onetime state senator (1812-1824) and Governor of Louisiana from November 15 to December 13, 1824

Pierre thought back to last year's final leg of his journey, and the very first local plantations he saw from the window of the express carriage. Fields stretching far into the distance, sugar cane thick and tall and green.

The first plantations that Pierre caught sight of from the express conveyance to Houma were St. Brigitte's and Balzamine near Schriever. Both fronted on Bayou Terrebonne not far from Terrebonne Station.

A chatty lady who was a fellow passenger on that trip asked him many questions about himself, and he was glad she spoke French. After he answered her questions about his home in France and a dozen other things, she must have decided Pierre needed education about the local area, because she talked to him the rest of the way to Houma.

"Young man, let me tell you about the grand homes we're about to see." She pointed out to Pierre that St. Brigitte's had been the home of Henry Schuyler Thibodaux, onetime acting governor of Louisiana for whom Thibodauxville was named. He was already called the Father of Terrebonne Parish, and had established his home within Terrebonne's northern boundaries. Balzamine, across Bayou Terrebonne, was owned by Henry Schuyler's son Bannon Goforth Thibodaux.

"Isn't it just beautiful the way they keep the grounds, and how brilliant the two houses' white paint shines in the sun?" his self-designated teacher had fluttered. She leaned a little out the window until the houses were behind them.

She whispered conspiratorially, "I've heard that the young *Monsieur* Thibodaux even commissioned the artist Persac to paint the two homes and grounds." Whoever this Persac was, Pierre decided, he must be an important man. And this Thibodaux, even more important to hire the artist. *One of these days, maybe....*

Northern Terrebonne's well-tended, bountiful fields were as appealing to Pierre now as they had been when he first set eyes on them. *I wonder if Barbazan and all the Hautes-Pyrénées ever made it past the crop failures and the vineyards' blight. It was so hard to watch everything dying, and families trying to get by on the little they could grow to feed themselves.* Pierre wondered for the hundredth time if his brothers and sister thought about him as much as he thought about them. *Maybe one day I'll be surprised by a letter from home. It would be good to know if Dominique and Jean settled back into civilian life. Or if I have more nieces and nephews in Barbazan by now. I may never know.*

He turned back into the bakery, but not before he caught sight of *Monsieur* Charles Fanguy from Grand Caillou heading up the street with a young lady on his arm. He had met the man only once before, on one of his infrequent visits to town. They were clearly headed this way, so once inside, Pierre smoothed his hair and mustache, and straightened his collar just in time for him to take his place behind the counter and see them enter the door. Jean-Marie Dupont joined him at the counter. *"Comment ça va, Monsieur Fanguy? Comment ça va, Mlle. Victorine?"* As Jean-

Marie introduced father and daughter to Pierre, he bowed his head in his best gentlemanly manner. *Monsieur* Fanguy's own head nod kept the father from spying his daughter's furtive second glance at Pierre through dark eyelashes from properly downcast eyes. Her acknowledgement of the introduction, *"Bonjour, Monsieur Cenac,"* was correctly sedate.

"Ah, Victorine. *Un joli nom pour une jolie fille,"* he thought as Jean-Marie placed into a money pouch the four *sous* M. Fanguy had paid him for the two *baguettes* they bought.

Pierre brushed from the counter the crumbs that had fallen from the *baguettes,* but he looked up just in time to catch Victorine's glance in his direction as she stepped out the door. Her clear blue eyes were made all the more vivid by her hair's nearly black fringe. Pierre watched her tall frame and straight shoulders walk away until another customer came through the door.

Balzamine, home of Bannon Goforth Thibodaux by Adrien Persac 1857; across Bayou Terrebonne from St. Bridgitte

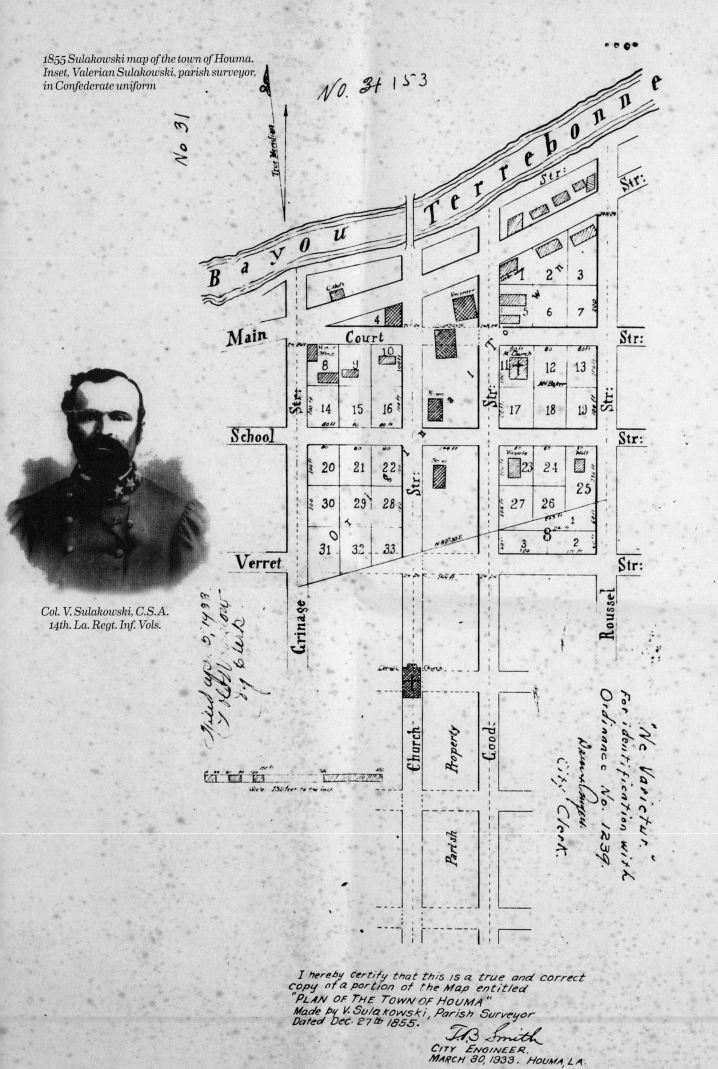

1855 Sulakowski map of the town of Houma.
Inset, Valerian Sulakowski, parish surveyor,
in Confederate uniform

Col. V. Sulakowski, C.S.A.
14th. La. Regt. Inf. Vols.

I hereby certify that this is a true and correct
copy of a portion of the Map entitled
"PLAN OF THE TOWN OF HOUMA"
Made by V. Sulakowski, Parish Surveyor
Dated Dec. 27th 1855.

F. B. Smith
CITY ENGINEER.
MARCH 30, 1933. HOUMA, LA.

CHAPTER 8
A Lush Paradise

Pierre Cenac's Terrebonne Parish consisted of a lush combination of vast cultivated lands, thick stands of timber, and undeveloped wilderness. Louisiana's bayou country was not an "Eden...as Longfellow and his successors have claimed, but a dense and forbidding semi-tropical jungle."[1] One directory of the late 1800s described Terrebonne's topography:

"Less than one eighteenth of the parish [approximately 1,808 square miles total] is high land; the balance is marshes, swamps, low prairies, bayous and lakes.

"The cultivable land is composed of the ridges along the banks of the different bayous, rich alluvial soil that is highly productive and easily cultivated. The principal bayous are the Terrebonne, Little Caillou, Grand Caillou, Black, Dularge and Blue. The space between the ridges of the different bayous is mostly swamps of cypress timber. Numerous lakes, bays and islands form part of the parish, and its southern limits are washed by the waters of the Gulf of Mexico."[2]

Many early-comers to Terrebonne in the late 1700s and very early 1800s had obtained Spanish land grants, most of not more than 640 acres, some being granted as early as 1787.[3] Among names recorded as receiving such grants were Edmund Fanguy, Joseph Hache (Achee), and Etienne Billiot. The Billiot land relatively soon (1824) was sold to J.B. Duplantis, and later to Euphrosin Hotard.

Early crops in southeast Louisiana included indigo, rice, and cotton. By the 1860s, sugar cane reigned supreme in the more southerly/coastal parishes of Louisiana, as opposed to King Cotton in Louisiana's central and northern regions, as well as in most of the Southern states. The swaying green landscape which Pierre evidenced was broken by crops of farmlands and animals of pasture lands, and by forested areas, as well as houses where one cluster of a sometimes-grand planter's home and workers' (often slave) dwellings lay at some distance from the next cluster.

The Civic Guard newspaper printed an account in June 1866 that gives a detailed description of Bayou Black plantations, a landscape representative of what Pierre would have seen upon first arriving in Terrebonne Parish:

Woodlawn slave cabins, Terrebonne c. 1870

Revered artist John James (Jean Jacques) Audubon was already famous for his expansive Birds of America *volume when he chartered a boat and sailed along the coast of Terrebonne Parish in 1837. He collected 104 different bird species on Caillou Island and 125 species on Isles Dernieres.*

THE CIVIC GUARD.

OFFICIAL JOURNAL OF THE PARISH OF TERREBONNE.

| VOL. III. | HOUMA, TERREBONNE, LA., SATURDAY, NOVEMBER 25, 1865. | NO. 15. |

*Above, horse-powered sugar cane mill c. 1860.
Below, sugar boiling kettles at Winter Quarters,
Terrebonne Parish, 2011. Bottom, an ad in the
Louisiana Coast Directory of 1857*

"In former times, the plantations on this bayou produced great crops of sugar. In the winter of '60 and '61, we remember the whole crop of this parish was estimated at some 16,000 hhds [*sugar hogsheads:* barrels or casks that each contained an average of 1,000 pounds], 8,000 of which were produced on bayou Black alone. The planters, overseers and slaves all vieing with each other, in a laudable desire to excel, not only in making large crops, but also in improvements and in opening and clearing up new lands. The sugar houses on the large plantations cost from $50,000 to $100,000 and when viewed at a distance, in connection with the great numbers of other buildings near them, resembled towns and villages. The buildings were almost always kept whitewashed and had a pleasing effect. The fences and bridges were generally kept in excellent repair and all the ditches nicely cleaned out. In fact, the reputation of a manager depended much on these things...."

As a matter of record, more than 1,200 plantations were producing Louisiana's sugar crop in the year 1861. Terrebonne Parish was home to numbers of sugar cane plantations and was a substantive sugar producer at the time Pierre arrived.

Planters by the 1850s were beneficiaries of two earlier important leaps in the industry. In 1795 Etienne de Boré initially developed the process for granulation. Fifty years later, Norbert Rillieux, son of a white planter/engineer and a freed slave, invented the multiple effect vacuum evaporation technique that replaced the open kettle process. Rillieux was a graduate of the École Centrale in Paris. When Pierre arrived, most Terrebonne parish planters used their own individual sugar houses and mills, some using the older and some the latest processes.

A list of sugar planters along each bayou area, along with production statistics, indicate the capacity of Terrebonne's growers. Most of the years' lists (beginning with 1844 and ending with the 1860-61 season) are segmented into planters along Bayou Terrebonne, Petit Caillou, Grand Caillou, Bayou Black, Bayou Dularge, and Bayou Chacahoula.[4]

As early as 1844-45, Terrebonne Parish was home to 42 sugar houses producing 12,661 hogsheads of sugar. By 1851, Terrebonne had a total of 110 plantations with 80 sugar houses. They produced annually from 12,000 to 13,000 hogsheads of sugar and approximately 20,000 barrels of molasses.[5] For the year 1858-1859, Terrebonne had 81 sugar houses, 62 with steam power and 19 powered by horse, with a total production of 22,815 hogsheads of sugar. Seventy-six planters or partnerships/farms produced that total. For 1860-1861, instead of all planters being listed, only the leading planters were included by the source for all years. Terrebonne's totals for 1860-1861 were reported as 87 sugar houses, 66 run by steam power and 21 by horse power, with a total production of 16,220 hogsheads. Only 18 "leading planters" appeared on that year's list.[6]

Population figures over the decades are important to understand that the place Pierre Cenac made his home,

although agriculturally progressive by the mid-1850s, was nevertheless just emerging from a relatively recent status as frontier land. The earliest inventory of population within the approximate boundaries of the territory which would become Terrebonne Parish was a census conducted in 1785, indicating that only 353 lived in what became known as the Lafourche Interior. Terrebonne was carved out of the *lower* Lafourche Interior (which formed Lafourche and Terrebonne civil parishes) in 1822. According to an annotation of the census of Terrebonne Parish in 1840, the entire parish in that year consisted of only 367 households.[7]

By 1848 the first pastor of St. Francis de Sales Church (parish established 1847, first church completed 1848), the Rev. Z. Leveque, documented that the number of houses in the parish seat of Houma was only 40. In 1850, only a dozen or more buildings were grouped in the "business district" east and west of the Court Square.[8] In marked contrast to the port city of New Orleans (with an 1860 population of 168,675), Houma was a village of only 429 people, according to census records for that same year.

Pierre was part of an increase of about 160 people in the decade of his arrival. By 1870 Houma's population had grown to 593.

A few other Terrebonne Parish communities grew principally at the confluences of bayous or along navigable waterways. In fact, at the time of the establishment of Terrebonne Parish, other communities (Schriever and Dulac) situated along bayou extremities rivaled the population of what was to become the parish seat. Terrebonne Parish Police Jury Proceedings record that a place in northwestern Terrebonne called Williamsburg,

Photograph of downtown Houma taken 1866, believed to be the earliest extant photo of the town

Poling a small boat on Bayou Terrebonne c. 1870

St. Francis de Sales Catholic Church, est. 1848, antebellum photo

Features of the Hache grant c. 1823;
note town of Houma location at center

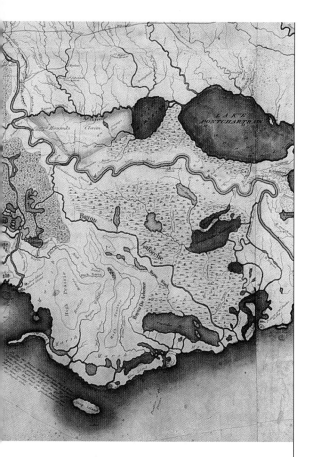

The Ludlow Map c. 1817 showing "Bayou de Arbonne"

Marie Seraphine Thibodeaux Theriot and Michel Eloi Theriot

Live Oak sugar mill, Dulac, c. 1906

now known only as Bayou Cane, served temporarily as a police jury meeting place at the home of Alexandre Dupre after Terrebonne became a separate parish. In 1825 a jail was authorized to be built there after William S. Watkins divided out lots in the area, the first attempt in the parish to form a town. When Watkins died after but few lots had been sold, the town faded away. The location for the jail was rejected by the Police Jury in 1831 before a courthouse and jail were to be constructed.

Houma had become the location of the parish seat years before Pierre Cenac arrived, following its incorporation in 1834, four years before Pierre's birth in France. Hubert M. Belanger and Richard H. Grinage donated land in Houma, from property known as the Haché grant, for the parish government's center that year. This original donation consisted of an arpent front on Bayou Terrebonne (one arpent equals 191.8 linear feet), by a depth of ten arpents on the right descending bank of Bayou Terrebonne. This location was a logistical practicality by virtue of the small town's location more or less at the hub of five bayous that spread like fingers southward, and one east-west bayou, the Black.

The parish seat received its name from a suggestion by the wife of Terrebonne planter Tobias Gibson, who urged that the community in this way commemorate the Houmas Indian tribe which had settled in the area sometime in the 1700s.

Terrebonne Parish's name has been variously attributed to its literal French translation as "Good Earth" or "Good Land," or to the parish's possibly taking its name from that of a family named Derbonne (alternately D'Arbonne or Darbonne), settlers in the area possibly as early as the late 1700s. That family is documented as having located in the coastal area, perhaps having made their arrival by sea. Another possible explanation for the parish's name could be that the head of a Dupré family was called by the *dit nom* Terrebonne. The Dupré family received a land grant in the area in the year 1795; this may have been among the first Spanish land grants within the confines of the current parish. In consideration of variations in spelling proper names in documents at the time, there remains the possibility that the above families could have been one and the same.

The present Bayou Terrebonne is designated on the Darby map of 1816 and the Ludlow map of 1817 as "Bayou De Arbonne." One of the first maps that give the waterway its current name is that of 1833, which details the meanderings of Bayou Terrebonne, as well as designating bayous Grand Caillou and Little Caillou, respectively, as "Grand Chio" and "Petit Chio." The Acadian French word *caillou* means *gravel* or *pebble*. However, Basque scholar Michel Nicolas held in a 2010 interview that the word *caillou* derives from the Spanish *caillo* and/or the French *caillou*, meaning "small port." He further identified the proper name *Caillou* as being a common family name in Europe.

Other parish communities included Gibson, originally named Tigerville, in northwest Terrebonne. Bourg, southeast of Houma, had its beginnings in the early 1800s as Newport; Hubert M.

From left, down: Oyster Bayou Light c. 1904; Timbalier Light at Little Pass (1895-1917); Ship Shoal Light erected 1859

Belanger founded a four-street community (Main, Front, Market, and Cypress) there in 1830, and for a time the entire community was known as Canal Belanger, until the turn of the twentieth century. Farther down Bayou Terrebonne about 15 miles from Houma was Montegut, first settled in the early 1800s; by the mid-1800s its environs took in several plantations and sugar mills, as well as a sizeable village below Madison Canal. Little Caillou, also known as Chauvin, developed around the fishing industry. Dulac, on Grand Caillou, developed around the sugar cane and timber industry, as well as being a fishing community. Along Bayou Dularge, Michel Eloi Theriot established the first plantation there after his marriage in St. James Parish in 1839. A major sugar cane production section of the parish was located along Bayou Black.

An early widespread local commercial crop, indigo, enjoyed dominance until the first part of the nineteenth century, when it faded in profitability. After indigo, large plantations' land was converted to sugar cane production, which became the parish's main economic base. Other important crops were cotton, rice, corn and citrus. This was the case when Pierre arrived.

Among the segment of the population who lived along Terrebonne's more southerly reaches, many ran often-smaller landholdings than did their plantation-owning neighbors.

Because even the southernmost stretches of land along the bayou communities had not as yet succumbed to subsidence or present-day high-water encroachment, many residents of these areas cultivated sugar plantations and operated sugar mills as well. In fact, the high-and-dry nature of even the most southerly farmlands which have now become marshlands is attested to by the fact that Dulac's large plantations, Live Oak and Dulac, in 1858-59 produced higher yields than any of the other major plantations of the parish.

Most bayou dwellers' homes hugged the bayous, and more often than not these people made their living tilling their lands and using their boats. Seafood—fish, shrimp, oysters—was plentiful in bayous, bays, lakes, and in the open waters of the Gulf of Mexico, and was there for the hard-working mariners to harvest—just as plantation workers harvested cane. Maritime traffic was busy along the Terrebonne coast. In the bays of the parish's coastline, the U.S. Government had constructed lighthouses at two locations a few years before Pierre's arrival in the area. The first Timbalier Bay lighthouse was built on

Ads from (above) the Terrebonne Patriot of April 30, 1870 and (below) the Civic Guard of October 28, 1865

Timbalier Island in 1856, using East Coast-style architecture and materials. After it fell over in an 1867 hurricane, a skeleton framework with a low-level keepers' dwelling was finished in 1875. Channel scouring caused this structure to fall on its side in 1894, and a temporary pyramidal structure replaced it on the north side of the island in a suitable depth of water. It would be replaced by yet another structure in 1917. The Ship Shoal lighthouse, a screwpile metal structure, was built in the Gulf of Mexico in 1859 south of western Terrebonne Parish waters. Later in his lifetime, Pierre was witness to the construction of the Oyster Bayou lighthouse, which marked the easternmost entrance to Atchafalaya Bay beginning in 1903.

Farming and trapping furbearing animals often also contributed to the lower Terrebonne people's livelihood. Many types of furbearing creatures inhabited the marshes, streams, and woodlands, including muskrat, mink, raccoon, otter, squirrel, rabbit, and opossums. Some families also gathered moss for market, since Spanish moss was a common stuffing at the time for upholstered furniture and mattresses. In 1876, moss was purchased at three cents or three and one-half cents per pound.[9] Alligators, turtles, and frogs were also hunted locally for market.

The bayou-dwelling segment of the population was described in differing accounts: "Encouraged by the mildness of the climate and the fruitfulness of the soil, many...set about with vigor to clear and prepare the land for agriculture. As houses were built and improvements made, the thickly settled bayou banks took on an aspect of progressiveness. Replacing an area heavily wooded or overrun with brush were small farms, little homesteads, well cultivated, producing enough to supply the family. To obtain the necessities they could not produce some of these people 'employed themselves...during the winter and spring of the year, in boating' and in killing 'vast numbers of duck and other game, both for use and market.' Many of these Creoles were agreeable and intelligent, 'speaking both French and English fluently and seemed to understand the politics of the day quite as well as some politicians...The old folks are pleasant, quaint old people; the young ones, sociable and intelligent.'"[10]

An alternative assessment is less kind. "Here, in this Eden upon earth, these people continued to live in a simplicity of primitive ignorance and indolence scarcely to be believed by any but an actual observer. Their implements of agriculture were those of two centuries before...Their wants were few, and were all supplied at home. Save a little flour, powder, and shot, they purchased nothing. These were paid for by the sale of the produce of the poultry yard—the prudent savings from the labor of the women—to the market-boats from the city."[11] The author did add that these people circa 1830 in Louisiana were "amiable, kind, law-abiding, virtuous and honest, beyond any population of similar character to be found in any country...a suit for slander or an indictment for malicious mischief, or a case of bastardy not known or heard of once in ten years. This will seem strange when we reflect that at this time schools were unknown, and not one out of fifty of the people could read or write." These people's physical description was recorded by this same source: "...many of their females are extremely beautiful. These attain maturity very early, and are frequently married at thirteen years of age...I have known a grandmother at thirty.... This precocious maturity is followed with rapid decay."

Although these sources referred to this segment of the population as Creoles, they were no doubt Acadians of Canadian descent, as well as other ethnic groups. (Acadians and Creoles are of two entirely separate derivations and histories, and the term *Creole* does not apply accurately to both groups, although Acadians were frequently identified as Creole in the antebellum period.) Opinions of the bayou people mirror the isolationist attitudes, independence, and *laissez-faire* policies of Acadians' ancestors in Canada, which had led to their eviction by the British.

Pierre stepped into this land of a burgeoning village and a lush, productive landscape, but he had adaptations to make in a humid environment that buzzed and crept with creatures he had never had to face in his native land. An account of a Union soldier quoted by *The Courier* newspaper describes nuisances that Pierre was first faced with during the same decade as Connecticut soldier Andrew M. Sherman, who was stationed in nearby Boutte:

"The mosquitoes...were so numerous and troublesome during the nights that the only way we could sleep at all was by inclosing our bunks with mosquito netting....I sometimes debated the question in my mind which was the greater evil, the mosquitoes or the stifling air of the inclosed bunks....It really seemed to me some evenings that I should be eaten alive by these infernal insects...." *The Courier* quotes Sherman as objecting to "tank water," since he seemed not to have known the word *cistern*. His revulsion was in part because he and his comrades saw "millions" of what they called "wrigglers" in their "tank water." Sherman indicated no knowledge that these were the larva of the "infernal insects" that plagued him at night. Another creature Sherman disliked was summarized in his statement, "...I very much prefer sleeping and living in a part of the country where lizards are unkown." One of the worst "pests" Sherman wrote about encountering were alligators, who "stealthily emerged from near-by woods."

Highlander Pierre Cenac must have at first had the same reactions as did Sherman to these creatures native to southern Louisiana.

Current residents might be surprised at the variety of other wildlife hunted long ago locally—"bear, panther and deer" detailed in E.C. Wurzlow's directory of the late 1800s. Terrebonne Parish Police Jury records show that in 1825 the government offered a bounty for each "tiger" destroyed. (Different sources surmise these to have been wildcats, bobcats, panthers, jaguars, or cougars.)

An early Terrebonne Parish map shows a Buffalo Bayou

Ads from the Terrebonne Patriot *edition of April 30, 1870*

Brooks and Tennet Store on Main Street, Houma c. 1860

An exceptionally large alligator c. 1880

(Bayou Dularge). A journal was kept by John Landreth, a U.S. Army engineer who charted the coastal area of Louisiana from 1818 to 1819. His guide Page Billiot described "an abundance of bald eagles, wolves, tigers, and buffalo in the area now known as Terrebonne Parish." It is also known that buffalo were hunted at Bayou Terre aux Boeufs in present-day St. Bernard Parish, as well as at Manchac near Lake Pontchartrain, for sale at the French Market in New Orleans.

Louisiana has had a history of bountiful wildlife resources. An Ursuline postulant, Sister Marie Madeleine Hachard, wrote to her father from New Orleans of the 1720s that her community lived on "wild beef, deer, swans, geese and wild turkeys, hares, hens, ducks, teals, pheasants, partridges, quails and other fowl and game...enormous fish...." She wrote, "Hunting lasts all winter, which commences in October. It is made at ten leagues from the city. Wild oxen [bison] are caught in large numbers....We pay three cents a pound for that meat, and the same price for venison, which is better than the beef or mutton which you eat in Rouen." [12]

Besides similar good hunting in Terrebonne Parish field and forest, almost all of the local population took advantage of the rich delta soil to grow produce, as well as keeping cattle and poultry, to supply their own tables. No doubt when Pierre first laid eyes on northwest Terrebonne's cultivated land from the stagecoach or express, he saw the homes encircled by expanses of sugar cane, but also closer to the houses were crops and farm animals that most landowners had as staples: corn, fruit trees of various kinds (most importantly oranges), potatoes, other vegetables grown for cooking; cattle, pigs; and some cotton and rice.

Migratory fowl has always been abundant, since Terrebonne lies along the Mississippi Flyway. Many varieties of ducks and geese abound during seasonal migrations, as well as tropical birds such as cranes and other species. A magazine edition of the *Houma Courier* as late as 1906 contained an assessment of this

An Indian mound at Dulac c. 1926

"hunter's paradise": "The bays, lakes, lagoons and shallow waters afford a vast feeding ground for the myriads of ducks that come here every winter. Quail, doves, snipe and other small game birds are to be had in season. The Houma market is well supplied with ducks and other game, and large quantities are shipped to the New Orleans market."

One deviation to the typical local landscape must have proved to be a curiosity to Pierre when he explored his adopted parish. "In the Parish of Terrebonne there are at least fifteen or twenty ... [Indian mounds], situated on the Bayous Grand and Petit Caillous, Terrebonne, and the Black, of various sizes, and from appearances, of various dates. But the most remarkable of these is at Tigerville, about twenty-five miles from Houma, on the Bayou Black."[13]

Jean Pierre Cenac had relocated to a land vastly different from his own High Pyrenees, but one which was becoming, despite the disruption of the Civil War, transportation-accessible, livelihood-friendly, and even surprising in some particulars of its tranquil landscape.

NOTES

1. Carl A. Brasseaux. *French, Cajun, Creole, Houma*

2. E.C. Wurzlow. *A Directory of the Parish of Terrebonne*, 1897

3. *American State Papers*, Public Lands, III

4. Marguerite Watkins. *History of Terrebonne Parish to 1861*, a thesis submitted to the graduate faculty of Louisiana State University Department of History, 1939

5. The Story of Terrebonne 1822-1972. Sesquicentennial Celebration Parish History

6. P.A. Champomier. "Statement of Sugar Made in Louisiana, Annual Reports, 1844-1862."

7. Phoebe Chauvin Morrison. Annotation of the 1840 Terrebonne Parish Census, published by the Terrebonne Genealogical Society, 1988

8. R.A. Bazet. *Houma—An Historical Sketch*, 1934

9. The Morgan City Historical Society. *A History of Morgan City, Louisiana*, 1960

10. Issues of *The Civic Guard* June 1866; Pierce's "Historical and Statistical Collection of Louisiana, Terrebonne" in *DeBow's Review XI*, 1851

11. W.H. Sparks. *The Memory of Fifty Years*, 1870

12. Richard Campanella

13. DeBow's Review, 1851

Above, advertisement from the August 28, 1909 issue of Field and Stream. *Below, from* The Outlaw Gunner Harry M. Walsh. *Price list c. 1900*

J. C. JACKSON WHOLESALERS
POULTRY AND WILDFOWL
BALT. MD. EST. 1786

SHIPPING PRICES

NAME	PRICE/PAIR
Buffell Head	$.30 – 50
Brant	1.25
Black Duck	1.25
Whistler	.30 – 50
Butterballs	1.00
Broad Bills	.50 – .50
Goose	2.00
Red Heads	2.50
Canvas Back Prime	5.00 – 7.00
" " Regular	2.50 – 5.00
Old Sauaw	.70 – 90
Ruddy	.90 – 100
Coot (beater)	.50
Sprigtail	.50
Widgeon	.50
Yellowlegs	1.00
Curlew	3.00
King Rail (per Dozen)	.70 – 100
Blackbirds	.25 – .75
Reedbirds	1.00

A duck hunter using a sculling float c. November 1885

CHAPTER 9
February 14, 1862:
The Baker's Plans

St. Valentine's Day is much more important here than in the Old Country, Pierre decided as he put the finishing touches on special pastries he and Jean-Marie had made for the day's customers. *Many of* les Americains *placed their orders as long as a week ago. Even in the middle of a war, some of them still have enough to spend on a few treats for their sweethearts and children. After two years in this country, I can still be surprised by these people.*

Since he had a few minutes before beginning a batch of bread, Pierre stepped out the door to get some air and to do the people-watching he so enjoyed. On good days, he caught drifts of conversations when people didn't think he could hear, or couldn't understand them. This watching and listening had helped him to know this place and the people better. He felt wiser in Terrebonne's ways since he first came over two years ago, not only from his direct contact with so many different people, but also from this indirect hearing what they were thinking and caring about.

Pierre saw the *grande dame* of a Bayou Black plantation bustling along the opposite side of the street, ignoring the children and shopkeepers who hastened to remove themselves from her path. He thought she wielded her parasol as a weapon, and her children followed her like the wake of a boat in full sail.

That femme *didn't surprise me, though. When most of her slaves ran away as soon and as fast as they could last month, she was not sad and afraid, but* furieuse. *I heard her talk about "outrage that they would abandon her and her plantation."* Sapristi! *What did she think they would do? I heard the stories about how that family treated their Negroes, much different from some of the other good families around here.*

Pierre had heard many conversations among planters' wives, most of them *Americains*. Their husbands and sons had joined different regiments of the Confederacy in the early days of *la Louisiane* joining the Confederate states. Mr. McCollam's oldest son Andrew was serving in the St. Mary's Cannoniers, so Ellendale was minus one child at their table these days. Two of the Shaffer boys, Thomas J. and John J., were both in Confederate ranks. Duncan Minor was off fighting in Virginia, and his brother Stephen was in a prison camp in Kentucky.

Henry Ellender of lower Bayou Terrebonne was in service to the Confederacy. The five sons of Concord Plantation were all away at war. Elisha, Abraham, young Holden, Thomas, and William had already been in Virginia and Pennsylvania battles. Mr. Wright, Sr. had received word not long ago that William and Thomas were in Yankee prison camps. Many other planters had gone away, leaving their families behind. *But when I hear these* mamans *talking, they speak of their worries for their husbands and sons more than their own discomfort, not like that woman across the street. She thinks she has a right to be treated better.*

Pierre was reminded of the few members of the French aristocracy he had encountered during his stay in Bordeaux. *It's the same attitude, except for one it's by birth, and for the other it's by money that they make their claims.*

He had stayed outside the shop long enough, and went back inside to begin baking *baguettes*. While his hands automatically shaped the loaves, he had a lot of time to think. *Poor Monsieur Blanchard. He thought he had made such a good deal when he sold all those acres bordering one* Americain's *plantation for fifty dollars. He was so busy rejoicing about having so much money at one time, nobody had the heart to tell him the land was worth at least three hundred dollars. After just a short time in the parish, I saw that it was an old pattern here. Small Acadien and other farms gobbled up by large landowners, and* les Acadiens *moving farther and farther from the choicest ground down into the bayou areas where only ridges accommodate them.*

But the majority of these people still seemed content, Pierre decided. *Most of them have no grand ambitions, and want only to have enough food on their tables and to be left to live their lives with no interference. When I first asked Philippe Lejeune if he was thinking of joining up, he laughed in my face. "Pierre, what would I want to do*

Charles Frederick Whipple family photo c. 1895. From left, George Whipple, Charles "Willie" Whipple, Caroline Whipple (seated), nephew Walter, Jr. at her side. Standing in rear, Sarahlene Falgout Whipple; Mary Augustine Mars Whipple with grandson Eugene beside her; standing, Mark McCool Whipple; bearded Charles Frederick Whipple, Thomas Andre Whipple and Walter Whipple

that for? What would I be fighting for, anyway? So les Americains around here can buy more silverware?"

Pierre knew a few of *les Acadiens* who worked large farms and lived more genteel lives, but they were exceptions, he decided. *I want more than Philippe Lejeune wants, though. I don't have to have silver, but I would like chairs that are upholstered and books to read on winter nights. I can see Mr. Daspit through his windows in the lamplight when I stroll down his street in the evenings, and he is always bending over a book. That's a nice sight.*

Pierre caught sight of Mr. Wakbespask, and chuckled as he slid the loaves into the open-air oven. Mon Dieu, *we have a lot of different kinds of names here. Let's see...Haché, Belanger, Boudreaux, Dupont, Viguerie, all French. Then there are the Germans: Berger, Loevenstein, Wurzlow. English and Scots, Duthu, McWilliams, Watkins, Wallis. The Italians, Medrano. The Swiss Sprague. And I don't know where some of them come from...Lum, Roddy, Hinar. I thought I had seen a lot of foreigners in Bordeaux, but this small place beats everything. Then there are the black people and* Les Indiens *with their dark skin and coarse hair. I didn't expect these differences once I left New Orleans.*

Fritz Berger called out to him from the *banquette* on the way to his store and waved. *"Bonjour, Pierre, mon frère,"* he said with a small laugh at his rhyme in a language that was not his own. Pierre laughed too, and waved back.

Yes, this was a different world, and even though the war was always looming large in his worries, Pierre told himself for the thousandth time that this parish was the place he needed to be. *I just need to get my hands on some land of my own, and there's a lot of it out there below town. A little more time here,* puis je m'en vais. Adieu, *Houma.*

The Dr. Hugh Maxwell Wallis family and home c. 1890. From left, Ethel Wallis (later Munson); Mrs. Hugh Maxwell Wallis, Sr.; Morley Wallis and his wife; (seated) Percy Wallis; the white-bearded Dr. Wallis, Sr., onetime Houma mayor; Mrs. Hugh Maxwell Wallis, Jr.; Claude; (seated) Ida; Granville; Helen (later Bazet); and Ellersley

Above, Holden E. Wright (1792-1868), probably at Concord Plantation on Bayou Black
Left, Abraham Wright and Mary Ann Callahan Wright with their twelve children and two others: (in no order) Eva Marie, Ida, Holden Otis, Joanne Laura, Laura, Abraham Elisha, John Edward, Nancy Charlotte, Margaret Florence, Maria Elia, Lester E. and Ellen, c. 1886

Acadians saltmarsh haying in Nova Scotia c. early 1700s, by Nova Scotia Museum artist Azor Vienneau, 1996 Right, thatched roof dwelling in lower Terrebonne Parish c. 1900

CHAPTER 10
Tangled Roots

When Pierre Cenac and other immigrants arrived in southeast Louisiana in the early 1860s, they found the dominant economic group in the rural landscape of southeast Louisiana to be Anglo-Americans. This was not because of their numbers, but by virtue of their being by far the largest landowners in the mid-nineteenth century.

Les Americains began to arrive after the Louisiana Purchase in 1803, and came in ever greater numbers after the War of 1812, but they were by no means the first non-native Americans, nor those of the greatest numbers, to settle here.

According to a local historian, "The first settlements in this parish were made during the closing decade of the eighteenth century by French, principally from the older colonies of Louisiana. Some French, Americans, Spaniards and Germans also made this their home....During that period various grants were made to divers persons by the Baron de Carondelet, then Governor of Louisiana, which was then a Spanish colony. Reference is made in the public records of 1828 to a tract of land on Bayou Grand Caillou, near Quitman's Lake, as 'the locality known by the name of the ancient encampement Derrebonne.'"[1]

These earliest European-derived settlers were met by Native Americans currently identified with the Houmas tribe that had lived in the area for generations. Although formerly located in more northerly sections of the state, the Houmas had migrated south for a variety of reasons.[2] "By 1776 so greatly reduced were they in number that they sold...ninety-six arpents of land in the district of the parish of the Ascension or La Fourche."[3] *La fourche* is French for *the fork*, which refers to the bayou's headwaters at the Mississippi River at Donaldsonville.

The Houmas were still located there in 1784, and "Finally this declining tribe drifted down Bayou Lafourche and into present day Terrebonne....There is no record to show the time of their advent into the latter parish or their exact location, but it is known that the remnants of the Houma tribe established a camp at a place called Ouiski Point located at the intersection of Bayou Cane with Bayou Black...." at a point of high ground.[2]

The tribe spoke the Muskogean language when its people were known as the Houma Chikchiuma (red crawfish); this people later were referred to as the Ouma or Houmas. Intermarriage

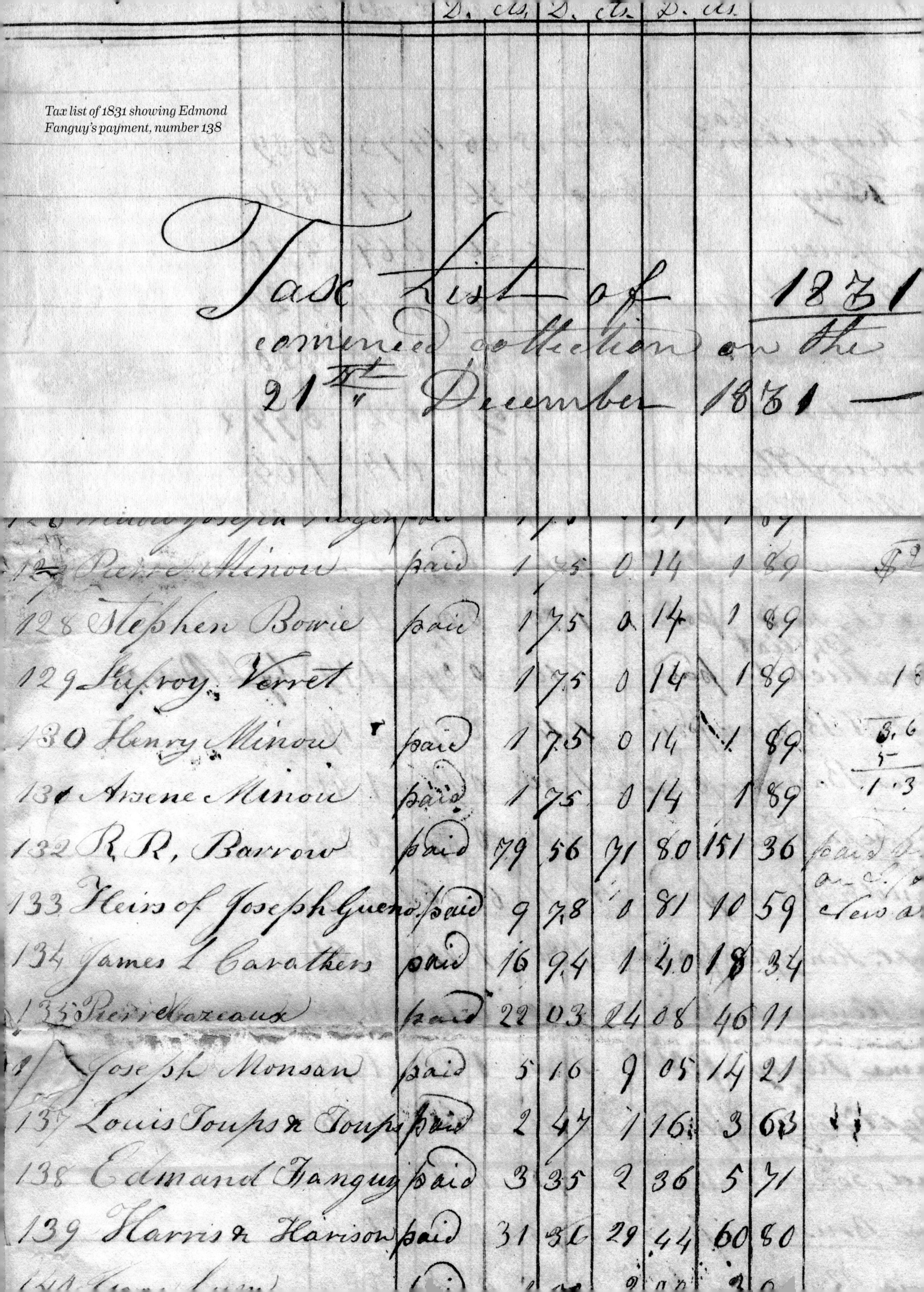

Tax List of 1831
commenced collection on the
21st December 1831 —

No.	Name		D.	Cts.	D.	Cts.	D.	Cts.	
127	Pierre Minou	paid	1	75	0	14	1	89	
128	Stephen Bowie	paid	1	75	0	14	1	89	
129	Lufroy Verret		1	75	0	14	1	89	18
130	Henry Minou	paid	1	75	0	14	1	89	
131	Arsene Minou	paid	1	75	0	14	1	89	
132	R. R. Barrow	paid	79	56	71	80	151	36	paid
133	Heirs of Joseph Gueno	paid	9	78	0	81	10	59	
134	James L Carathers	paid	16	94	1	40	18	34	
135	Pierre Hazeaux	paid	22	03	24	08	46	11	
136	Joseph Monsan	paid	5	16	9	05	14	21	
137	Louis Toups & Toups	paid	2	47	1	16	3	63	
138	Edmand Fanguy	paid	3	35	2	36	5	71	
139	Harris & Harison	paid	31	36	29	44	60	80	

with whites and blacks in the 1800s diluted the tribe's identity, and in Terrebonne Parish they eventually settled at the farthest limits along the coast.[3] Their long isolation from ancient ties, as well as intermarriages, caused their widespread adoption of the language of the Acadians, and by the early 1900s the Houma had lost their linguistic integrity.[3] They became known by the derogatory name Sabines. One Houma word that has survived in Terrebonne Parish is *ouisky* (as in Ouiski Bayou, Ouiski Point). In the Houma language the word meant *cane.*

In the 1850s Houmas descendants had relocated to Isle de Jean Charles below Montegut and other southerly bayou reaches after a swampland purchase in 1859 by a pure-blood Houmas woman named Rosalie Courteaux. One online Terrebonne Parish history indicates that the earliest Indian settlements in the parish were along bayous Terrebonne and Little Caillou, later spreading to Pointe-Aux-Chenes and Bayou Dularge. A 1907 count included 175 at Bayou Salé [and Bayou LaButte] below Dulac, 160 at Pointe-Aux-Chenes, 117 at Isle de Jean Charles, about 90 at Bayou Dularge [and Bayou Mauvais Bois], and 65 at Pointe au Barré.[4]

Rowing in a standing skiff using a "jourg" or yoke to row

During Pierre's time, many families bearing Houmas bloodlines lived below Bayou Salé south of Dulac. Family names identified with Houmas include Billiot, Dardar, Dion, Fitch, Francis, Gregoire, Naquin, Parfait, Solet, Verdin, and Verret, most of the surnames associated with French derivation. In 1830 the tribe as it had been was declared extinct, but descendants remained in the local area, educationally deprived and socially shunned by the wider community.

During the 1820s and 1830s a new wave of settlers came from many different places to the local area, such as from Mississippi, North Carolina, and points north and east in the United States.[5] Some American families found their way here from as far away as New England. East-coast, Midwest, Southeastern, or other "American" families that made their way here from Natchez and elsewhere are found in old local names McCollam, Barrow, Watkins, Bisland, Krumbhaar, Minor, Shaffer, Smith, Wallis, Hellier, Cage, Rhodes, Aycock, Sanders, Parr, Connely, Foolkes, and McBride.

A palmetto house in the lower reaches of Terrebonne's coastal region c. 1861-1865

Among other families originally from the Continent which have long Terrebonne histories are those with the names Belanger (from France's Paroisse de Touque via Quebec), Duval, Frederick, Brien, Henry, Hotard, and Fields.

Not far away, in Plaquemines Parish, Croatians and Slovaks made their homes as early as the 1820s. Many German families settled in St. Charles parish upriver from New Orleans; St. Charles has long been known as the German Coast.

Along the west bank of the Mississippi near New Orleans, and along Bayou Lafourche, Canary Islanders ("Islenos" of Basque and Spanish descent) settled in large numbers, one group as early as in 1779 and another the next year. Some from the upper Lafourche community of Valenzuela near present-day Plattenville in Assumption Parish migrated to Terrebonne

Parish in the late 1820s, at first to the Little Caillou area. Among Terrebonne Parish family names that descend from the Isleño immigration are Castille, Domingue, and Segura. Another Spanish family name in Terrebonne Parish is Fabregas, the family having its origin in Barcelona.

After their native land's potato famine of 1845-1847, Irish immigrants made their way into the Lafourche region from New Orleans. Two Terrebonne families with Irish origins are the Brady and Wright families.

Later on, Czechoslovakians and Polish immigrants, many of them professionals, settled in Houma and its environs. East European names Jastremski and Zelenka appeared locally in the late 1800s, and still later the Russian Bojarsky, as did other Continental merchants such as the Blum, Blahut, Elster, Heymann, and Ferber families. Earlier, German immigrants were the Ellender (by way of Ohio, then Pennsylvania), Whipple, Zeringer, Walther, Kohman, Drott, and Berger families. Middle Eastern names are still represented by the Saadi, Haddad, Samaha, Fakier, and Mohana families.

Asians—Filipinos and Chinese—began to arrive in the state in the 1850s, settling in the southeastern coastal area of Louisiana, particularly Barataria Bay, Manilla Village, and Bassa Bassa.

At the time of the Anglo-Americans' immigration to the Lafourche-Terrebonne region, "it became apparent to them that all the rich farmlands fronting the many bayous of the district were in the hands of small landowners, such as the exiled Acadians. With their wealth and ease of credit, the Anglo-Americans began buying up large tracts of property from these people. Many of the poorer landowners, who were forced to sell their property, principally the Acadians, moved further down the bayous of Lafourche and Terrebonne or migrated to the *brules* [ridges along marshes or swamps] looking for new land to settle and cultivate."[6]

What many Anglo-Americans fashioned from their vast land purchases were huge sugar plantations, which they ran with large numbers of slave labor. At the start of the Civil War, approximately 180 sugar-producing plantations hugged the banks of Terrebonne's bayous.[5]

The season 1858-1859 was the high year for sugar, the second most valuable crop handled in New Orleans, when "257,225 hogsheads of sugar and 353,715 hogsheads of molasses reached the New Orleans market" from plantations via steamboats, river schooners, or by railroad (after 1854).[7]

By the time of the Civil War, some 21,176 slaves resided in Lafourche, Terrebonne, and Assumption parishes, compared with 19,820 whites, 315 blacks (free men and women of color), and 103 Native Americans (who by 1800 had been "essentially displaced from their lands and relegated to the back lands of the district.")[6]

Large plantation owners had the most to lose depending on the war's outcome. Economic survival, besides the principle of states' sovereignty, was one overriding motivation for many of the

Manilla Village Store in Barataria Bay c. 1915

landowning class to support the Confederacy.

One author wrote, "For the most part, the Acadian and Spanish, along with the earlier migrants from Germany, Switzerland, and France who came and settled the southeastern portion of the state, were small farmers, predominately Roman Catholic in faith, and poor. The principal cash crops at the turn of the nineteenth century were rice, corn, and other vegetables, indigo, and some cotton, which the settlers used to clothe themselves. The Acadians largely owned few slaves; there was no need as they were traders, fishermen, and small farmers by trade and economically poor. Nevertheless, there were a few affluent inhabitants in the region, like the slave-owning French from the Caribbean...[and] French Creoles."[6]

Acadians, as well as other nationalities occupying the same status as that of Acadians, were looked down upon by the large Anglo-American planters and Creoles. They did not have the same economic incentives as did the large slaveholders to fight in order to maintain lifestyles.

Anglo-Americans were most often Protestant and more wealthy than Acadians and most other local ethnicities. Creoles, although Catholic, as were Acadians and many other local ethnicities, considered themselves socially and culturally superior. Anglos and Creoles often "clashed with the Acadian people on many regional and state issues as the district expanded and local political brawls spilled into state politics."[8]

French-speaking Acadians had an entirely different history from that of the Foreign French immigrants of Pierre's generation. Acadians had already lived in southern Louisiana for almost 100 years when Pierre and other French immigrants arrived. Because of their numbers, and because of Pierre's eventual close connections with this culture, their story is important to Pierre's story.

Acadians received their name because they belonged to a colony in Canada termed *Acadie* in French (*Acadia* in English), which is thought to be derived from a term for a rural Eden (*Archadia* from Greek myth, the name credited to Italian explorer Giovanni da Verrazzano and given to a section of the U.S. northeast coast). A map published in 1586 clearly applied the name *Arcadie* to the Nova Scotia peninsula.

In order to understand Acadians' long history, one must understand their place in the sequence of the earliest permanent North American colonies. Contrary to most American history textbooks' emphasis, it was not the English who founded the first permanent colonies on the continent. Saint Augustine in Florida was founded in 1565 by the Spaniard Don Pedro Menendez de Aviles.

Canada's Acadia colony of the early 1600s was a result of France's religious warfare, according to Dr. Carl Brasseaux of the Center for Louisiana Studies.[9] After French Huguenots' failed attempts to establish colonies in the New World beginning in 1555, "French colonization along the Bay of Fundy grew out

Early Acadians in Nova Scotia c. 1750 by Azor Vienneau

Acadians repairing saltmarsh dikes c. early 1700s, by Nova Scotia Museum artist Azor Vienneau, 1996; note aboiteaux *opening at bottom of levee*

of an attempt by Huguenot Pierre du Guay, sieur de Monts, to exploit the fur trade in eastern Canada beginning in 1603. Port Royal on Nova Scotia was evacuated in 1607, de Monts' monopoly was revoked, and in 1610 Port Royal was reoccupied by Jean de Biencourt de Poutrincourt, acting governor of Acadia during de Monts' proprietorship. This laid the foundation for a permanent settlement there.

The colony was proprietary, operated by the Company of New France, when most of its colonists arrived in the Bay of Fundy Basin between 1632 and 1654. "At least 55 percent, and possibly as much as 70 percent, of Acadia's seventeenth-century immigrants were natives of either the Centre-Ouest provinces of Poitou, Aunis, Angoumois, and Saintage or Anjou Province, in an adjacent geographical region. All of these ancient régime provinces were located southeast and east-southeast of Brittany." Recruited families exhibited "remarkable fecundity" in the New World, thereby perpetuating their demographic dominance. "By the twentieth century this core group's descendants had come to constitute between 80 and 90 percent of the total Acadian population in the Canadian Maritimes and a corresponding proportion of Louisiana's Acadian community."

Seventy-six percent of the 1671 census of Acadia were *labourers*, France's designation of the nation's "most prosperous peasants...constituting a kind of peasant-aristocracy...noted for their industriousness." This begs the question of why they had left their native land. The answer lies in the fact that much fighting in the religious wars occurred in their provinces, followed by years of "unseasonable weather [which] brought famine and...epidemics."

In Acadia, colonists had to "adapt to harsh new surroundings with virtually no outside assistance. The Acadian colonists found strength in their remarkably cohesive families." In dealing with authorities, they practiced techniques they had learned in their experiences as Old Country peasants, namely "passive disobedience,...and the transplanted *labourers* used them quite successfully against French, and, later, British colonial authorities." Because of frequent changes in colonial domination, geographic isolation, and neglect by the mother country, the Acadians developed a spirit of independence and became the first group of European colonists to develop a distinctive North American identity.

Significantly, Acadians were among the only New World immigrants who reclaimed land rather than merely cutting and clearing forests. Acadian farmers in Canada reclaimed marshlands using *aboiteaux*, or sluices carved from tree trunks, at key points along dikes, to divert and drain water from marshy areas to make them cultivable. In 1636, "*sauniers*, or saltmakers, from the La Rochelle area" were imported to *Acadie* because they were expert at draining marshes to recover salt for the preservation of fish. "Other Acadians traced their roots to the Poitou region, where freshwater marshes were drained and cultivated."[10]

Sauniers in Loire, France extracting salt from sea water

Acadia eventually consisted of Nova Scotia, New Brunswick, and Prince Edward Island, Canada. "They [Acadians] established a string of coastal settlements and built dikes to reclaim fertile marshland for their farms. Their population exploded, from a few hundred in the mid-1600s to more than 15,000 a century later. The frontier molded them into a new, distinct people....They were proud, stubborn, self-reliant, and bound together by blood and marriage. They were progressive, electing deputies to represent their communities and asserting a sense of independence that exasperated a succession of governors. They asked only to keep their Catholic faith and to be allowed to remain neutral in time of war, but geography and history conspired to trap the Acadians in the crossfire as France and Britain fought for supremacy over North America."[10]

Acadie fell under British rule in 1713 when most of what was called *Acadie*—now the Nova Scotia mainland—was ceded by France to Britain. When Acadians were given an ultimatum but refused to swear allegiance to the British, they were banished from their homeland beginning in 1755.

Le Grand Derangement continued until 1763. Of the deportees, 1,000 were shipped to England where they were held as prisoners of war. Thousands of others were dispersed to the Caribbean, Guiana, the Falkland Islands, and along the American colonies on the U.S. east coast from New England to the Carolinas, as well as to France.[10]

Their names included Arceneaux, Aucoin, Bergeron, Blanchard, Boudrot, Bourg, Bourgeois, Breaux, Broussard, Comeau, Daigle, Dugas, Foret, Gautreau, Giroir, Guidry, Hache (originally from St. Sevan, France), Hebert, Junot (originally from Burgundy, France), Landry, Lejeune, LeBlanc, Marchand, Martin, Melanson, Michel, Prejean, Richard, Robichaud, Savoie, Templet, Terriot, Thibodeau, Trahan, and many other family names, with spelling variations, still common in South Louisiana. Other families whose origins were in France but who arrived here after years in Canada were the Eschetes, Belangers and Caillouets (Normandy), Chauvins, and Gagnés. The Dill family also made its way to Louisiana via Canada.

Of the more than 10,000 people whom the British deported, at least half died in exile. "Refugees in the American colonies and most of those repatriated to France gathered [over time] in southern Louisiana," beginning sometime after 1750, with 1785 as the peak immigration year.[10]

In the Louisiana New Acadia, "the typical pre-dispersal Acadian cherished land, family and personal dignity above all else. Having emigrated from France prior to the rise of capitalism, they were not materialistic in the modern sense of the term. Indeed, the Acadians sought only a comfortable existence, producing agricultural surpluses in order to acquire European manufactured goods to ameliorate their often harsh existence—never for conspicuous consumption."[9]

In the Louisiana rural agricultural society, the "fiercely independent" Acadian, "who had sprung from peasant stock and

who had spent 150 years casting off the shackles of feudalism...
bitterly resented the efforts of white Creoles to cast them in
the role of a colonial peasantry....First-generation Acadian
immigrants remain unimpressed by the aristocratic trappings
incumbent upon slave ownership." Later, however, "Outside of
the plantation areas only a small minority of Acadians owned
slaves, and most landholders continued to engage in small-
scale farming and ranching. In addition, the *petit habitant's* (or
yeoman farmer's) lodging remained the one- or two-room cottage
developed in the 1760s and 1770s."[9]

A century later Pierre Cenac was surrounded by descendants
of the exiled Acadians and Basques when he settled in
Terrebonne Parish.

The language of the Acadians had been cut off from the
mother tongue for many generations by the expanse of the
Atlantic Ocean, one reason for its becoming a classification of
its own derived from the French mother tongue. The Acadian
patois probably sounded quaint to Pierre. But it was French
nonetheless, and he could converse in his own language among
Terrebonne's Acadian population—as well as all other ethnicities
which had adopted the Acadian language as their own.

Another important part of Terrebonne's population at the
beginning of the Civil War, of course, was the large numbers of
slaves of African descent. Although the U.S. Congress banned
importation of slaves five years after the Louisiana Purchase of
1803, the numbers of slaves in the South had increased through
natural propagation and through transfer of slave populations
from one region to another. (The term "being sold down the
river" was used as early as 1837 as a reference to slaves who
caused "trouble" in northern slave states being shipped down the
Mississippi River for sale to plantations in the lower Mississippi
Valley—which were perceived as allowing harsher conditions for
slave labor. The term could also be a reference to New Orleans
and Mobile, located "down the river," being major sites of sale for
slaves who worked more northerly plantations.)

Terrebonne Parish was among areas in the South in which
slaves were in the majority in the year 1860. Census statistics for
that year record that Terrebonne Parish had a white population of
5,131 and a slave population of 6,785. Additionally, census figures
included 103 Indians and 72 "free people of color," bringing the
total parish population to 12,091.[2]

Houma city proper was the only location in the parish at
which slaves did not outnumber whites at the approximate time
that Pierre arrived in Terrebonne—425 whites, four blacks.
However, the courthouse in Houma served as a slave purchase
and sales site, with auctions being held until the beginning of
the Civil War.[2]

In the year Pierre came from France, one source documents
Terrebonne residents as owning a total of 5,069 slaves (a slight
inconsistency with the above census records). It is interesting
to note that only 14 of the 44 major slave owners were listed as

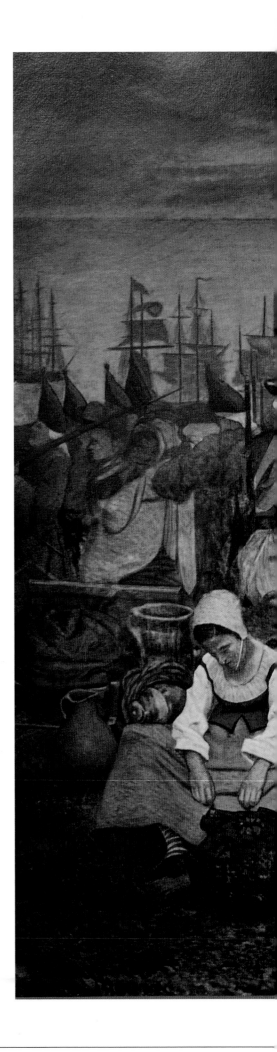

Dispersion of Acadians by Henri Beau, depicting events of September 5, 1755

having been born in Louisiana, and that six owners on the list were not residents of the parish.[11]

The state of Louisiana in 1860 was "only seventh among the states in total slaves," and "only tenth in number of slaveholders," but the state was fourth "in the number of slaveholders with fifty or more slaves."[11] Although Terrebonne Parish's slaves outnumbered the white population in that year, it was not among the parishes which "led the state in ratio of slaves to free inhabitants" at the time. "In Concordia Parish, 90.9% of the population were slaves."[11]

Slaves were regulated by what was known as *le code noir*, both in Saint-Domingue and Louisiana. The code is defined as "the body of law applicable to the colored population...The regulatory statutes everywhere were frankly repressive. They forbade slaves to possess weapons, to beat drums or blow horns which might serve to convey signals, to strike any white person even in self-defense, to be out of their quarters after curfew, to travel singly without written authorization, to travel in groups without a white escort, to assemble at night unless a white person were present; and rural citizens in their capacity as militia were embodied into squads to patrol their designated beats and chastise any slaves caught in transgression."[2]

Pierre stepped into a Terrebonne Parish of the early 1860s that was a conglomerate of ethnicities and accents, a place which was still sifting and shifting relational and societal differences before it could settle into a cohesive whole. Along with fellow immigrant Frenchmen and other nationalities, Pierre had to feel his way toward what would become his place in the community he had chosen to become his home.

The slave block in the rotunda of the Old St. Louis Hotel, original postcard photo partially captioned, "...frequently used by the auctioneers of the city when they had slaves to sell up to the time of the Civil War. Now located in the State Historical Museum." Below, the Code Noir book cover, 1743. Opposite, ad in Louisiana Coast Directory of 1857

NOTES

1. Marguerite Watkins thesis

2. Primary source, Swanton, *Bureau of American Ethnology, Indian Tribes*

3. John Swanton, *Bulletin 43*

4. Thomas A. Becnel. Ph.D.

5. Christopher G. Pena. *Scarred By War: Civil War in Southeast Louisiana*, Author House, 2004

6. Robert Reinders

7. Christopher Pena. *Scarred By War*, referencing original source Stephen S. Michot, *Bayou Society Embattled: Sectionalism, Secession, and Civil War in Louisiana's Lafourche Region* (Blytheville, Ark., 1994)

8. *French, Cajun, Creole, Houma*, Louisiana State University Press, 2005. This authoritative, definitive work following 30 years' research by author Dr. Carl A. Brasseaux is the reliable source for all history of the Acadians which follows (either quoted directly as indicated, or indirectly), except as otherwise noted.

9. Dean Jobb. *The Cajuns, A People's Story of Exile and Triumph*, John Wiley & Sons Canada, Ltd., 2005

10. Joseph Karl Menn. *The Large Slaveholders of Louisiana—1860*, Pelican Publishing Company, 1964

CODE NOIR,

O U

RECUEIL D'EDITS,

DÉCLARATIONS ET ARRETS

C O N C E R N A N T

Les Efclaves Négres de l'Amérique,

A V E C

Un Recueil de Réglemens, concernant la police des Ifles Françoifes de l'Amérique & les Engagés.

A P A R I S,

Chez les L I B R A I R E S A S S O C I E Z,

M. DCC. XLIII.

CHAPTER 11
Early May, 1862:
Witness to War

"Union soldiers." Pierre said it in a low voice to Jacques Benoit, whose neck was craning out the boarding house window next to Pierre's. Both their nightshirts billowed in the early May breeze. They stayed in place at their windows, stretching their necks around the sweet olive trees just outside, and above a low house across the street. Both young men focused their eyes in the dim moonlight toward the oblique view of their street's intersection with Main Street a block away. Yes, those were indeed blue uniforms, and then they heard marching orders shouted out in unfamiliar accents.

The two of them hesitated only a minute before withdrawing into their separate rooms. Each could hear the other close his window, each knowing those closed windows would not keep away what they had seen.

Pierre, Jacques, and several other residents of the boarding house had awakened to unfamiliar noise and had gone to their individual north-facing windows when the sounds began. Feet tramping in unison about a block away, in the direction of Main Street. Wagons, too. "It's just after two in the morning!" one of them had relayed down the line.

The whole place stirred until the landlady served an early breakfast. At the long table, Pierre absorbed details from other men's comments. "About 75 men, the blacksmith said..." "Confederate blockade runner..." "Little Caillou..." "No, Bayou Grand Caillou..."

Pierre heard more as bakery customers filled in a few details throughout the day. The troops were on their way to capture that blockade runner *Fox* the townspeople knew had entered the mouth of Bayou Grand Caillou a few days before. *All right, then. They'll capture it, or miss it, and then they'll go away.*

But that night, just as he had finally settled in, someone stage whispered, "Pierre! Pierre!" He opened his door to Jacques and Etienne in the middle of the night. "Men from town killed some Union soldiers this evening. Ambushed them and shot them dead. Got prisoners, too. Mr. Tanner...you know, Room 7...he was out late, and saw them come back into town."

Pierre sat back down on the bed. "You know what this means. They'll come for revenge."

"But it won't affect us," Etienne said without conviction. "We're never going to be soldiers, we decided two years ago. We haven't done anything. It's not our war, remember?"

Jacques and Pierre gave each other knowing glances. "Yes, the regiments did not call us up. And we speak bad English," Pierre answered. "But Etienne, you were far away from the wars back home, weren't you? They have a way of catching up with you, whether you're for one side or the other."

"Then, do we head out of town? Or do we stay? Where would we go?" Jacques' usual calm was shaken.

The three looked at each other, and Pierre said what they all knew. "We have no place to go. No families, no friends out in the country yet....Not much we can do, except just try not to be noticed."

What could not go unnoticed were the events of the next day. Both mesmerized and repulsed, the three young men stood at the back of the crowd near the courthouse when the townspeople's ambush party brutalized two Union soldiers' bodies, then forced blacks to bury them in the square a few feet from the market house. No coffins. Just a blanket to cover them and dirt heaped in a mound to remind passersby what had happened to the Yankees.

That afternoon and into the night, they watched families closing up houses and heading out of town on whatever conveyances they had, some even on foot. The men had worried faces, the children looked excited, and some of the women sniffled as they passed by the bakery shop where Pierre could see them. He was struck by how little they took with them.

In the early morning hours the next day, word got around to the remaining few citizens that a new Federal regiment was heading to Houma from Terrebonne Station. Pierre heard the bluster of their arrival around mid-morning, and braced himself. Not much later, he heard someone shout from the sidewalk that Colonel Bisland and other town leaders were being rounded up and arrested.

The three Frenchmen stayed inside as much as they could, into the following day. Since their shops were not open on Tuesday, May 13—Pierre would remember the date always—the friends closed their curtains and stayed together in Pierre's room. They talked softly, and found stale bread and a little butter for a small breakfast in Mrs. Gaston's deserted kitchen. The house was silent. But not for long.

Boots thudded down the hallway of Mrs. Gaston's house around noon. Three soldiers shouted, "Out of here! Come with us!" They grabbed Pierre, Jacques, and Etienne by the arms and shoved them out the front door toward Main Street.

"*Mon Dieu! Ils vont nous tuer?*" Etienne gave voice to their common thought.

Instead, the soldiers lined up the three of them and countless other Houmans who hadn't fled the town to follow behind two new coffins containing the unearthed remains of the two Union soldiers. The enforced funeral cortège walked slowly down Main to Church Street and into the graveyard behind St. Francis de Sales Church. As they approached the church, Pierre removed his hat and others

Top, campsite of the 159th New York Regiment and the 13th Connecticut Volunteers in Thibodaux, Louisiana c. 1864 Bottom, Civil War Regimental Band, 16th Indiana Mounted Infantry at Thibodaux Courthouse c. 1865 Opposite, Civil War Camp Hubbard of the 13th Connecticut Volunteers Regiment in Thibodaux, Louisiana c. 1863 (spire of St. John Episcopal Church visible in background)

followed his gesture. They stood, still and silent, in the cemetery, soldiers at attention with their guns right behind them. A Federal officer said words over the bodies. At the end, one soldier spat out a chew of tobacco near Pierre's shoe. Pierre clenched his fist and looked into the soldier's eyes. Through a red beard, the soldier grunted so that the commander couldn't hear, "Do it, Frenchy. Give me a reason." Pierre inched his foot away and unclenched his fist.

After the soldiers released them with hard voices, Pierre heard most of the people around him breathe sighs of relief. The crowd all disappeared into houses or into shops below homes. When Pierre walked into the door of Mrs. Gaston's quiet house, he looked down the street. Empty.

"Horses stomping down the street and soldiers shouting, day in and day out." It was three days after cortège duty. Jacques was getting grumpy from lack of food. Their seats at the dining room table reminded him and Etienne how much they wanted Mrs. Gaston to return and cook her sturdy stews and soups. "Where did Pierre go, anyway?" Jacques whined.

A few minutes later, Pierre came running up to the house. "Come and see! They can't find the rebel leaders, so they're burning Main Street!" At that moment, a dense cloud of black smoke drifted past the window.

Maybe les Acadiens *have the right idea. Living down the bayous. Maybe that's the smartest thing.*

A few minutes later, two soldiers hustled them out of the house again to watch most of the town go up in flames. Everyone left in Houma had been corralled onto the street near the town square. Pierre saw the faces of the town leaders flinch when soldiers hitched a team of horses to harness and lassoed an entire wall of the unfinished courthouse. As the wall crashed down, the ground shook beneath their feet.

Smoke thickened as shops, mills, stables, and houses were torched one by one. Ash rained down, and tears streaked grown men's faces. Soldiers threw personal possessions into a heap in front of the crowd and set them ablaze. A man lamented, "No, not my books," and a woman brave enough to have stayed in town wailed, "My papa made that baby crib!"

Pierre saw the men's bodies taut with frustration, and felt his own helplessness. *It's the same everywhere...*la guerre.

Thibadauxville November 26th 1828

on or before the first of March
next I Promise to pay R P Bowie
or order the sum of twenty
five thousand dollars
for Value Received ——

James Bowie

CHAPTER 12
The War Comes to Town

As national political strife became more heated in the late 1850s and early 1860s, Louisianans in all geographical regions became alert to the potential need for military readiness on their home ground. Terrebonne Parish residents were no exception to this heightened level of watchfulness.

During the late 1850s Terrebonne responded to the rising levels of dissent in the nation by organizing a Brigade of the Second Division of the state militia. By 1859 locals organized the Terrebonne Rifle Company in response to threats of war. "To further safeguard the residents of the parish the Grivot Guards and the Terrebonne Rangers were organized."[1]

By 1861 the Terrebonne Parish Police Jury authorized the purchase of a cannon "with equipments and ammunition...to be securely deposited in the town of Houma." Volunteers joined either the state militia or military units in other states. Women of the area formed a Ladies' Aid Association to supply local volunteers with winter supplies.[1]

In preparation for possible local Union aggression, Confederate troops constructed an earthenworks fort at the junction of bayous Grand Caillou and Dulac in June 1861. Its location was strategic to any attack from the Gulf, and the fort was the only installment the Confederacy built in lower Terrebonne. The fort was first named Fort Butler, and at one time was staffed by five Confederate officers and 140 enlisted men. Soon thereafter, the name was changed to Fort Quitman. Relatively early in the war, in April 1862, the fort was abandoned after the fall of New Orleans to Union forces.[2]

The fort was named for Natchez planter, state legislator, U.S. Congressman and Mississippi governor John A. Quitman. His connection to Dulac was that he owned and operated Live Oak plantation at the confluence of the two bayous near the fort's location, having bought the land in 1828 and 1829 from James Bowie of Bowie Knife and Alamo fame. Quitman's plantation and subsequently the fort were across Bayou Grand Caillou from Dulac Plantation. He had constructed a stately home in the Georgian style fronting on the bayou at Live Oak, a site which today is the location of the U.S. Coast Guard Station-Dulac. (The home was, in 1877, to be the birthplace of Marie Adelphine Michel, the future wife of Pierre's second son, Albert. Her family

James Bowie of Bowie knife and Alamo fame moved to Terrebonne Parish around 1819, where he and his family purchased large land tracts in Dulac and along Bayou Black. They later lived in neighboring Lafourche Parish, where they acquired Acadia Plantation's sprawling expanse. Above, Acadia Plantation c. 1885. Prominent Mississippian John A. Quitman bought Live Oak plantation in Dulac (opposite) from Bowie in 1828 and 1829.

Marie Adelphine Michel Cenac, born at Quitman plantation house in 1877

Below, Union General Benjamin Butler and flyer protesting his proclamation (part of which is quoted) that outraged New Orleans citizens in defense of women of the city

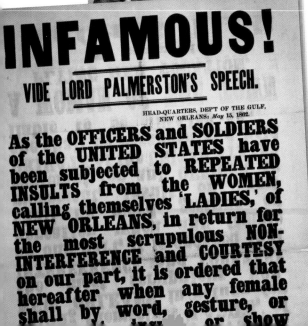

had taken refuge there in a hurricane the night before, and she was born in the storm's aftermath.)

Preparations for conflict charged the atmosphere when young Pierre Cenac stepped onto Terrebonne Parish soil for the first time. He left New Orleans before its 1862 Union occupation, which spared his having to apply for a military pass to allow his travel to Terrebonne and averted his being cooped up in the city for the war's duration.

The smaller town of Houma probably seemed less vulnerable to war's worst, but who could be sure what Union soldiers would target? Nor was it any easier in the town than in the city for a new immigrant to decide whether action or inaction was called for—morally and practically—in such turbulent times. For a young man newly arrived from a world away, a world long afflicted by wars, Pierre had to be daily plagued by forces tugging at his conscience.

The year 1862 probably brought Pierre and other local non-soldier immigrants their most personal conflict, because of war action in their own town. A Confederate blockade-runner, the steamer *Fox*, arrived on May 7 at Bayou Grand Caillou 30 miles south of Houma. Commander of the Union occupation of New Orleans, General Benjamin Butler, received word from federal informants in the area, and sent an order for the *Fox*'s apprehension. Colonel James W. McMillan led a company of 65 men who rode the Opelousas Railroad from Algiers and arrived at Terrebonne Station (Schriever) during the night of May 8-9.[3]

Pierre may have been one of the townspeople who were awakened at around two o'clock in the morning on May 9. The troops had marched the 13 miles down the right descending bank of Bayou Terrebonne and crossed the Barataria Canal Bridge to enter the small town. The sound of marching federal foot soldiers with their equipment and their wagons marked their progress through Houma on their way to Grand Caillou.

Fifteen to 20 local men set out after the Union troops, but realized they were severely outnumbered, and headed back to town. But by late evening May 9, they received word that four sick Union soldiers were being transported in wagons back toward Terrebonne Station for passage back to Algiers. One and a half miles south of Houma at Honduras Plantation, the locals ambushed the wagons and killed two of the soldiers, wounding the two others. Union Pvt. Miller, one of the wounded soldiers, escaped. The local posse drove the other wounded man, Pvt. Morris, and two bodies to Houma.

The badly beaten corpses were buried in the open square a few feet from the market house, directly in front of the courthouse. They were buried without coffins, with only a single blanket and a mound of earth covering their bodies.

Members of the local band of activists included Thomas Albert Wood, a former Confederate lieutenant Morelle, E.N. Dutrail, B. Cooper, Gilbert Hatch, D.W. Crewell, an overseer of Mulberry Farm Plantation named Edwards, Howard Bond and his young brother W. Bond, F. Gatewood, Dr. J.L. Jennings, and William H. Hornsby.

On May 10, another 65-man company commanded by Capt. Elihu E. Rose of the 21st Indiana was dispatched from the New Orleans area. They met the two surviving soldiers near the rail depot at Terrebonne Station, Miller having escaped and Morris having been released by his Houma captors. From New Orleans General Butler dispatched 240 additional soldiers under command of Lt. Col. John A. Keith of the 21st Indiana, who also had charge of 30 additional men and artillery from the 6th Massachusetts Battery.

The new Union commander began to investigate the shootings and ordered the exhumation of the bodies for Christian burial in a prominent churchyard. The leading citizens of the town were arrested and placed into a makeshift prison at the corner of Main and Church streets in the Winder building. After burial of the two Union dead, Sgt. Jesse Frakes and Pvt. Charles Geisendorffer, in St. Francis de Sales Catholic Church cemetery, the lieutenant colonel threatened to destroy Houma and all surrounding plantations if the guilty were not given up within 48 hours. The imprisoned gave some names of those involved, and though most had fled the area, some were seeking nearby refuge. Those known as having harbored the men, such as G.F. Connelly of Mulberry Farm, had their animals and wagonfuls of forage confiscated. The Union leader realized it was futile to look further for the guilty men, who by then had had time to escape far away.

Residence Plantation, c. 1887

On May 16, 1862, the Union commander forced locals to watch while he and his men torched houses, stables, barns, stores, newspaper offices of the Houma *Ceres*, jailhouse, sugarhouses, cooper and blacksmith shops, a buggy, a steam saw and corn mill, and hundreds of personal items and books. Soldiers also destroyed the courthouse which was under construction. Because of this and other war and Reconstruction conditions, it was not completed until 1875. Union troops commandeered scores of cattle, horses, mules, and oxen, along with harness, wagons filled with forage, a separate buggy, and a chest of tools. The *Ceres*, founded at least a decade earlier, closed forever when Union troops threw its type into Bayou Terrebonne.

On May 17, the battalion began its march back to Terrebonne Station on the Terrebonne Road along the right descending bank of Bayou Terrebonne. The original mission against the *Fox* proved successful when the initial Union company dispatched from Algiers, led by Colonel McMillan, captured the steamer on May 16.

From May 7 until May 17, Houma and Terrebonne residents who entered the bakery where Pierre worked must have been buzzing with the latest developments each day, the troop movements and reprisals. He could not have helped but witness

Pre-Civil War Mulberry Plantation in Terrebonne Parish

CAPTURE OF FORTS JACKSON & ST. PHILLIP.

Pensacola. Richmond Kineo. Flag Ship Hartford in Collision with fire Raft. Mississ...

VARUNA Capt Boggs. Brooklyn. 2 IRON CLAD BATTERIES BY UNION FLEET UNDER COM. FARRAGU...

Cayuga. nine knots and the Ships seemed to be fighting

wn by C. Parsons. Gun Boat Winona.

FORT JACKSON.

AND ENTIRE DESTRUCTION

An Officer writes "The sight of this night attack Entere...

...AY, MAY 8, 1862.

THE CAPTURE OF NEW ORLEANS.

FULL PARTICULARS

Forts Jackson and St. Philip Bombarded 6 Days and 6 Nights.

THE FORTS SILENCED.

Eleven Rebel Gunboats Destroyed by Our Navy.

TERRIFIC NAVAL COMBAT.

Louisiana regimental fatalities at the Battle of Antietam, September, 1862; Union coat button recovered in present-day Schriever, Terrebonne Parish; illustration depiction and newspaper accounts of the 1862 capture of Forts Jackson and St. Philip, at the mouth of the Mississippi River

FIVE CENTS

Eng.d by Geo. E. Perine N.Y.

...troying "Hollins Ram."
FORT St. PHILLIP.

...IL 24 1862.
...y amidst flames and smoke.

The steamer Ceres, *commandeered by Union forces during the Civil War*

The New Orleans, Opelousas & Great Western Railroad's, (owner of the Ceres), *request for monetary compensation following the steamer's capture and sinking*

the burning of so many buildings in town on May 16, and perhaps was one of the townsmen forced to march in the two deceased soldiers' funeral procession several days before.

After 1862, Houma itself escaped further damage from federal troops, but many Terrebonne plantation owners suffered losses to Union forces through confiscated crops, goods, and valuables as homes were pillaged. Many civilians in Terrebonne, as in all the Southern states, suffered from hunger and diseases for which there were only rudimentary treatments. Because of protracted hunger and the lack of doctors, women in large numbers succumbed to complications following childbirth during this time period. Families were often forced to forage for food, since many homes were bereft of men, who were in military service. The war years saw an increase of sickness and non-combat mortality for these reasons. During the war years 1861-1865, typhoid fever killed 187,000 North Americans.

As for service to the Confederacy, military duty did not become law until conscription was enacted by the Confederate Congress in April 1862, encompassing men ages 18 to 35. By September the same year, the Confederate Congress made conscription official for men up to the age of 45. However, forcing men to serve was a difficult matter in Louisiana, where in October 1862 draft dodgers, runaways, conscripts or deserters numbered 8,000 under Confederate General Richard Taylor's domain. Between April and October of 1862, the parishes of Assumption, Lafourche, and Terrebonne had 1,696 men inducted into the Confederate army.

One more or less traditional battle in the area about which local residents received detailed stories was that of Lafourche Crossing in June, 1863, which was a significant and prolonged action. Since Thibodaux was larger than was Houma at the time of the Civil War, and since the railroad line ran north of Houma toward Brashear (now Morgan) City, much of the area's conflicts were in those locales.

The battle at Kock's Plantation near Donaldsonville in mid-July of 1863 was another important conflict between the opposing armies in south Louisiana. It "marked the last hurrah between organized units from the North and South. From July 1863, until the end of the war, no further battle cries were audible. Though combat fought in large-scale battles ceased after July 1863, a different kind of warfare took over. Its ferocity was no less tense for those who fought or lived in southeast Louisiana." This "different kind of warfare" was the advent of guerilla tactics, which proved to be effective for locals in southeast Louisiana until the end of the war.

The relative commitment of area troops was described by one Union officer, who participated in a battle near Labadieville. He spotted whom he thought were "Terre Bonne militiamen...mostly of French stock and not very zealous Rebels" who "opened a hasty sidelong fire" toward the federal troops and then quickly "broke for the neighboring thickets, disappearing like young partridges."

Guerilla warfare continued until the end of the war.

The Confederacy unofficially ended in April of 1865 when General Robert E. Lee surrendered to Major General Ulysses S. Grant at Appomattox. However, in Louisiana, guerilla warfare had escalated in 1864 and 1865 and had proved effective against Union forces, who had a decided disadvantage in the terrain so familiar to local men.

One Terrebonne Parish incident indicates the extent to which Union soldiers went to capture particularly troublesome Confederate soldiers. Lt. Omar Boudreaux and his band of "renegades" were tracked to "Bayou DeLarge to the rear of J. Terrion's plantation." Boudreaux was wounded and his group dispersed, without "time to get their clothes on before departing the area." This was on May 27, 1865, but "there were still reports of at least two Confederate guerrilla parties roaming the area near Houma" on May 31.

At the end of the war, statistics proved that "in both lives and property, southeast Louisiana perhaps suffered greater proportionally than any other region in the state. In the Lafourche district, in particular, 18 percent of the white population, some 3,500 men, served in some degree in the Confederate army prior to the fall 1862 Union occupation. In 1862, that represented 79 percent of the estimated 4,428 eligible males of military age from the district. Only 61 percent of eligible males in the collective states of the Confederacy served in their army. In the North, only 35 percent of eligible males served.

If Pierre and other recent immigrants agonized about not "joining up" for a war they couldn't claim as their own, they were certainly not alone—even among native Southerners and Northerners—in their decision to remain out of uniform.

NOTES

1. Marguerite Watkins thesis, 1939

2. Casey A. Powell. *Encyclopedia of Forts, Posts, Named Camps and Other Military Installations in Louisiana, 1700-1981.* Christopher Pena. *Touched By War: Battles Fought in the Lafourche District*

3. All accounts and factual statistics of Civil War action in southeast Louisiana which follow are quoted either directly (as indicated) or sourced indirectly from Christopher Pena's detailed book, *Scarred By War: Civil War in Southeast Louisiana.* His book contains extensive research and comprehensive crediting of original sources for anecdotal and factual information.

A sketch in Harper's Weekly *of Union troops foraging in lower south Louisiana during the Civil War*

A rendering of the meeting between Union General Ulysses S. Grant and Confederate General Robert E. Lee at Appomattox, Virginia on April 9, 1865

The Rev. Jean-Marie Denece, founding pastor of Sacred Heart Church in Montegut, who performed Pierre and Victorine's marriage ceremony

CHAPTER 13
August 9, 1865:
The Future Smiles

Father Jean-Marie Joseph Denece turned toward the little church's tabernacle and genuflected, his long vestments skimming the altar's raw wood floors. He began to intone the Latin marriage rites that Pierre had heard so often at his brothers' and cousins' weddings in the old stone church of Barbazan-Debat. Pierre pictured the worn stones the priest in Barbazan trod upon there, stones that had seen generations of country couples wed.

Pierre stood stiff and tall in his dark suit. His starched white collar scratched his neck as he made the slightest movement to glance at Victorine beside him. She was wearing the wedding dress her mother made for her last year before the young couple jumped the broom in the front yard of Victorine's family home on Grand Caillou. Today, she wore part of the tulle veil from that occasion draped over her shoulders as a shawl.

Pierre tenderly looked down at Victorine's burgeoning abdomen. Victorine and Maman "Zelide" had to make some adjustments to the dress for this church wedding, but his bride looked even more beautiful today. *It will be soon now that we will be parents. Moi, papa. Un garçon, j'espère.*

Father Denece brought Pierre's mind back to the ceremony when he began the questions familiar to every Catholic who had ever attended a wedding in the Church. Victorine smiled up at Pierre. He recognized that look of joy. Pierre remembered how excited she was when she heard Montegut had opened its own church just recently, in time for their wedding before the baby was born. A distance they could travel instead of the longer, difficult trip to Houma's St. Francis de Sales.

A black tendril had escaped her upswept hair arrangement, and Pierre had to suppress an impulse to caress it back into place while he repeated his own vows after the priest. He knew better than to make such a personal gesture on the altar.

Fr. Denece gave the couple a final blessing with the flair of a young priest. The two turned to walk down the aisle, silent, before receiving the congratulations of the few guests who had followed them to just outside the front door of newly-built Sacred Heart church. Papa Charles Fanguy shook Pierre's hand while Maman Azelie kissed Victorine's cheek. Witnesses Uncle Edgar

Fanguy, Bernard Monthieu, and Baptiste Artigue followed with their own circumspect respects to Victorine and hearty ones to Pierre.

The small family group would have to begin the journey back to Grand Caillou right away if they wanted to arrive at their homes before too late in the evening.

As he helped Victorine up into the carriage, Pierre's mind went back to last year's celebration after they had performed the custom that seemed so strange to him when he first moved into the country from town. He was more than happy to jump a broom to declare their commitment to the world, because he wanted to marry Victorine with no further delay. Two years of courting was enough, in his mind.

But he agreed with his bride then that it was a sad thing, these only-occasional mission trips of priests from Thibodaux to bless marriages and to baptize babies along Terrebonne's lower coastal communities. This had been going on since at least the 1840s, his future father-in-law informed him. It was just an accepted thing they had learned to work around, according to *Monsieur* Fanguy.

The Fanguy family—and there were many of them—turned out last year in large numbers to wish them happiness. There had been homemade cakes and blackberry wine, and even a fiddler on the porch to play a wedding waltz Pierre had never heard, but which Victorine hummed as they danced.

Pierre had never shaken so many hands before, but he decided that he liked it.

After Maman, Papa, and Uncle Edgar began to doze despite the carriage's lurches and bumps, Victorine took Pierre's hand and placed it over her belly. The baby was kicking hard and strong. The couple grinned at each other, and Victorine whispered, "It won't be long now."

*Fire brand and registration of
Pierre Cenac dated January 31, 1865
and registration of Edmond Fanguy
dated March 7, 1833*

CHAPTER 14
From Artisan to Entrepreneur

Jean Baptiste Cenac was born on August 30, 1865, at the Cenac home in Dulac, or possibly at the home of Pierre's father-in-law. It was common practice at the time for young couples to move in with one set of parents before becoming established themselves. The Charles Fanguy house may have been a temporary residence for the newlyweds.

Sometime between 1862 and the time of his marriage, probably in 1864, Pierre relocated to lower Terrebonne near the confluence of bayous Grand Caillou and Dulac, after living for a time in Houma. This decision to move there probably took primary impetus from its being the home place of Victorine and her family.

Victorine's great-grandfather Edmond Fanguy was a veteran of the Revolutionary War. He had a Spanish land grant on Bayou Terrebonne which predated the Louisiana Purchase in 1803 (ownership confirmed by the U.S. government in 1812 when Louisiana was granted statehood[1]). He is listed as Edmond Fanguille in the first census taken of Terrebonne Parish residents in 1830.[2] Some of the Fanguy family relocated at an unknown time to Grand Caillou.

The Fanguys and Pierre had in common their Basque heritage. Basque expert and researcher Michel Goitia-Nicolas found that the Fanguy surname comes from the French Soulé state in Basque country (seven total: three states in France, four in Spain). Soulé is the only state to use the prefix *fan* meaning *to go*, whereas the universal Basque word for that phrase is *joan*. The suffix *guy*, as well as *gue and gui*, essentially means *place through the mountains*. The name Fanguy means "mountain pass," or "a place to go through the mountains."

Pierre, his wife, and in-laws, then, probably shared capability to speak in both Basque and French dialects, as well as generations of customs and common ties in the Old Country.

Even as a young man, Pierre began acquiring property in Grand Caillou and continued over the next several decades. However, Pierre's first recorded land purchase was on February 9, 1865—five months before he married, and not in Dulac, but "in town." On that date Pierre bought half of Jean-Marie Dupont's lot on the corner of Main and Barrow streets in Houma. Pierre's half was bounded by Barrow Street and the now non-existent Short

Street, which at the time was the back boundary of the Dupont holdings there. Short Street intersected Barrow on the opposite side from still-existent St. Matthew's Episcopal Church, between the church's location (before destruction by fire on November 11, 2010) and Main Street.

Pierre paid $1,500 in February for the southern half of the property on which the (greatly expanded) Dupont store building still stands. It was designated as Lot 2 Block 14 in the document of sale. Just nine months later, on November 25, Pierre sold this same property back to *Monsieur* Dupont at the exact price he had paid for it.

Just a few days before that first venture into property ownership, on January 31, 1865, he was granted a cattle fire brand according to records in the Houma courthouse, recorded at the time by Alfred Rougelot. The brand was numbered 499, and consisted of his initials connected by a bar: P—C. This was the earliest transaction recorded for Pierre Cenac in the official documents of Terrebonne Parish.[1]

In Dulac he acquired his initial long-term landholdings by purchase or via patents and quitclaims, in one of the southernmost undeveloped spots in Terrebonne Parish. Purchase of "patent certificates"[1] from the state of Louisiana was a type of transaction the state began in 1850. This procedure granted the holder up to 640 acres of land after Congress passed the Swamp Land Grant Act of 1849. By this act the federal government transferred to the state all marsh and overflowed land, some of which had previously been part of older land grants to individuals.

In the Grand Caillou area, Pierre's early purchases were of property adjacent to and south of Dulac and Live Oak plantations, and included land along Bayou Salé (Salty Bayou), Bayou Four Points and Bayou Grassy, in a part of the parish that was primarily raw land at the time.

Besides his wife's being a resident of the area, also important to Pierre's move was the fact that Dulac had traditionally been a large settlement and not just a remote outpost in the hinterlands.

Pierre's patent certificate No. 256 from November 12, 1867

1830 Terrebonne Parish Census

The Fanguy (Fanguille) name was one of only 167 family names listed in the 1830 parish census. Of those, seven households bearing the same surname was the most numerous in repetition. Family names were: Adams, Albararo, Arsineaux, Arseneaux, Ashley, Aucoin, Babin, Baille, Barras, Bastane, Batey, Barrow, Boudoin, Belanger, Belangier, Benjamin, Benois, Berjean, Bergeon, Bell, Billeaux, Blanchard, Bonvillien, Boudreaux, Boudloche, Bourgue, Brasowell, Brunet, Buford, Burrett, Butler, Calotte, Casson, Calvey, Carl, Carr, Chambers, Charpentier, Chataignier, Chaisson, Clark, Clifton, Cazeau, Collette, Comeajain, Comos, Collinsworth, Crochet, Daigle, Dazy, Darses, Davis, Dubois, Dugas, Duplanty, Dupre, Eaken, Ecliff, Ellis, Fanguille, Field, Fontineaux, Foster, Fuqua, Gans, Gautier, Garey, Gautreaux, Gauber, Gibson, Goodwin, Green, Gregoire, Greenage, Guidery, Hauk, Hammond, Haynes, Hebert, Henry, Hinar, Holdman, Hunter, Imelle, Keys, King, Laby, Laflin, Lancon, LeBlanc, LeBouef, Lejeune, Lum, Lambert, Lapeiruse, Leday, Leroux, Lirette, Lyman, Maiseille, Marlborough, Malbrough, Maronde, Marone, Marrow, Martin, Mars, Mead, Medrano, Miller, Millehomme, Mellor, Moncon, Monier, Montogudean, Moore, Moreau, McCoy, McLaughlin, McWilliams, Naquin, Osbern, Payne, Phipps, Pichauf, Picou, Pitre, Porche, Porter, Ratcliff, Ready, Richard, Robichaud, Roddy, Rodrigues, Richardson, Rountree, Rousseau, Sathens, Savoy, Shelden, Shield, Signe, Squeyers (Squires?), Sterit, Tyvet, Tabour, Tanner, Thibodeaux, Tirguy, Toups, Torrero, Tulaire, Tyson, Veret, Verdin, Vannoman, Wade, Waggoner, Wakbespask (Waguespack), Watson, Watkins, Welsh, Westbrook, Wood, Wright. List is from Sherwin Guidry's Explorin' Terrebonne, a collection of newspaper articles by Mr. Guidry.

Another source, the publication "Pioneers" edited by Phoebe Chauvin Morrison in 1984, gives the following statistics for 1830: 237 household heads listed; population of 1,063 whites, 25 free Negros and 1,033 slaves, for a total of 2,121. Number of families by origin: 74 Acadian French; 74 American; 29 French (apart from Acadian and Canadian); 19 German; 18 Canadian French; 8 Irish; 4 Spanish; 4 Indian; 3 English; 2 Scots; 1 Swedish; 1 Canary Islands family.

Grand Isle, Louisiana c. 1932

Bayou Salé c. 1944

Although much of the surrounding land was undeveloped, a considerable community had sprung up over the years near the natural deep water channel to the Gulf at Bayou Grand Caillou. Adjacent bayou lands were prime for many potential undertakings when the 22-year-old Frenchman arrived on the scene 40 or so years after the founding of Terrebonne Parish.

Discounting any considerations of the Civil War's potential aftermath in any part of Terrebonne, Pierre had weighty enough reasons to locate there—besides his wife's connections firmly entrenched there—by virtue of the number of residents of similar ancestry and common language, the deep-water port, and its fertile lands.

An 1849 description of Dulac Plantation gives a perspective of the area where Pierre later resided: "...situated at or near the mouth of the Caillou, the last plantation on this route to the sea coast, commands the admiration of all. The land being narrow, on account of its proximity to the marsh, the plantation is proportionably long, seven or eight miles. Several bayous lie contiguous, and the tide water passes through the ditches, but does not interfere with cultivation. Very beautiful scenery is spread out before the eye here. A lake and sea march in one direction, which extends nearly to the limit of vision. Large live oaks line the shore of the bayou, a shell road running along it: the rural residence of the hospitable and intelligent proprietor; the garden of tropical evergreens and fruits; the quarter romantically situated near the bayou; the bridge which spans the bayou—these views, connected with the influence of the sea air, which comes from the Gulf, makes one feel, indeed, 'There is not in this wide world a valley so sweet.'"[3]

Coastal erosion was not a factor in Terrebonne's southernmost communities in the mid-1800s. Dense cypress and hardwood forests stretched far behind cleared farms and homesteads. Land in Dulac was high and dry, with extensive natural ridges reaching far back from bayousides. The topography was an agricultural jewel for anyone whose desire was to work cultivable land. The semi-tropical climate and waterways were sources for all requisite irrigation. The community's size provided neighbors with whom to transact business.

It was a perfect spot for a young, ambitious man to begin his business life and his family. Beginning in 1865 there is evidence that Pierre transitioned in short order from being a *boulanger* to becoming a property owner operating several types of his own business interests a distance from Houma, in both Grand Caillou and Little Caillou.

The birth of their first child only 21 days after Pierre and Victorine's church marriage was not an uncommon occurrence, nor a morally scandalous one, for bayou couples at the time. Factors contributing to this situation included Dulac's relative remoteness from the parish seat, the difficulty of overland transportation with minimal or no road system, and Grand Caillou's lack of a Roman Catholic church of its own until many years later. In 1864 and 1865, Houma remained under Union domination, probably discouraging the couple from having a civil ceremony at the courthouse there. Few, if any, records remain from the Civil War years because of the federal troops' destruction of the courthouse; if Pierre and Victorine did manage to have a legal ceremony there, the records have been lost.

The young couple probably had performed a ceremony many Catholic rural inhabitants resorted to in order to declare their married status until they could have the benefit of a priest's blessing. "Jumping the broom," (*sauter le balai*) witnessed by family and friends, signified couples' pledging their lives to each other until a priest performed a (usually annual) missionary trip to the bayou communities.

The earliest mission trips down Bayou Terrebonne followed Father Charles Menard's appointment as assistant pastor of St. Joseph Church in Thibodaux in 1842. That church parish, founded in 1817, had jurisdiction over all of Lafourche and Terrebonne civil parishes to the Gulf of Mexico. Appointed many years after St. Joseph was built in Thibodaux in 1819, Father

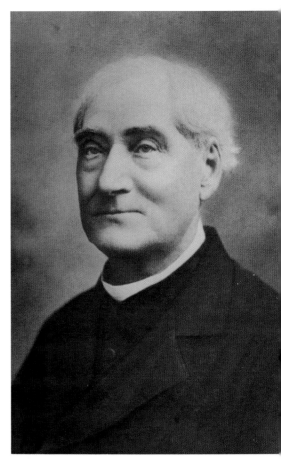

The Rev. Charles Menard, born 1817 in Lyons, France, was called the "Apostle of the Bayous." He was vicar, then pastor, of St. Joseph Church in Thibodaux 54 years (1842-1896)

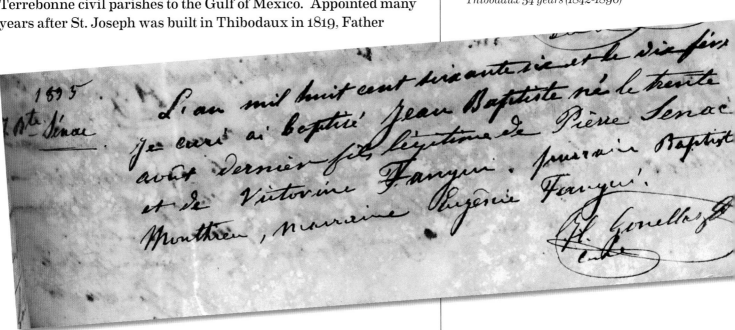

Baptismal certificate of Jean Baptiste Cenac dated February 10, 1866

Menard became known as the "Apostle of Bayou Lafourche and Bayou Terrebonne" for his zeal in providing spiritual services to the outlying areas as well as to Thibodauxville, as the town was known at the time. Before establishment of Terrebonne's earliest church parishes, bayou residents relied on the occasional visits from missionary priests for performance of marriage ceremonies and baptisms along the course of one trip.

Father Jean Marie Joseph Denece was appointed as first resident pastor for the people of lower Terrebonne. He had made the crossing from France aboard the ship *Sainte Genevieve* at the same time as one Msgr. Odin, who was soon to become Archbishop of New Orleans. The people of "Canal Belanger" (Bourg), Montegut, Little Caillou, and Grand Caillou were his flock beginning in 1865. He oversaw the development of Montegut's Sacred Heart parish and served as pastor there until his death in 1890.

Father Denece and other early priests to local Catholics endured considerable hardships to serve their parishioners. The priest wrote, "The people of my parish were in majority very poor and could not help very much, so I was obliged to sacrifice all my savings....I passed five years without a fire, not even having a chimney in my poor house. In order to keep warm, I would work in my little garden."

In another record entry, Fr. Denece wrote, "One day I traveled in four different manners. I left Bayou Plat at 9:00 in the morning in a pirogue; at noon I left Bayou Salé on horseback; at 2:00 I crossed Fredric Parfait's woods on foot; at Bayou Lacache I got into a buggy at Jean Larrieux's house; and at 4:00 p.m. after having celebrated Onesippe Robichaux's wedding, I was brought back to Bayou Lacache in a buggy and walked the rest of the way. I was home finally at 7 p.m."

Sacred Heart Church was a considerable distance from Dulac but was more accessible to people of the Grand Caillou area than was St. Francis de Sales Church in Houma. The church building was newly established when Pierre and Victorine said their formal vows before Father Denece that August day in 1865.[1]

Jean Baptiste was the first of 14 children Pierre and Victorine brought into the world over a period of 26 years. From 1865 until 1891, the Cenacs of Dulac gave birth to eight boys and six girls. All 14 were born during the family's residency in Dulac.[birth certificates 1] (Victorine was 21 and Pierre 27 when they delivered their first baby. She was 47 and he was 53 when Victorine gave birth to their fourteenth child.)

One of Victorine Cenac's irons and (below) one of her washboards

During the period 1865-1880, Pierre and Victorine became parents to their first 11 children while Pierre was forging lifelong professional contacts and forming numerous business ventures. They were halcyon years when their family flourished, and when Pierre's businesses grew in number and profitability. According to later newspaper articles, Pierre's reputation within the parish community rose in stature beginning with this period. The Cenacs of Dulac seemed to lead a charmed, happy life within the context of their time and place.

Their first 11 children and years of birth were: Jean Baptiste, 1865; Marie, 1867; Albert, 1868; Marguerite Laurentine, 1870; Theophile, 1871; Victorine Aimée, 1872; Jean Pierre, Jr., 1874; Jean Charles, 1876; Paul Michel, 1878; Marie Anne Celestine, 1879; Josephine, 1880.

As to his first business affiliations, a 1914 article about Pierre read in part, "The early part of his life was spent in the fur business and in cane planting. He owned a large number of oyster beds also, which paid him a lucrative income." In 1926, a newspaper account about Victorine stated, "...she and her husband the late Pierre Cenac, owned a small sugar plantation...." State records indicate that Pierre "Senat" ran a wooden sugar house and used the open-kettle process to produce sugar at Bayou Salé.[4]

These cursory assessments of the couple's business interests touched only on what stood out in retrospect, decades after they had begun as newlyweds to work both land and waters, and to build their family. The couple's methods of "earning a living" eventually became almost as numerous as were the children they brought into the world together.

Abstractor Herbert Wurzlow said of Pierre, "the biggest part of his land on Grand Caillou he bought from Robert Ruffin Barrow."[5] Conveyance records in Terrebonne Parish's courthouse clarify that, after the 1865 transactions with Jean-Marie Dupont, Pierre's next land purchase was on May 9, 1866, from Baptiste Vito *et al*, in Little Caillou. In 1868, on August 15, he bought his first patent from the State of Louisiana, 640 acres in Grand Caillou.[1] That was followed by another purchase in this manner of another 640 acres on January 9, 1871.[1]

In later years Pierre also traded for land, and acquired other tracts via quitclaim and at tax sales.[1] At the time of his death in 1914, he had accumulated approximately 4,000 acres.

The Cenacs' family life in Dulac was described by Pierre and Victorine's daughter-in-law Gertrude Laurentine Bourgeois Cenac for a newspaper interview. Her description portrays a world of self-sufficiency and hard work. She said the family "raised pigs to make lard, sausage (boudin) and salt meat. They had cattle and always boiled their milk....There were always lots of fresh eggs and they had their fill of garden-fresh, vitamin-rich vegetables. They raised cane and made their own sugar and syrup. They churned their own butter. They made coal by burning wood in deep holes.

Above, Perfection Brand kerosene stove Ivanhoe Model 259 c. 1900 belonging to Marie Madeleine Bourgeois Cenac. Below, A. Bouchereau's report of 1877. Bottom, clothes boiling kettle of the period

Eleanor Monthieu Bourgeois and Bernard Jean-Pierre Caliste Bourgeois with baby Marie Madeleine and children (from left) Louis Caliste, Eugenie Octavie and Gertrude Laurentine. Photo from September 1885. Below, Caliste Bourgeois fire brand and its June 26, 1885 registration

"They had no ice, but ...put watermelons in big sacks and lowered them into a 15 foot deep well....They had their cisterns under the same roof as the house to keep the water clean and cool.

"They washed their clothes on wash boards or boiled them in big black iron pots. They made their own soap....They ironed with black irons heated on a charcoal furnace or in the chimney place.

"They made their own mattresses and quilts and clothes. In winter they slept on feather beds. In summer their mattresses were made of Spanish moss, dried, or corn shucks and their beds were covered with big net mosquito bars."[5]

Considering their self-sufficiency, the family must have had fruit tree orchards as well, which most families cultivated for their own use.

Important to their family life during their years in Dulac were ties the Cenacs developed with four families: the Bourgeois, Carlos, Carrere, and Gatewood families. Two Cenac daughters would marry two Carlos brothers and one daughter became the betrothed of a third Carlos brother. Another Cenac daughter later married a Carrerre who was reared in the same community. Two Cenac sons went on to marry two Bourgeois sisters from Houma, and the oldest Cenac son married a neighboring Gatewood daughter. The intertwining of these families was extended by the fact that three Carlos brothers married three Carrere sisters, and a Gatewood sister married yet another Carlos brother. (Marie Cenac, one of the Cenac sisters who wed a Carlos, was the second wife of Salvador Carlos, Jr., whose first wife, Josephine Constance Marie Carrere, died at age 17 during the birth of their first child.)

Cultural norms of the day, the stay-at-home nature of bayou residents' existence, and the proximity of these families must have prompted many a *veillée* (evening visit) among these families at each other's homes.

Even as a young newcomer to Dulac, and when his family was just being formed, Pierre exhibited a wide range of interests which did not stop at subsistence livelihood. "Jean Pierre and his family...ran a grocery store and operated a syrup mill," according to one genealogical organization's account.[6] Pierre must have rejoiced in the rich earth of Terrebonne when he remembered the unyielding lands which had failed to produce crops in the *Hautes-Pyrénées* when he left France.

Most residents of the area, both in the bayou communities and "in town" (Houma), maintained chicken yards and milking cows. It was probably a considerable number of chickens, as well as a substantial vegetable garden, that were required to furnish the Cenacs' many children with daily meals and to supply their general store with the extra vegetable and fruit produce.

The "fur business" referred to in the 1914 newspaper article referred to the prevalence of the seasonal occupation of trapping muskrats, otters, and other furbearing animals in the marshlands along the coast. Although no written source or family records give details, this probably took the form of Pierre's brokering the buying and selling of pelts. The Cenac sons helped to furnish the family's own necessities as well as supplying goods for market. They were skilled at hunting and fishing, and no doubt trapping was also a part of their existence, as it was for most of the families living in that environment.

Another assumption is that as the Cenac sons got older, they may have at one time engaged in hunting birds with decorative plumes such as egrets. These were coveted by the women's millinery industry at the time these young men were growing up. Many across the South hunted such specimens for market until the practice was outlawed in the early twentieth century when some species were in danger of extinction.

Among Pierre's enterprises was the operation of a broom factory during the Dulac years. The family grew what was known as "broom corn" on his lands to provide material for the brooms. (Broom corn grows tassels, and the dried tassels become the straw for the sweeping part of the broom.) When he moved to Houma many years later, he re-established the broom-making business there. Little Caillou native Aurelie Eschete remembered buying brooms from Pierre when the factory was located north of Bayou Terrebonne on East Park in Houma. The exact site of the factory is lost to history.[5]

Terrebonne Times *ad of July 17, 1897. Below, John James Audubon print from* Birds of America, *1827-1838*

Still-functional broom-making machinery originally used by Pierre Cenac at Dulac and later Park Avenue in Houma, "broom corn" (a variety of sorghum grain) tassel atop the machine

Below, raw material and finished product

The machinery which manufactured Pierre's brooms at first remained in the family. After Pierre died, Victorine's brother Charles Fanguy first used it, and then his son, also Charles, made brooms in the Grand Caillou community using the equipment. After the younger Fanguy died, Ivy Vice of Bayou Dularge bought it from a Fanguy cousin, and the Vices made brooms as a part-time business. Pierre's broom-making equipment is in storage on Bayou Dularge, in the ownership of Ivy Vice's son Bobby. To the credit of everyone who used it, the machinery is still operable after about 130 years.

One favorite—and long-lived—occupation Pierre began soon after his marriage was that of trading and selling horses and mules. This began during his Dulac years, and continued after he much later moved "to town."

During this period, Pierre began purchasing oyster beds, and his sons and sons-in-law were initiated into methods of cultivation and harvesting of the bivalves.

Consistent with the surrounding terrain and the family's ventures, Pierre's family owned boats while they lived at Dulac. Some of them were the *Generosity, Defender, Terrebonne,* the *Rosalina* (all one-mast luggers), and the two-masted schooner the *Peter Casano. La Casanne,* as French-speaking people used to call the *Peter Casano,* apparently created a lot of excitement when it sailed down the bayou because of its two masts' billowing sails, as opposed to the more common sight of single-mast boats.[5]

The Cenac family's domestic lives in the bayou community were closely tied to the fertile soil and the productive waters that anchored and surrounded their homestead. It is possible that the

Cenac homestead was known by a name Pierre might have given it, as was common practice at the time by sugar-cane growers of more than subsistence acreage. An informal note by Olympe Labit Cenac, wife of Pierre and Victorine's grandson Arthur, records information about the original Terrebonne Cenacs. The note makes mention of "House La Cordaire on bayou." Therefore, it may be that the Cenac home was referred to as the name "La Cordaire." Although it would have no meaning in the French language, Basque scholar Michel Goitia-Nicolas explained that in Basque, the name could have its origins in the word *Cordoaire* or *Kordoaire*, meaning "place on high ground." In Pierre's case, it would be a reference to the high ridge upon which he built his family's home.

La Haute-Garonne, France c. 1880

A large part of their family's cultural heritage was language-based. By the mid-nineteenth century, Victorine's extended family had been absorbed into Acadian culture, with vestiges of her Basque heritage. This, added to Pierre's upbringing, meant that the Cenacs of Dulac spoke a form of French as their primary language in the home, according to more than one of their surviving grandchildren. The family's entrenchment in French heritage is evidenced by the fact that the thirteenth child Dennis, as an adult Houma resident with eight children of his own, prayed in French when he awoke each morning.[7] He spoke both English and the French his parents had taught him until his death in 1965, a full 105 years after his father arrived in the parish.

Adenise's daughter Marion Williams Charpentier, and William Jean Pierre Cenac's children Olga and Donald all also attested to the fact that French was commonly spoken in their homes. Because of William Jean Pierre's having married Marie Madeleine Bourgeois, whose grandparents and mother, Eleanor Monthieu, had also immigrated directly from France (Carbonne, Haute-Garonne), the French spoken in their home probably was a mixture of the French standard language and the local *patois*.

Pierre must have also had a strong command of the English language to have been a successful businessman. Although many of his neighbors and business clientele spoke a form of French, many of the larger Terrebonne community were Anglo-Americans who conversed in English only. Pierre had to adapt to this requirement in order to become a community leader and a business success.

Another important adaptation for Pierre, especially when he began to have children of his own, was the separation from his family of origin. While he was building his family and enterprises, he must have wondered about what was going on in the lives of his siblings a world away. During the years of the Civil War, which did not end until Pierre had made his move to Dulac, the conflict had to have forced thoughts of his two younger brothers, both soldiers in his native land. Genealogical accounts of his French family document that one of the soldier-brothers, Jean, died at 27 years of age in 1870. The other soldier among his brothers, Dominique, died at age 33 in 1873. Pierre was an ocean away, and his only contact was in daydreams about their fate.

One particularly poignant piece of correspondence is in Pierre's descendants' possession. The letter was addressed to Pierre's brother Jean from a Louisiana man in response to Jean's apparent inquiries concerning his emigrant brother's whereabouts. It is addressed from the civil *Parish of St. John the Baptist* to *Mr. Jean Senac of Barbazan Debat* and dated November 7, 1867, seven years after Pierre's disembarking at the port of New Orleans (and at a time when over 3,000 had died of yellow fever there).

Sir, I received your letter dated last August 25. If I am late in responding it is because of the yellow fever, which has decimated the population of New Orleans, along with cholera. One must not be familiar with this country in order to abandon our own and come to die far from one's family. As for your brother, I have lost sight of him for about five years. One told me that he had left for Mexico, another told me that he lives in New Orleans. I wrote to him in care of general delivery in New Orleans, but I have not yet received any response. I wrote to several friends asking them to investigate as much as possible. I just learned that he has left New Orleans and that he has moved to the country. That is all that I could gather for the moment. As soon as I know where he is I will write to him to communicate your letter. I always make it a duty to do for my fellow man what I would like [done] when I need. If you need to write to me here is my address: Mr. F. Abadie/St. John the Baptist/United States of America, Louisiana/ Edgard Peret Post Office. I would like to know the man about whom you are seeking information from me. I am your very humble servant, F. Abadie.[1]

No evidence exists as to whether Jean was ultimately successful in finding Pierre, or whether Pierre initiated correspondence to his siblings in France at all, either from New Orleans prior to his leaving there, or from his new home in Terrebonne Parish. Between the time he left France and the date of Jean's letter attempting to locate his brother, at least one

Letter in French from F. Abadie to Pierre's brother Jean in background this page. Right, St. Thérèse of Lisieux, late 1800s

of Pierre's siblings, his sister Jacquette, a novice, died in 1862 at age 16. She probably succumbed to tuberculosis, which was documented as being present in the Lisieux Carmelite convent (later made famous by St. Therese of Lisieux) at that time.

Later court documents and conveyance records exhibit Pierre's strong, even penmanship, which proves his literacy. There being no barrier, then, to his writing home, one can only wonder whether Pierre ached for knowledge about his family, whether there indeed existed correspondence that has since been lost to history, or whether it was out of emotional self-preservation that he may have severed all ties with his French family.

Monsieur Abadie's letter is in possession of the Terrebonne Parish family, so either Mr. Abadie himself forwarded a copy of it to Pierre when Mr. Abadie eventually ascertained Pierre's whereabouts, or Pierre may have received it as an enclosure with other correspondence from his brother Jean who initiated the search, once he was able to determine Pierre's place of residence.

While the Cenac family in Terrebonne Parish lived their daily lives in Dulac, the wider community changed and shifted as the years of Reconstruction beginning in 1865 intensified and subsided.

Postwar labor relations between planters and freedmen laborers were tense, and sometimes radically contentious. Freedmen applied for "government lands" in accordance with Circular No. 10, Headquarters Bureau Refugees, Freedmen, Abandoned Lands, State of Louisiana. (Such applicants were freedman David Curley, of "St. Bridgett Plantation," in Terrebonne Parish on September 11, 1865, for 250 acres of land; Grandison Hunt for the 800 acres composing "the whole of the Ranche Plantation" in Terrebonne Parish; Grandison Hunt for the 3,000 acres composing "the whole of the Woodlawn Plantation in Terrebonne Parish; Grandison Hunt for lease of 800 acres, composing "the whole of the William Besland Plantation" in Terrebonne Parish. A number of other freedmen in nearby Lafourche Parish applied for the rental rights on different parcels of acreage on Vick Plantation and Leighton Plantation that September, as well.)

One important episode that indicated the contentiousness between laborers and planters was the Terrebonne Parish strike of January 1874. The labor disturbance occurred early in the crop season, and violence was averted. However, in 1887 the "Thibodaux Massacre" became the second bloodiest labor action in American history, after plantation workers (black and some white) conducted a three-week strike organized by the Knights of Labor in Iberia, Lafourche, St. Mary and Terrebonne parishes. The strike ended in the death of more than 30 blacks during a confrontation in and around Thibodaux, and with thousands of plantation laborers homeless.[8]

These prolonged upheavals to the pre-war status quo were but one change to which Pierre Cenac and his generation of emigrants had to adjust.

A note dated January 30, 1897 from Pierre explaining that he is ill, and requesting that Clerk of Court Aubin Bourg allow Pierre's son Jean Charles to represent him in the transfer of a piece of land to John R. Scott

U.S. Mint in New Orleans, c. 1858

Emile Daigle, Sr.

Steam engine "Old George"
of the Houma Branch Line Railroad
sometime after 1872

One earlier indicator of the tides of change was that of currencies Pierre had to use in the few short years after his arrival in New Orleans. During the time he spent in the city, francs (coins), U.S. coins, and Spanish coins were still in circulation. Employers would have paid him in either U.S. coin or Louisiana-issued money. The U.S. Mint in New Orleans remained in operation until the state joined the Confederacy, at which time Montgomery, Alabama, and subsequently Richmond, Virginia, became the sources of Confederate currency. After Pierre's move to Terrebonne Parish, business was conducted using not only Confederate money, but also corporate-issued script, money printed by the local government, commercial script, and commercial tokens "good for" a certain monetary value of merchandise or services. (Tokens are still in use in such venues as amusement arcades and the like.) When locals found themselves with no capital of any kind, they resorted to the barter system to exchange goods or services.

Tides of the literal sense that Pierre encountered for the first time belonged to the surges pushed inland by hurricanes at this building time in his life. Tales of the 1856 hurricane that destroyed Last Island off Terrebonne's coast, killing more than 200 people, were oft-repeated legend by the time Pierre arrived in Terrebonne in the early 1860s. The first major storm he actually experienced was that of July 1866, and then another, a month later in August. Such extreme weather events were entirely new to him, and as he witnessed battering winds and rising waters he must have feared for his little family's survival. Only five years later, another hurricane hit, in June 1871. The old people probably advised him to see these storms as inevitable in the life of southern Louisiana. Since he did not move his family farther inland after these initial experiences, he must have resigned himself to this fact of coastal life.

In 1870 when Jean Baptiste was only five years old, the parish seat, Houma, had expanded to a population of 593. The same year, Madison Canal was dug to connect Bayou Terrebonne to Lake Barré (which means "enclosed lake" in French); before the canal was dug, the area was called a *portage* because boats had to be carried overland between the bayou and the lake. Gradually, local citizens were seeing improvements to their terrain and some improvements to their lifestyles.

The *Terrebonne Republican* newspaper, under the headline "Terrebonne Progressing," effused in their issue of Saturday, June 24, 1871, "We are informed that one of our wealthiest, most influential and enterprising citizens [Emile Daigle] has gone to the Crescent city for the purpose of purchasing a steamboat to navigate in the different water courses of Terrebonne. The proposed plan is this: to run the boat from Houma down Bayou Terrebonne, to Bayou Lacache, through the last named bayou into Little Caillou; from Little Caillou to Grand Caillou by the way of Robinson's Canal, the object being to put the Houma branch of the Railroad in direct communication with the many plantations

THE TERREBONNE REPUBLICAN.

FREEDOM OF SPEECH—LIBERTY OF THE PRESS—JUST ENFORCEMENT OF THE LAWS.

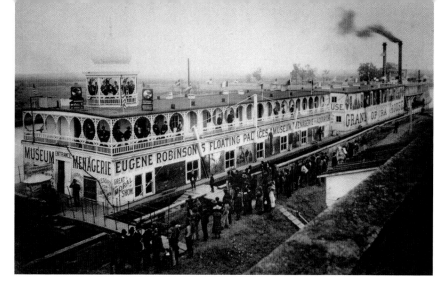

which dot the above named bayous....What benefit will be derived by Houma from this line of steamboat running in connection with the Railroad is inestimable."

The primary impetus for favorable change was the 1872 completion of a railroad spur from Schriever to Houma, when the long-awaited transportation link became a *fait accompli*. The name Houmans gave the steam-engine drawn branch train was "Old George," for its engineer George Williams, no relation to Adenise's husband George V. Williams. The railroad spur, in its first year, brought Robinson's Circus to town, the first of such magnitude to be seen by locals. This banner year also saw the establishment of the Houma Volunteer Fire Company No. 1 on Church street. It was in the same block as the first public school (the McMaster school), which had been built in the early 1840s at Church and School streets.

The first floor of Houma's second courthouse building was completed in 1875, replacing the first which had begun construction in 1834 and was subsequently destroyed during the war.

Houma's early progress was not without its setbacks. The first major conflagration after that of the Union army's retribution to the town in 1862 was on June 14, 1876. Almost all buildings in the square bounded by Bayou Terrebonne, Main Street, Roussell Street, and Barrow Street were rendered a total loss. Two men, J.N. Starnes and a Mr. Walter, were charged with arson, but a grand jury returned a finding of "not a true bill." The men were later released and left the parish.

In 1877, a new jail replaced the first one that had also been burned by Union soldiers. In 1877, Terrebonneans probably rejoiced with the rest of the state's residents when United States Army units were withdrawn from Louisiana, ending the longest occupation of any Southern state.

Eugene Robinson *showboat, above left, in Bayou Lafourche near Labadieville, c. 1887. Ad for Robinson's Circus in the* Houma Courier *of October 13, 1917*

Houma Volunteer Fire Company No. 1 c. 1876.

Left, the McMaster School on Church and School streets. Above, E.C. Wurzlow's rendering of the first completed Houma Courthouse c. 1875

B. No.____ &. No.____

La Parisse St. Martin — The Parish of St. Martin

WILL PAY

ONE DOLLAR after date

to the order of the Comptroller at the Office of the Parish Recorder, with eight per cent interest from maturity until paid, and receivable when due for all debts due the Parish of St. Martin

St. Martinsville,_____186_

Julien Babi Parish Treas.

L. T. BURNETT, PRINTER.

SECURED BY ____ WAR TAX FOR THE REDEMPT___

Richmond   Feb. 1st 1864

Fifty 50 Cents

1st SERIES

The Confederate States of

Will pay FIFTY CENTS

No. Tyler

REGISSER   TREASURER

VERMILLIONVILLE, JUNE 2nd 1862.   No 5222

Corporation of Vermillionville.

The Treasurer will pay to Bearer, on demand the Sum of

5 FIVE CENTS, 5

In Confederate notes, when presented in sums of TWENTY DOLLARS.

Treasurer.   Mayor.

Receivable in payment of the ad valorem taxes due to this Corporation and to the Guion Academy.

10 No. 3   B X

THE TOWN OF THIBODAUX,

Will pay to Bearer

TEN DOLLARS

Redeemable in current funds, bearing Eight per cent. per annum interest from date until paid. THIBODAUX, La., May 25   1863

Thompson Treas.   Jos. Nicol Mayor

25 D   THE   No. 658   25

PARISH OF IBERVILLE

Will pay to bearer, on demand, at the Treasurer's Office, the sum of .... TWENTY-FIVE CENTS, ... when demanded in sums of Five Dollars.

Plaquemine, January 20 1862

Pres't. Police Jury.

Treas'r.

TWENTY-FIVE CTS.

25 CENTS.

25   25

Iberville.

Dec. 20, 1861.

THE CORPORATION OF THE

Town of Houma

WILL PAY TO BEARER,

TEN CENTS

Secured by pledge on Corporation Taxes

10 Cts.   10 Cts.

Treas.   Mayr.

CIVIC GUARD PRINT.

THE STATE OF

WILL PAY TO BEARER

at the Treasurer's Office

BATON R___

FOR AUDITOR

2 DOLLARS $2.00

THE PARISH OF ASSUMPTION

No.

Receivable in payment of all debts due the Parish which mature after the 1st April 1863.

Promises to pay to the Bearer

TWO DOLLARS

on demand in Current Funds.

TWO DOLLARS

Fifty Cents. 50

IVE MONTHS

E. H. DE

OF THE PARISH OF ST.

Will pay FIFTY C

In Current Funds, with Eight per Cent. In in sums of Twelve Dollars

FRANKLIN, LA., JANUARY 1st 1863

Le Courrier De Houma.

Houma was reincorporated in 1878, and the same year *Le Courier de Houma* newspaper was founded by former Confederate soldier "Lafayette" Bernard Filhucan de Bazet.

In the early 1880s, Pierre was operating his bakery and livery stable in the 600 block of Main Street, next door to the Presti Shoe Shop. At this point Pierre continued to run his Dulac businesses as well as those he owned in town.

By this time, Wells Fargo Express Company and Western Union Telegraph offices had opened in Houma and Schriever, as well as post offices in both places.

By 1880, Jean Baptiste was 15 years old and the eldest of 11 Cenac children. One can imagine that Pierre took some or all of his growing family to "town" occasionally, if for no other reason than to accompany him while he conducted business, but probably to see the town's growth and progress, as well.

Some of the new faces they saw in the community included Italian, primarily Sicilian, immigrants who began to arrive by 1880, when planters needed inexpensive labor to replace the former forced labor of slaves.

From the more than 1,200 plantations which had produced Louisiana's sugar crop in 1861, that number had dwindled to 175 operating plantations by the year 1864.[9] By 1870, "at least half the planters were either Northern men or were supported by Northern money" in Louisiana.[9] A dramatic decline in native Louisiana plantation owners was the order of the day in the aftermath of the Civil War. State government and railroad company officials, as well as planter groups, advertised for and recruited many of the Sicilians.

Far from causing friction with the pre-war labor force, "The chronic labor shortage in the sugar industry prevented the immigrant from becoming a threat to the black American's job." However, this association, the author notes, forced "Sicilians to a marginal position in the larger society" which many immigrants worked hard to overcome. One indicator of the marginalization of Italians is that a planter in St. Mary Parish classified workers on his payroll as "Whites, Dagos and Darkies," in February 1904.[9]

Assessment of Sicilian laborers by Ridley LeBlanc of nearby Raceland in Lafourche Parish was that they were "very good workers in the fields...They were good gardeners, raised goats, made and baked their own bread, made and formed their spaghetti, made cheese and made their clothes. They were self supporting and saved nearly all of their small earnings and quickly went into their own successful business."[9]

Terrebonne Parish attracted some Italian immigrants. Among the earliest in Terrebonne include the family names Jaccuzzo, Fazzio, Crispino, Morello, Scurto, Catanese, Elardo, Fesi, Cefalu, Cangelosi, and Strada. A personal connection

"Lafayette" Bernard Filhucan de Bazet, founder of Le Courier de Houma *newspaper, c. 1890. Houma Courier newspaper of January 18, 1879, printed in both French and English*

65.........Rue Decatur........65

—IMPORTATEUR DE—
VINS, COGNAC, LIQUEURS, FRUITS
A L'EAU-DE-VIE, VERMOUTH,
HUILE, SARDINES,
ABSINTHE.

Seul agent pour le Sud et l'Ouest de W. H. CZUBA & CO., Cognac; de la célèbre marque des vins de A. SELLIER & CO., Bordeaux; CHAUVET FILS. Un assortiment général de liqueurs du pays.

BITTERS DES ARABES

Superieur a tout autre.

Les propriétés toniques stimulantes et digestives de ce bitter agissent sur le système nerveux et en font une boisson extrêmement agréable et bien faisante. Comme apéritif le BITTER DES ARABES fait le plus grand bien aux estomacs faibles et délicates et combat efficacement la dyspepsie.
VERGNOLE
Propriétaire. Nlle-Orléans.

ARABIAN BITTERS

This agreable and wholesome beverage is extracted from the plants known for its great tonic property and is combined with the choicest brandy, thus rendering it THE LAST REMEDY for the immediate restoration of the enfeebled organs.

It is to be remarked also that the use of this Bitter as a drink is of a great efficacy in preserving from epidemic diseases.
VERGNOLE
Proprietor. New-Orleans.
Feb. 21

between French immigrant Pierre and the son of a Sicilian immigrant was forged when Russell Strada came to Houma looking for a job at the Presti Shoe Shop. Strada's father, Joe, immigrated to Thibodaux around 1872 and taught Russell and brother Salvador leatherwork, specifically shoemaking. When he was in his nineties, Russell Strada told an interviewer that the Cenacs treated him as family when he first moved to Houma, even providing sleeping accommodations in their home. Another courtesy the Cenacs provided Strada was the use of a horse-and-carriage "limousine" for his wedding.[5]

The first 15 years of Pierre and Victorine's life together were unmarred except by the usual vagaries of everyday life. In 1880 the family was healthy and prospering in a parish where the population of Houma had grown to 1,084 residents. Pierre was a successful 42-year-old businessman, a friend to both prominent and humble community colleagues, and a man enjoying the bustling family he had fathered.

NOTES

1. In the Cenac Collection of the Nicholls State University Archives

2. See sidebar on page 127.

3. Article in DeBow's Review in 1850 "written at Oak Grove on Bayou Black on November 14, 1849"

4. A. Bouchereau, "Statement of the Sugar and Rice Crops Made in Louisiana" 1877-78, 1878-79

5. Helen Wurzlow. *I Dug Up Houma-Terrebonne*, Volumes I-VII

6. Jess Bergeron. "Terrebonne Life Lines" Terrebonne Genealogical Society

7. Louise Violet Cenac Bourg, daughter of Dennis J. Cenac, in a 2007 interview

8. John C. Rodrigue, *Reconstruction in the Cane Fields*, Louisiana State University Press

9. Jean Ann Scarpaci. *Italian Immigrants in Louisiana's Sugar Parishes*, Ph.D. dissertation, 1980

A Dago Stabbing.

Two dagoes became involved in a difficulty on Bayou Black last Saturday night, which resulted in the free use of a knife by one of the participants. The wounded dago was badly stabbed; but it is thought that the wounds will not prove fatal. Dagoes can stand a great deal of stabbing. For generations back they have stabbed each other until they have about gotten used to it.

Article from Houma Courier *of January 23, 1897*

Pierre Cenac (on right) pictured in front of his livery stable present day address 7937 Main Street, c. 1900. From left, Russell Strada and Eddie Evest

CHAPTER 15
1883: The Cradle Falls

Steady, solemn murmurs filled Pierre and Victorine's living room in Dulac. Black muslin covered the walls from the chair rail to the baseboards, fastened there by the older girls in solemn preparation for tonight's wake. All the chairs the boys could fit in had been arranged along the walls.

Whenever one of the Cenac children approached the small coffin on one side of the room, sniffles interrupted the murmurs, and a collective intake of breath was audible.

Pierre and Victorine stood near the head of the homemade wooden casket. Every now and then, Victorine leaned over to adjust the netting-and-lace veil that was draped from the open lid to the front side where mourners came to pay their respects.

Pierre stood erect and still next to her, automatically shaking men's hands as they were extended. But he did not speak.

Before everyone arrived, he had taken a long last look at his three-year-old child lying there, behind that coffin veil. The women had prepared Celestine for tonight's wake and tomorrow's burial, but Pierre left the house while they placed his little girl inside. As he had stood there earlier, looking at her tousled curls spilling over her small pillow, he allowed himself a few moments of shoulder-shaking grief.

He still found it hard to believe. This tenth child had the same robust look of the other children at the same age. There had been no warning, no sickliness. She giggled at her brothers' antics and shrieked with delight when one of the older girls tickled her just to hear the sound of her high-pitched laugh.

The fever had been sudden and fast. He and Victorine had called in a *traiteur,* but Celestine's sickness just got worse. There was nothing even the doctor, after his long journey from Houma, could do for her.

Every few hours during the long night of the wake, he went into the kitchen for coffee before returning to his post beside Victorine. While he sipped the strong black brew, he kept telling himself, "Pierre, you're 45. You can't let these other men think you're weak. You can't let them see you vulnerable."

Around one in the morning, two men standing across the room from him were confirming his thoughts in whispers Pierre never heard. One of his neighbors said, "Pierre sure is tough. Did you hear he bought the Toups family land for less than it's worth because poor Toups needed to sell out quick? Look at him tonight. Hard as rock. I don't know how he does it."

The other man leaned in conspiratorially. "He is buying up land like he can't get enough."

"You're right. He is honest, but a hard bargainer. Strange, though...he's always been generous to my children, sharing his pecans, Japan plums, and vegetables we don't grow. I know he does the same with your family. *C'est étrange, non?*"

After the hard night of staying awake while friends came and went, the Cenac family made a funeral cortège to Sacred Heart Church in Montegut. After the priest intoned the requiem ceremony, Pierre hoisted the small coffin onto his right shoulder and carried it to the graveyard.

Victorine and the children stood near the gravesite until the cemetery workers threw the first shovelful of dirt over the wooden box. When Pierre had caught sight of the men approaching, he moved away and stood near the carriages. He could hear his wife and daughters weeping. He wouldn't cry, but he knew he'd never forget the weight of that coffin.

Victorine joined Pierre for the journey home, clustering her children around her. All but one.

Baptismal certificate of Marie Anne
Celestine Cenac dated March 13, 1879

Opposite, St. Eloi Catholic Church, Bayou Dularge, built in 1875. The founding pastor, Fr. Jean Goffry, celebrated Mass there for the first time that year during Lent. Last Mass before demolition was November 13, 1971

CHAPTER 16
Progress and Heartbreak

From the time they were married until the early 1880s, Pierre and Victorine with their ever-growing brood lived a boom time of family well-being and business growth. Of their 11 children born by the beginning of that decade, their daughter Josephine was the youngest, born in 1880. That year, the population of Terrebonne Parish was 17,957 and the City of Houma's was 1,084.

However, Pierre and Victorine were bringing children into a world that had no medical answers to many sicknesses and diseases. They must have heard with fear, for example, about the *fièvre jaune* (yellow fever) epidemic that began in July 1878 in Morgan City some 30 miles west of Houma. During the following four months, 600 persons contracted the disease and 109 died.[1] Statewide in 1878, yellow fever killed more than 5,000 people, and a total of 13,000 in the lower Mississippi Valley.

Other medical scourges of the time were typhoid fever (*fièvre typhoïde*, pronounced tee-foe-EED), scarlet fever, measles, diphtheria, smallpox, tetanus, and cholera. Epidemics took their toll on local populations at many different periods in the parish's history. Livestock, which played an important role in most households of the day, likewise did not escape the perils of disease. Anthrax felled many cattle, beasts of burden, and other animals in periodic outbreaks during this historical period.

After 17 years of childrearing that went undisturbed except by the common childhood health issues, Pierre and Victorine were abruptly, and grievously, reminded about the fragile nature of surviving to adulthood during the time in which they lived. Their tenth child, Marie Anne Celestine, lived only to the age of three years. She died of an unknown sickness in 1882. Pierre and Victorine laid her to rest in the cemetery of Sacred Heart Church in Montegut, in a burial site which can no longer be identified. Some local residents say that the original cemetery lies under the current roadbed of the highway that parallels Bayou Terrebonne at Montegut.

Two years after Marie Anne Celestine died, Victorine gave birth to their twelfth child, William Jean Pierre, in 1884. Another son, Dennis, was born in 1887, and in 1891 Marie Azelie Ademise became the Cenacs' fourteenth child. (Later in life, she legally changed her name to Adenise Marie, probably because she had always been known by that name rather than her official one.)

Baptismal certificate of William Jean Pierre Cenac, dated March 17, 1884

Family name	Given name or names
Cenac	Pierre
Address	
Terrebonne Parish, Louisiana	
Certificate no. (or vol. and page) Nat. Papers,	Title and location of court 19th. Jud. Dist.
folder in steel file drawer	Ct., Terrebonne Parish
Country of birth or allegiance	When born (or age)
France	Not shown
Date and port of arrival in U. S.	Date of naturalization
No date or port shown	I/O -- July 12, 1880
Names and addresses of witnesses	
Peter Berger	
Andrew Zeringer	

U. S. Department of Justice, Immigration and Naturalization Service.   Form N-415 (Old 1-IP)

Sandwiched among all these personal events was another type of milestone for Pierre in the year 1880. On July 12, he became a naturalized citizen of the United States. This entailed renunciation of his native country's citizenship and oath of allegiance to American citizenship. The brief ceremony took place at the Terrebonne Parish Courthouse in Houma. Two witnesses to his becoming a citizen of the country he had adopted 20 years before were Peter Berger and Andrew Zeringer, both of whose families were prominent Houma residents at the time.[2] Becoming a U.S. citizen was another step in Pierre's cementing his place in the community.

However, family was always the first line of concern in the busy household, and seven years after their youngest child entered the world, Pierre and Victorine's family suffered a heartbreak that was perhaps even more tragic for them than the loss of Marie Anne Celestine. Josephine was 18 years old in 1898, a young woman looking forward to her marriage to fiancé Charles Barthelemy "Bahya" Carlos. He was the brother of her sister Marie's deceased husband Salvador Carlos, Jr., and also brother to her sister Marguerite's husband Eugene Prosper Bertrand Carlos.

Above, Charles Barthelemy "Bahya" Carlos, betrothed to (below) Josephine Cenac at the time of her death. Right, an oath of the type Pierre would have had to declare at his naturalization

STATE OF LOUISIANA,
Parish of Lafourche.

Before the undersigned C. J. Barker Clerk of the District Court, for the 18th, Judicial District of Louisiana, sitting in and for the Parish of Lafourche, (being a court of record with common law jurisdiction.) Personally came and appeared George Cousin an alien, now residing in the parish aforesaid, who being duly sworn according to law, declares, on oath, that he is a native of France is now 36 years of age, and that he arrived in the United States in the year of grace 1871

And the said George Cousin further declares, that it is "bona fide" his intention to become a citizen of the United States of America, and to renounce forever all allegiance and fidelity to all and any foreign prince, potentate, state and sovereignty whatever; and particularly to the Republic of France

Sworn to and subscribed at the Parish and State aforesaid, on this 13th day of Dec A. D. 1897, before

So help him God!

Geo Cousin

On February 5, 1898, Josephine's brother Theophile, 11 years her senior, and his wife Sylvia Bourque Cenac became parents of a daughter, Marie Isare. They asked Josephine to be *marraine* (*nainaine*) of the infant. The baptism took place two months later, on April 9, at St. Patrick Church in Gibson.[2] The baby's maternal uncle, Alcee Adam Joseph Bourg, served as Isare's *parrain*. Josephine and her brother Dennis traveled from Houma via carriage to the christening ceremony in Gibson. On the trip back to Houma, they were caught in a rainstorm.

Josephine contracted pneumonia soon thereafter, and died in Houma on May 3. It had to be with great sorrow that her parents arranged for her to be laid in her coffin wearing the wedding dress she had prepared for her imminent nuptials. She was buried in Prevost Cemetery in Grand Caillou, and according to family lore, was also wearing the ring her fiancé Charles had bought for their wedding. The funeral cortège proceeded from St. Eloi Church on Bayou Dularge on May 4, 1898 to the upper reaches of Bayou Grand Caillou at Ashland by horseback and buggies. Mourners then accompanied Josephine's coffin down Bayou Grand Caillou by boat to the cemetery. Transporting coffins by boats—large (in the bayous) and small (in *traînasses*)—was a common practice at the time, considering the time's inadequate or nonexistent roadways.

The deaths of these two daughters brought considerable emotional pain to the Cenac household, which was probably always bustling with activity by the sheer numbers of children under one roof at any given time. According to family members, a strict work ethic was impressed upon the Cenac children by Pierre and Victorine. The children all had chores, and all were expected to participate in gardening, tending livestock, and learning various skills. Aside from what was likely personal belief in hard work, the family's size and the culture of the time no doubt reinforced this requirement.

A further early family crisis involved the twelfth Cenac child, young William, whose life-altering accident occurred within the year of, or the year immediately before, Josephine's death. Although most agree that he was 13 or 14 at the time, in either 1897 or 1898, varying retellings give different ages for him when his trauma occurred, as well as some differing details. The following is from a published account of his upper left arm being severely wounded by a shotgun blast. The source for this article was an interview with William's daughter Rita Mae Cenac Hoffmann:

"The accident happened when a group of duck hunters were unloading their pirogues near Jean Pierre's home on Grand Caillou...They rushed the lad into the house to try to stop the bleeding as best they could. They had no telephone to Houma then. His brother Charlie and a friend named Lottinger mounted mules bareback to ride to Houma to get the doctor.... Charlie...made it.

Theophile Cenac and his wife Sylvia Bourque (Bourg) Cenac

April
25
Isaure
Marie
Sénac

On this, the ninth of April 1898, I baptized Isaure Marie, born on February 5th, of Théophile Sénac and Sylvia Bourg. Sponsors: Alcée Adam Joseph Bourg and Josephine Sénac.
H. F. Chastt

Marie Isare Cenac's baptismal certificate dated April 9, 1898

Dr. L. H Jastremski,

Funeral on Lower Bayou Terrebonne

Fr. Joseph M. Coulombe, pastor of Sacred Heart Church on lower Bayou Terrebonne (Montegut), often performed funeral services in which he had to travel by boat and then smaller pirogues, the same means of transportation often used for the deceaseds' coffins. On these pages, photos of a funeral in lower Terrebone Parish c. 1922-1937.

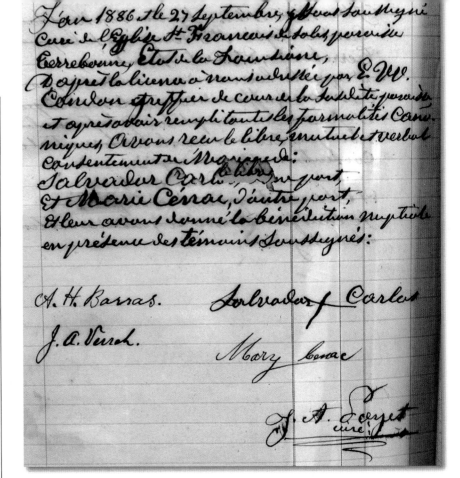

Salvador Carlos and Elvire Heloise LaGrave Carlos above. Middle, Marie Cenac Carlos. Bottom, Salvador Carlos, Jr. Above right, Marie and Salvador, Jr.'s marriage certificate dated September 27, 1886

"Dr. Leon H. Jastremski and Dr. Charles Menville came down, but they had no way to get there except via horse and buggy. All this took hours from late morning one day to early morning the next. Meanwhile, the young patient had to bear his pain while his family ministered to him as best they could...."

"They had to take the arm off," said Rita Mae, his daughter, according to the same account. He lost his left arm below the shoulder. "They operated right there at the house. They did put him to sleep with ether for the operation....When he had to come to Houma to have his wound dressed, they would put him on a mattress in an open cart, mule-drawn, and drive to town. They would stay at the old Durand hotel for several days."[3]

Because of the lack of antibiotics and other medicines, it was an anxious time in the Cenac household while they took care of him as best they could. To their and his credit, William not only recuperated, but overcame his handicap stoically.

After all those years of robust health among the family, in just a year or so they became subject to two gripping experiences that could shake anyone's sense of well-being. On the other hand, William's accident and the death of Josephine may have cemented even further the family bonds being formed as the children grew up, some well into adulthood at the time. Baptiste, born in 1865, was a family man of 33 the year his teenaged sister died. Youngest sibling Adenise was only seven years old.

As in the case of Theophile, many of the Cenac children had grown to adulthood and married, beginning in the mid-1880s. All the Cenac children were married in civil ceremonies at the Houma Courthouse, and then at Catholic churches in religious ceremonies.[marriage certificates 2] Jean Baptiste, the oldest, married Martha Frances "Fannie" Gatewood (age 19 years) on February 1, 1886, when he was 21. On September 27 that same year, second child Marie became the 19-year-old bride of 21-year-old Salvador Carlos, Jr. whose family lived across Bayou Grand Caillou from the Cenacs.

(The Carlos patriarch, Salvador Carlos, Sr., was born into a wealthy family of Barcelona, in the region of Catalonia, Spain. When he was 26, he sailed from Spain in the year 1856, and eventually settled in Dulac. He and his wife Elvire Heloise LaGrave (daughter of a Canadian medical doctor from Massachusetts) were the parents of nine before Elvire Heloise died in childbirth.)[4]

Four years after Marie's marriage, the sixth Cenac child, Victorine Aimée, married 24-year-old Jean Pierre Carrere on March 10, 1890 when she was 18. (Jean Pierre was one of 14 children and son of *Hautes-Pyrénées* native and stone mason Dominique Jules Carrere, born in Lomné-Esparros, France, who emigrated at age 23 on February 15, 1857 aboard the ship *Le Cabinet* and later married Pauline Rodrigue. He left France to avoid not only service in Napoleon's army, but also the threat of being beheaded because of not serving in the military.[5])

Fourth child and second daughter Marguerite Laurentine, at age 25, became the second Cenac girl to marry into the neighboring Carlos family when she became the bride of Eugene Prosper Bertrand Carlos, age 22, on June 13, 1895. Second son and third child, Albert, was 28 when he married 19-year-old Marie Adelphine Michel a year later, on May 12, 1896. Theophile, 26, completed the marriages of the six eldest children of Pierre and Victorine with his nuptials to Sylvia Bourque (later recorded as Bourg), age 22, on February 23, 1897. The marriage was celebrated in Stephensville at Sacred Heart Church. (Until two years before, the church had been called St. Clothilde. Later, the Sacred Heart Catholic Church name was assigned to a new edifice in nearby Morgan City.)

One indication of close family ties is that Baptiste and his

Eugene Prosper Bertrand Carlos at left, Marguerite Laurentine Cenac Carlos at right. Below, Dominique Jules Carrere's tomb cross marker from Dugas Cemetery in Montegut Far left, marriage certificate of Theophile and Sylvia Bourque (Bourg) Cenac. Left, Pierre and Victorine Cenac Carrere's marriage certificate. Below, St. Clothilde Catholic Church in Stephensville

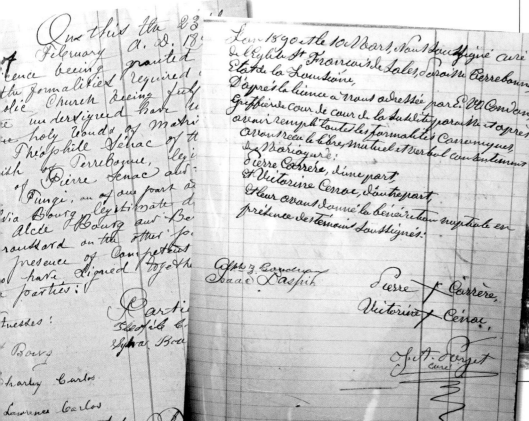

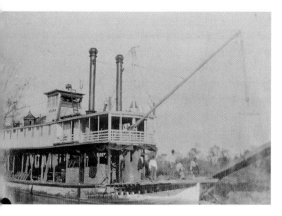

Top, the steamboat Houma *c. 1910. Right, the* N.H. Breaux, *which was used on the Atchafalaya and Mississippi rivers*

Jean Charles Cenac pictured in his store, present day 8053 Main Street, c. 1916

Eugenie Celeste Carlos on right, with an unknown friend, c. 1904

wife Fannie (whose father was born in Kentucky) lived in the house adjacent to Pierre and Victorine when the census of 1900 was compiled. He was an oyster fisherman and was an early purchaser of oyster bottoms nearby beginning in the year 1897 along with his brother-in-law, Salvador Carlos, Jr. The third Cenac son, Theophile, spent a time in residence at Morgan City working in the fledgling oyster industry there, but he returned to Terrebonne Parish after a relatively brief time. Most of the Cenacs lived close to Pierre and Victorine in Dulac, or in Houma.

The reason for many of the children, such as Baptiste, staying close to the home place of their parents was that the men participated in their father's business ventures or in related ventures of their own. For example, beginning in the 1880s some of the teenaged and young adult Cenac sons—Baptiste, Theophile, Albert, Jean Pierre, Jr., assisted by their brothers-in-law Salvador Carlos, Jr. and Eugene Carlos—hauled oysters harvested from their bedding grounds to the nearest packing plant, which at the time was in Morgan City. On the return trip, they brought home groceries for not only the families' own consumption, but also for sale in Pierre's store. These early experiences were to serve them well in future ventures in the oyster industry.

For the daughters, such as Marie and Victorine (known in the family as Tante Marie and Tante "Tile"), their husbands were not only natives of the area, but also fishermen (Marie's husband Salvador worked the sailing lugger *Young Camellia* that he purchased from his father), so they remained residents of the Dulac community. Jean Pierre Carrere, Sr. (known in the family as "Nonc Plotte") owned and operated his own farm and boat, the *Florence C.*

Marguerite's husband Eugene Prosper Bertrand Carlos was a steamboat captain on Bayou Lafourche, Bayou Terrebonne and the Mississippi River, so she stayed close to home to raise her children until her sons, in turn, plied the waters themselves. In later years, she joined her husband aboard the vessels he captained: the *Laura*, the *Harry*, the *Houma*, and the *Terrebonne*. Eugene continued as relief pilot aboard the steamer *N.H. Breaux* after his son Joseph Pierre Eloi, known as Edward, took over as captain. Eugene later owned the vessel *Good Hope.* Edward's brother Jimmy Morris (pronounced *Maurice*) was a licensed steam and diesel engineer aboard vessels. Their youngest brother, Randolph, had an unlimited pilot's license.

The older Cenac women were practicing midwives, delivering their many nieces and nephews. By the year of Josephine's death, 1898, Marie, Marguerite, and Victorine had been kept busy with the delivery of 19 grandchildren. By that time, Jean Baptiste and Fannie had five: Jean Albert, Edna Marie, George Lee, Joseph Cyrille, and James William Cenac. Marie and Salvador, Jr. also had five: Salvador Albert, Elvire Victorine, John Hubert, Marie Ida, and Helene Carlos. Albert and Adelphine had Lydia and Ursule (Cela) Cenac. Marguerite and Eugene had Inez and Eugenie Celeste Carlos. Theophile and Sylvia had Marie Isare Cenac. Victorine and Jean Pierre had Adam Ennis, Justilien, Lydie, and Josephine Carrere.

Adenise Marie Cenac (second from left) with her oldest brother Jean Baptiste's children (left to right) Joseph Cyrille, Edna Marie, James William, and George Lee Cenac, c. 1900

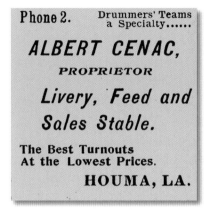

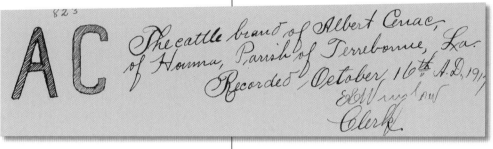

Above left, Albert Cenac's business ad in the Southern Manufacturer of November 1901. Right, Albert Cenac's fire brand registration of October 16, 1917

The adult sons who moved to Houma as young men during the late 1890s did so to work in businesses in which their father was either part owner or former owner, before they struck out on their own. Jean Charles was a butcher and served as a city alderman,[6] Paul ran Pierre's livery stable and was subsequently a butcher, and Albert owned a butcher shop and stable.

Jean Pierre Cenac, Jr. was still living with his parents at age 23, but was the first to break ranks by spending most of his married life on Little Caillou rather than Grand Caillou or in Houma. He became a shrimper/oysterman, and ran his own boat, *St. Agnes*, on Petit Caillou, where he raised his family until the early twentieth century, when the 1926 hurricane forced him to move to Houma.

Weather phenomena continued to play havoc with the area and affected the Cenac family into the 1880s. In 1881, local commercial citrus production, which for years had been a profitable enterprise, began to wane after a succession of hard freezes[6] which destroyed all but the trees in the most southerly reaches of Terrebonne. Another blow delivered by weather was the October 1886 hurricane which damaged crops not only along the coast, but also statewide in Louisiana.

Another hurricane the very next year (1887), again in October, was so large that its wind and rains lashed southeast Louisiana for a full four days. But in August 1888, an even stronger hurricane, which the U.S. Weather Service classified as the most severe storm since that of 1837, affected most of the northern

Below, Paul Michel Cenac in his butcher shop c. 1920, and his November 28, 1917 fire brand registration

Cenac or Senac?

Martha Frances Gatewood Cenac, wife of Jean Baptiste, with children James William and Marie Cornelia c. 1905

The Old Country spelling of Cénac, using the accent, indicates that the name was pronounced "say-NOCK." It should be noted that variant spellings exist, even in "official" documents, for the Cenac surname. Baptism certificates, marriage bonds, marriage licenses, and death certificates alone attest to errors common to this type of recordkeeping. Pierre's family members were variously recorded as Cenac, Senac, Cenag, Senat, Simiock, Cinnack, Cenan, Cenace, Cenacle and Senacle in official documents.

Baptiste's marriage bond, as recorded in the 19th Judicial District Court on January 26, 1886, erroneously spelled his surname Cinnack, (and his wife's name as Getwarde). These bonds served as a protection for the future children of the marriage, and to insure inheritance rights. According to Louisiana Parish Record Descriptions, "A bond obligated a prospective groom to pay the bond if he were discovered to be a bigamist or imposter or otherwise ineligible to contract a valid marriage. As long as the marriage was legal, the bond was void. Bonds generally include the groom's name, name of the surety, the sum [often $300], and the date of the agreement."

One of the children's marriage certificates is documented as Cenan, and a death record as Cenace. A local publication named Pierre "Cenag" as a member of the parish school board. Earlier, in France, Pierre's ancestor Dominique was named a Senac at birth and a Cenac at death.

Place names in France which could be erroneously associated with the Terrebonne Cenac family name include the town of Cenac, a small suburb of the port city of Bordeaux. Another town, Cenac-et-St.-Julien, is located near Domme on the Dordogne River, slightly east of Barbazan-Debat. However, the Cenac surname is not found in either area, confirmed by research in cemetery and church records, and by family members residing in France. Another town situated slightly northeast of Barbazan-Debat is named Senac, but the Cenac surname is not associated with this Hautes-Pyrénées village, either. The city of Pau had both Cenacs and Senacs, and the town of Benac recorded a Cenac family there.

U.S. census records provide even more aberrant spellings as both surnames and given names for various members of the Terrebonne Parish family. Census lists of 1870, for example, record the family name as Simiock. However, through the generations, the accurate Cenac name survived and is currently distinguishable from the local Senac name, which did not descend from Jean-Pierre Cenac.

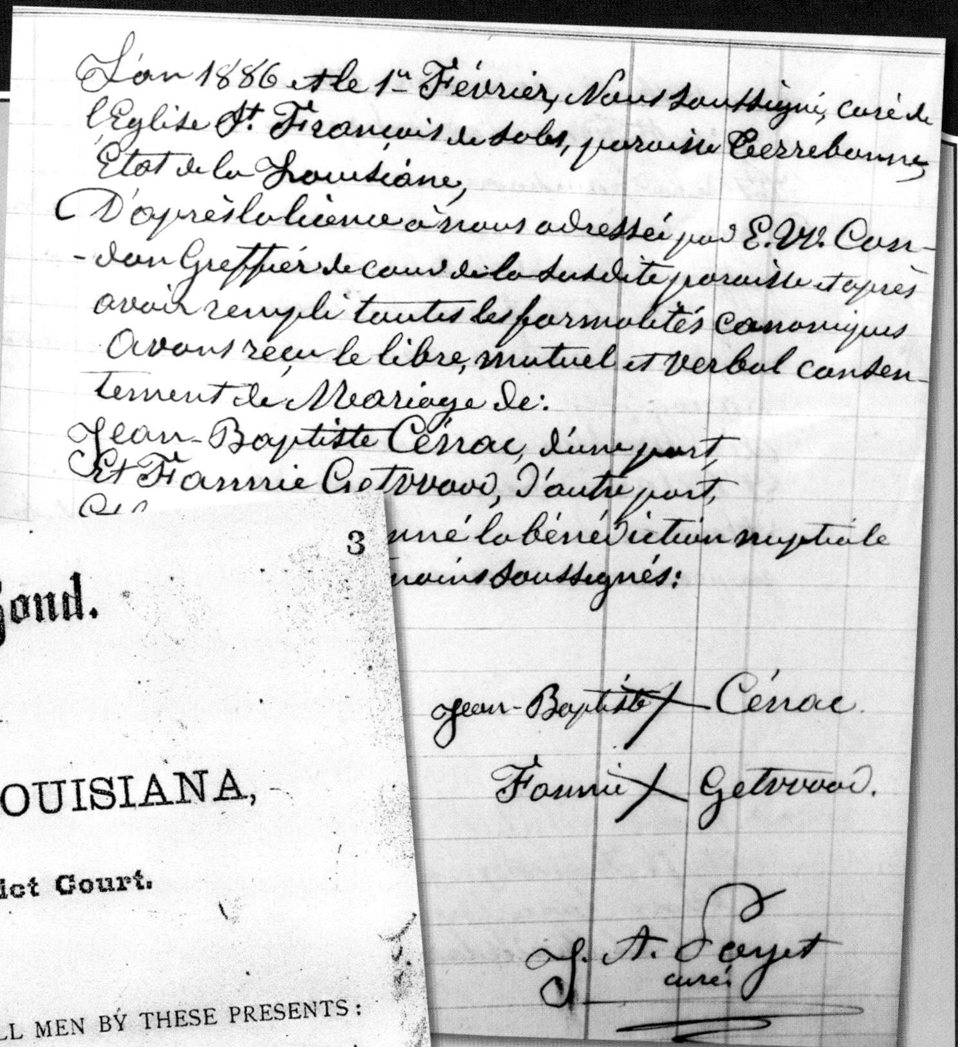

L'an 1886 et le 1er Février, Nous soussigné, curé de
l'Église St. François de Sales, paroisse Terrebonne
État de la Louisiane,

D'après la licence à nous adressée par E. W. Con-
-don Greffier de cour de la susdite paroisse et après
avoir rempli toutes les formalités canoniques
Avons reçu le libre, mutuel et verbal consen-
tement de Mariage de:

Jean-Baptiste Cénac, d'une part,

Et Fannie Getwoad, d'autre part,

Et... donné la bénédiction nuptiale
... mains soussignés:

Jean-Baptiste + Cénac.

Fannie + Getwoad.

J. A. Peyret
curé.

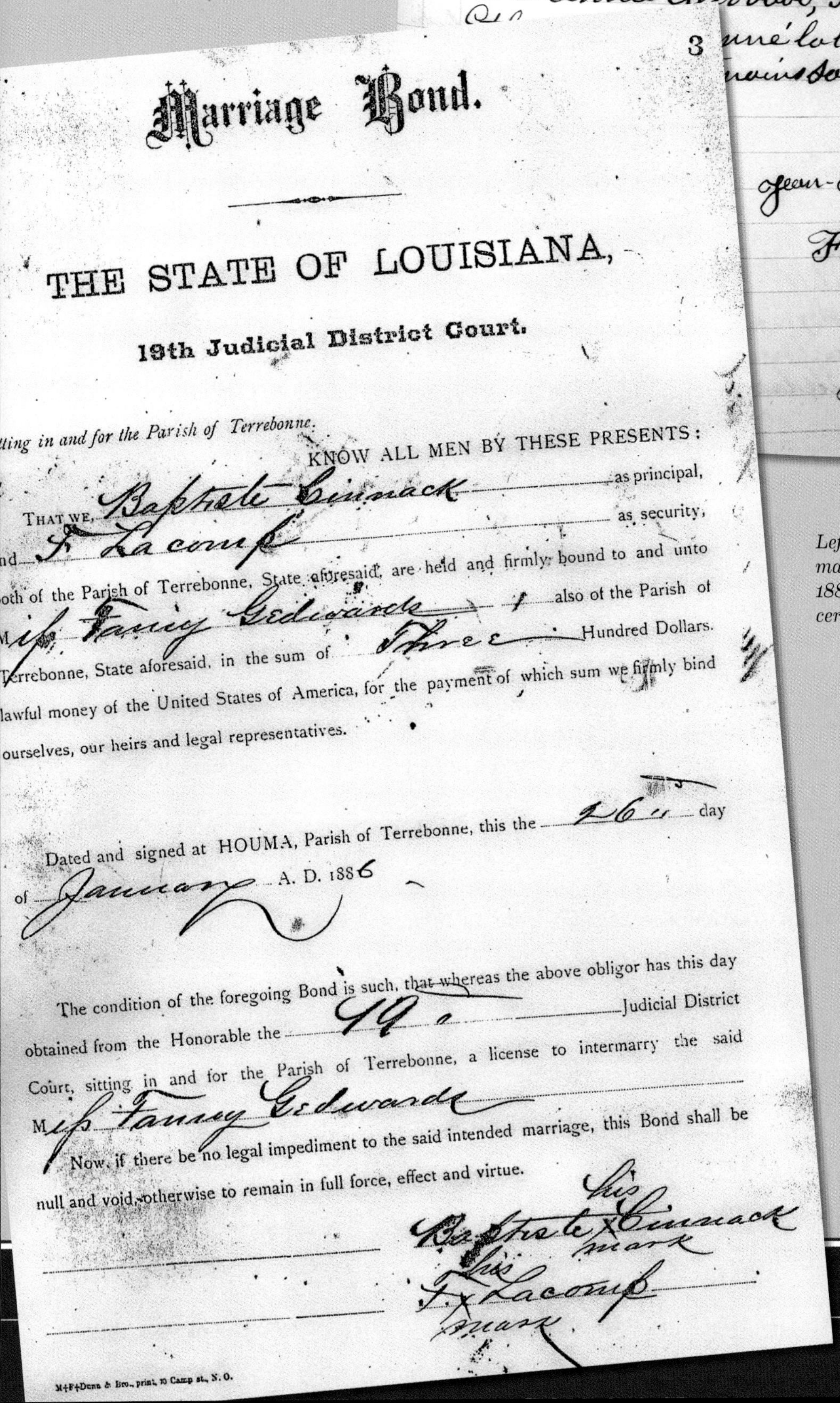

*Left, Baptiste and Fannie's
marriage bond of January 26,
1886. Above, their marriage
certificate of February 1, 1886*

Marriage Bond.

THE STATE OF LOUISIANA,

19th Judicial District Court.

Sitting in and for the Parish of Terrebonne:

KNOW ALL MEN BY THESE PRESENTS:

THAT WE, Baptiste Cinnack as principal,

and F Lacomp as security,

both of the Parish of Terrebonne, State aforesaid, are held and firmly bound to and unto

Miss Fanny Gedwards also of the Parish of

Terrebonne, State aforesaid, in the sum of Three Hundred Dollars,

lawful money of the United States of America, for the payment of which sum we firmly bind

ourselves, our heirs and legal representatives.

Dated and signed at HOUMA, Parish of Terrebonne, this the 26 day

of January A. D. 1886

The condition of the foregoing Bond is such, that whereas the above obligor has this day

obtained from the Honorable the 99 Judicial District

Court, sitting in and for the Parish of Terrebonne, a license to intermarry the said

Miss Fanny Gedwards

Now, if there be no legal impediment to the said intended marriage, this Bond shall be

null and void, otherwise to remain in full force, effect and virtue.

his
Baptiste + Cinnack
mark
his
F + Lacomp
mark

M+F+Dens & Bro., print, 10 Camp st., N. O.

LOWER TERREBONNE.

GREAT SUFFERING IN THE OVER-FLOWED SECTION.

Further Details of the Late Storm—The Second Relief Party from Houma Visits the Scene of Disaster—Scenes and Incidents.

HOUMA, La., Aug. 24.—It has been hinted before how terrible was the visitation that afflicted Terrebonne parish in the storm of Sunday last.

The details of the devastation yet remain to be written, and these make a chapter in the experience of the people hitherto unprecedented.

Let us for a moment conceive a region blest by every smile of heaven, where the Acadian exile more than a hundred years ago planted his vine and fig-tree, under the shelter of which, his children and their children have been born, have lived and died; where the husbandman's toil has been rewarded through all vicisitudes with abundance to supply every simple want; where the children's dower still was another house and portion of land as in the days of Evangeline; where hundreds of small farms supported as many large families, and ripening fields of corn and rice were waiting the fullness of time in the August sun to put the sickle in. And then let us turn from this picture of peace and plenty and happiness to realize the desolation that in a single day bring men, women and little children fleeing before the wrath of the storm, adrift and homeless, looking only for land, prayerful only for life and a haven of refuge, leaving behind them all the accumulations of a lifetime of thrift and persevering industry.

When these things are realized, then one can estimate how pitiless was the storm's wrath and how pitiable the condition of these people.

THE TIMES-DEMOCRAT'S correspondent spent a day and a night in this region. The pictures of desolation and misery require a larger canvas than the columns of a newspaper afford to paint them; but an outline at least may be given which may invoke "sweet charity's" aid in behalf of the suffering.

As soon as the news of the terrible disaster reached Houma a relief and investigating committee was organized, a steamer chartered and some forty citizens proceeded down Bayou Terrebonne with a small supply of provisions to relieve immediate want. They found that every house from Bayou Lacache, twenty-five miles below Houma, to the Gulf, had been swept away, that more than a hundred people were utterly homeless, that nearly a thousand people were in want of food, that relief was necessary at once to keep them from starving to death. Upon the return of the expedition, and the facts being made known, the police jury was convened and appropriated $750.

A mass meeting of citizens was immediately assembled, and committees on subscriptions and distribution of supplies appointed, as follows: Messrs. J. J. Shaffer, A. Bourg, Peter Berger, Thos. Turnbull, W. A. Bisland, Oscar Daspit, Aurelie Theriot, E. W. Condon, Dr. C. A. Duval, I. M. Price, Mesdames V. Berger, E. W. Glenn, E. Picou, V. Strauss, and P. Toujean.

Thursday noon the steamer Harry left Houma for the scene of suffering with supplies of food and clothing to relieve immediate necessities on Bayous Terrebonne and Little Caillou. Two ladies, Mrs. Valentine Berger, and Mrs. Glenn, and Messrs. Frank ...

Sugar Houses Damaged on the Teche.

The steamer E. W. Cole, which steamer arrived yesterday morning from the Teche, brings additional particulars of the damage wrought by the late storm. From Capt. W. T. Jones, of the Cole, it was learned that the following sugar houses on plantations lying along the bayou from Morgan City to St. Martinsville were more or less damaged:

Slightly Damaged—Point Pleasant, Glenwild, Riverside, Victoria, Live Oak, Luckland, Avelon, Calumet, Ricohoc, Buckeye, Schwans, Retreat, Susie, Alice C., Arlington, Franklin Refinery, Sterling, Trowbridge, Centennial, Pelican Rest, Oak Bluff, Belleview, Katie, Johanna, Harding, Des Ligne.

Badly Damaged—Fairview, Boy Blue, Lagonda, Tuttle Hope, Davenport, Mora, Shady Side, Oxford, Camperdown, Indian Sugar House.

Blown Down—Buccaneer, Pecan Grove, Grandwoods, Mound, Fairfax, Justine, Francis, Garden City, Baldwin.

Completely Wrecked—Oak Lawn, Linwood, La Estancin.

On Bayou Sale thirteen sugar houses were damaged more or less, the ones on the North Bend and Marsh plantations being blown down.

The Pharr & Williams' sawmill at Pattersonville, burnt a short time ago and just rebuilt, had its new iron roof entirely blown away.

Gulf coast, including Terrebonne Parish.

More devastation was to come in the year 1893. The hurricane of September 1893 was so damaging to Terrebonne and Lafourche communities that it partially destroyed Lockport in nearby Lafourche Parish. Only a month later, a violent hurricane roared into 500 miles of coastline from Timbalier to Pensacola; the U.S. Weather Service documented that the storm surge was 15 feet. This storm killed 900 people in nearby Cheniere Caminada in Lafourche Parish and Grand Isle, including half the women and nearly all the children.

Two other personal losses affected the Cenacs the year after the devastating October 1893 hurricane. Marie's husband Salvador Carlos, Jr. died of pneumonia on March 20, 1894, at only 29 years of age and only one month after the birth of their fifth child, Helene. He and Marie had been married eight years. By age 27, she was a widow with five children. Her youngest child, Helene, died in either 1895 or 1896 of croup, further compounding the widow's grief. The personal and physical closeness of most of her siblings and her parents provided Marie and the other four children with necessary aid and comfort until her remarriage on May 12, 1903, to Louis Collins when she was 36.

An unusual South Louisiana weather event was the snow of February 14-15, 1895, when a snowfall that left eight inches in New Orleans also blanketed the southeastern portion of the state. Terrebonne Parish residents, who were accustomed to viewing local snow as an almost once-in-a-lifetime occurrence, experienced another snowfall only four years later.

The most destructive of all these weather events during this time frame required aftermath periods of rebuilding, replanting, and general regrouping by the Cenac clan as well as all their neighbors who lived in the coastal communities most affected by wind and waters.

NOTES

1. The Morgan City Historical Society

2. In the Cenac Collection of the Nicholls State University Archives

3. Helen Wurzlow accounts

4. Angie Fonseca Trahan, *A Walk Through the Past: The Life and Times of Salvador Carlos, Sr., Elvire Heloise LaGrave and their Families*, 2008

5. Descendant James R. Carrere, personal account, 2009

6. Houma Centennial Celebration History Supplement, 1934

CHAPTER 17
December 24, 1898:
La Tristesse

Christmas Eve, and all Pierre could do was to sit by the fire and stare at the silent flames consuming logs until they split and folded over on themselves. *It would be easy to do that myself, but I have to be stronger.*

He re-crossed his legs and adjusted his frame in the rocking chair. Glancing over at William across the room playing a game of checkers with Dennis, he cringed a little when he saw the boy's left shirtsleeve flattened, folded, and pinned up onto his shoulder. It had been a whole year since William lost his arm, but Pierre was still sometimes startled all over again at seeing his son without it. William was adapting better than anyone else.

The boy wouldn't let anyone button his shirt or tie his shoes anymore. Pierre admired his strong will, but he had to stop himself as well as the females in the house every day from going to William's aid. He heard his 14-year-old son's hearty laugh at a mistake Dennis made in the game. William would be all right. But he would have obstacles the other children would not have to face.

The other children. Twelve, not fourteen as it should be.

First little Celestine all those years ago. Just a baby, really. That tiny coffin, but so heavy.

Then Marie's baby, Helene. And now Josephine. I thought Victorine would die herself from grief. And sometimes I thought I would, too.

Pierre accepted the cup of coffee Victorine handed him, and took a long sip. As his wife settled into her own chair opposite the fire, Pierre noticed again that she moved more slowly, with less grace than she had once forced her body to assume.

She smiled at him and whispered *"Joyeux Noël demain,* Pierre," but he could not bring himself to respond. Instead, he just nodded.

He thought way back to that first Christmas Eve midnight mass in New Orleans. *What a thing to remember tonight. The candles in the cathedral's chandeliers sparkled night lights such as I had never seen before. Festive holiday vestments of the bishop and a dozen priests on the altar. The choir, the pews packed with people smiling at each other. That was 38 years ago, and I can still smell the incense smoke the altar boys left behind them in the aisle.*

He forced himself to think about Josephine's last days only a

Adenise Marie and Dennis Joseph Cenac c. 1900

few months ago. Eighteen years old, and planning her marriage to the third Carlos boy to catch the eye of one of his daughters. She had sewn and folded her trousseau into a chest the older boys built for her. He walked into the room the day she was carefully laying a tablecloth she had embroidered with her favorite flower, daisies. "Look, Papa, do you think this is nice enough for Bahya to spill his gumbo on?" she said, with a mischievous look in her eye. They had laughed together while she closed the lid of the chest.

Not a month afterward, they were closing the lid of the coffin over Josephine, in the wedding dress she had not been able to wear down the aisle, and wearing the wedding ring her fiancé had not been able to place on her finger.

Adenise walked up to him, smiling her seven-year-old's gap-toothed smile. *"Papa? Tu est encore triste?"* The other children stopped their conversations, their reading, and their games. All heads turned toward him. He sat straight, put his cup down on the floor beside the chair, and lifted his youngest child onto his knees.

"Non, chère petite. How can I be sad with all of you to make me happy?"

THE UNITED STATES OF AMERICA.

* STATE OF * LOUISIANA *

STATE BOARD OF EDUCATION.

TO WHOM IT MAY CONCERN;

Be it Known, That by virtue of an act of the Legislature of the State of Louisiana, entitled "An Act to regulate Public Education in the State of Louisiana, to provide a revenue for the same," etc., approved July 12, 1888, the State Board of Education hereby appoint *Pierre Conrad* a member of school Board of the Parish of *Terrebonne* vice *E Picon failes to qualify* and he is hereby authorized and empowered to execute and fulfill the duties of that office according to law, and to have and to hold said office, with all the powers and privileges of the same, until his successor shall be duly appointed and qualified according to law.

IN WITNESS WHEREOF, The President of said Board has signed his name, and caused the seal thereof, to be affixed, at the City of Baton Rouge, this *twenty third* day of *March* in the year of our Lord one thousand eight hundred and *ninety four* and of the Independence of the United States of America the one hundred and *seventeenth*

Murphy J Foster

Governor of Louisiana and President of the Board.

State Superintendent and Ex-Officio Secretary of the Board.

Pierre's 1894 membership certificate on the Terrebonne Parish School Board and school transfer boats photo

CHAPTER 18
A Place of Substance

In the years coinciding with the oldest of the Cenac children marrying and leaving home, Pierre became more community-minded and politically involved. One newspaper of the time records that Pierre and Victorine's house in Dulac was the polling place for the Third Precinct of Terrebonne Parish's Fourth Ward. Pierre was the commissioner of election for November 3, 1890; his son Jean Charles was the clerk for the Fourth Ward. Jean Baptiste served as commissioner of election for the Cenac voting place on April 19, 1892.

The Houma Courier of March 15, 1890, described Terrebonne's Fourth Ward: First Precinct—"From upper line ward, to lower line Ashland plantation, polling place at Honduras..."; Second Precinct—"From lower line Ashland Plantation to Bayou DuLac, including the Live Oak Plantation, Polling place at E.J. Richard's School House..."; Third Precinct—"From Bayou DuLac and lower line Live Oak Plantation to the sea shore; polling place at P. Cenac's...."

Four years later, Pierre became a member of the Terrebonne Parish School Board, which was formed to address the shambles of the local education system that had been floundering since Civil War years. His certificate of membership is dated March 23, 1894, and is signed by Murphy J. Foster, governor of Louisiana and president of the state school board.[1]

Pierre, as the member from Dulac, joined other community leaders T. H. Casey, president, of Gibson; C.A. Celestin of Newtown (now Daigleville), superintendent, Houma; C. St. Martin of Theriot; D.O. Gautreaux of Houma; James D. Wilson of Montegut; J.O. Duplantis of Houma; E.B. Hebert of Schriever; Paulin Navarre of Ellendale.[2]

Parish leaders were trying to rebuild some semblance of a local education system after the long period of Reconstruction. Before the Civil War, the local public school system had received only sporadic support by the state, and relatively little interest from the citizenry. In 1849, "Of the 982 educable children in the parish only 236 attended school for an average period of five months and fifteen days."[3] Affluent families did not send their children to local public schools, but instead hired tutors or enrolled them in local private or out-of-state schools for their higher education during the years preceding the war.

Above, Houma Academy building on Point Street, later used as St. Francis School. Below left, listing from the Houma Courier *of March 1890 parish polling places, including Pierre's Dulac residence. Below right, Terrebonne Parish commissioners of election list for April 1892, including Jean Baptiste Cenac*

Right, the "Rooster" School, the firehouse building moved to Church Street in 1896; the first public high school in Houma after the Civil War

Terrebonne High School on Goode Street (first new building and the second public high school), c. 1909

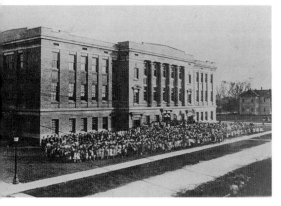

Terrebonne High School on Church Street (third high school building), c. 1919, with the St. Francis de Sales Boys' Elementary School on Verret Street at right

Ellendale School c. 1925

Bayou Blue School c. 1925

After the war, local public education was in disarray. The oldest of the 14 Cenac children seem to have received what little schooling they did at home, while the younger children did have the opportunity to have formal education. One evidence of the family's interest in education is that Jean Charles Cenac as a young man was serving as principal of Dulac School in 1897.[2]

Pierre and Victorine's younger children had educational opportunities the older children did not. From official documents we know that the younger children could read and write, but the two oldest sons and the three oldest daughters—Marie, Marguerite, and Victorine--could not. This did not prevent Jean Baptiste from having a successful boat-building business. Nor did it diminish the respect Marie, Marguerite, and Victorine commanded from practicing physicians of their time because of their skill as midwives.

A dramatic population increase continued, and extensive development of the downtown City of Houma occurred between 1890 and 1910, when the population rose to 5,024. Because of the added numbers, community leaders tried to provide more educational facilities in the town. In 1896, the city fathers applied for a charter to establish a high school in Houma, through the Louisiana Secretary of State's office. What was referred to as the "rooster school" (because of its rooster weathervane) was the donated firehouse building, which was slowly moved from the batture across Main Street from the courthouse to the block behind the courthouse. Elementary school students continued attending classes in the nearby old McMaster school building while the rooster school was reserved for high school classes. The rooster school was used as Terrebonne High School until 1909 when a new structure was built for as many as 400 secondary school students, facing Goode Street, in the block behind St. Francis de Sales Church. Terrebonne High became the second high school in the state (in 1914) to be accredited by the Southern Association of Colleges and Schools. Growing student population and consolidation necessitated the need for expansion in the decade following the opening of the 1909 school. A new building at a cost of $100,000 opened in 1918, on the site of the demolished rooster school facing Church Street (where the present-day Courthouse Annex was completed in 1973). Elementary school students inherited the 1909 building for use as Houma Elementary School well into the mid-1900s. The building which continues to be used as Terrebonne High School on Main Street north of downtown was completed in 1940; the 1918 building served first as Houma Junior High, then as Houma Central until its demolition to make way for the current Courthouse Annex building.

Rural schools had functioned across the parish for many decades. To encourage many of these students to attend classes in Houma, the parish provided transportation in the form of boat transfers to shuttle students along waterways to and from Houma. (This system continued until buses began adjunct service in the early 1930s, but the school boat transfers were not discontinued completely until the year 1958, when 32 boats still transferred 1,000 school children each day.)

A private school named the Houma Academy was organized in 1858, built on land donated by R.R. Barrow. The Academy building was designed by esteemed architect Henry Howard, and the contractor was J.B. Dunn of Houma, who owned a brick yard on Dunn Street. In 1870, the Marianite Sisters of Holy Cross bought the unused building when they arrived in Houma to staff the first local Catholic girls' school.

St. Francis Boys' Elementary School was founded in 1890, and for decades the two-story framed building stood on the site of the present St. Francis Cathedral complex's youth center and rectory on the corner of Verret and Goode streets. The current St. Francis co-ed elementary school building at the corner of Verret and Grinage was finished in the 1951-52 school year. The antebelleum structure of the old Academy on Point Street was repurposed in 1952 as St. Francis Boys' High School when Brothers of the Sacred Heart came to Houma to teach prep school boys. A year after Vandebilt Catholic High School opened in 1965 for education of both boys and girls, the Academy and longtime "Boys' School" building on Point Street was torn down to make way for a shopping center.

One native son of Terrebonne made his mark in education outside the parish, but merits mention because of the scope of his contribution. Randall Lee Gibson was the son of Terrebonne pioneer Tobias Gibson. Randall Lee studied at Yale University and graduated from the Louisiana University in New Orleans in law. After serving in the Civil War, he was elected to Congress and then to the U.S. Senate in 1880. At the bidding of wealthy New Orleans merchant Paul Tulane, Randall Lee Gibson guided Tulane's educational endowment and became founding president of Tulane University's board of administrators. Gibson Hall on the Tulane campus is a memorial to the Terrebonne native's contributions to this prestigious university.

Top photo, St. Francis de Sales priests' residence facing Verret Street on the corner of Grinage c. 1920s
Above, St. Francis de Sales Boys' School on Verret Street circa 1940.
Bottom, Gibson Hall on the campus of Tulane University in New Orleans

Above, plaque in Houma's Courthouse Square commemorating the Cenac Oaks. Below, the Terrebonne Parish Courthouse of 1898. In background this page, Police Jury minutes book reference to the oak trees' planting.

During the Cenacs' Dulac years, Pierre's connection to and regard for the entire parish took the form of an aesthetic project which literally lives on today in the center of Houma's downtown district. At the request of City of Houma officials, he uprooted 24 live oak trees from his property at Bayou Salé and, with his sons Paul and Jean Charles, took them by mule train to the Courthouse Square on Main Street to be transplanted during the winter of 1886-87. "Lafayette" Bernard Filhucan de Bazet, founder of *Le Courier de Houma*, planted the trees as documented in Minutes Book D, page 112 of the official records of the Terrebonne Parish Police Jury.

A sign of the town's lifestyle during those days was an early ordinance of the local government. Apparently some Houmans of the day allowed their cows, chickens, pigs, and other animals to feed at will in public places. The Terrebonne Parish Police Jury found it necessary to adopt an ordinance (Number 107) making it unlawful for anyone to place "stock of any kind in the Court House yard." The same ordinance protected the oaks by outlawing any defacing of or injury to the trees there.

Eight of the trees were removed for construction of a new courthouse in 1935. The 16 oaks surviving in 1989 were inducted into the Louisiana Garden Club's Live Oak Society. Two of these trees, 118 years after being planted, were removed because they were diseased, and replaced, in April 2005. Pierre's great-grandson Dr. Christopher E. Cenac, Sr., donated and planted two trees to replace them in April, 2005.[4]

Interestingly, the Cenac Oaks live on in many communities far from Houma and Dulac. Terrebonne Parish Clerk of Court Randolph Bazet used acorns from the oaks to plant new trees, which he distributed to other Louisiana clerks of court and to many U.S. communities. These trees presumably continue to thrive far away from the Houma Courthouse Square.[5] Local descendants of the Cenac Courthouse Square oaks can be seen on the campus of Honduras School on Grand Caillou Road.

While participation in community life was obviously becoming important to 42-year-old Pierre around the beginning of the 1880s, his livelihood and businesses were uppermost in his interest and energies, after family concerns.

Pierre's early acquisition of land had begun in 1865 with the short-lived ownership of half of the Dupont property on Main and Barrow. He followed this with a purchase of land in Little Caillou, and then purchase of patents (up to 640 acres per patent) from the state in November 1867, April 1870, and April 1882.

But the bulk of his landholdings were acquired during the years between 1880 and 1898. Pierre bought another piece of property on January 14, 1880, from the Duponts, plat numbers 13 and 37 in the present-day 7900 block of Main Street on the bayouside diagonally opposite the Dupont Building—where the Picone Building stood for decades until destroyed by fire in 2010. On that property, Pierre operated a bakery and a livery stable.[6]

With his various land and business purchases in the rural

areas of Grand Caillou and Little Caillou as well as in Houma, Pierre proved his philosophy of diversifying his holdings.

He next increased his Dulac properties for sugar cane production and other pursuits. His following purchase during this period was land in Grand Caillou from A.F. Gaubert on April 5, 1881. The next year Pierre bought 1,213 acres, plus 184 acres, located on Grand Caillou from Robert Ruffin Barrow and Volumnia Roberta Barrow, the sale dated January 12, 1882. Two days later, Pierre purchased property on Grand Caillou from John E. Pellegrin and Ely Pellegrin on January 14, 1882.

Pierre continued his purchasing spree when he bought 88 more acres in the Dulac area along Bayou Grassy and Bayou Salé, on August 6, 1883. Former owners were large landholders Robert Ruffin Barrow and his sister Mrs. Volumnia R. Barrow. (Their mother, Volumnia Washington Hunley Barrow, who married Robert Ruffin Barrow, Sr., was the sister of Captain Horace Lawson Hunley, who invented the underwater craft used by the Confederate navy. Barrow, Sr., had invested in the first prototype his brother-in-law built, the *Pioneer*.) Pierre further expanded his holdings in that area by buying 80 acres on Bayou Salé from Armand St. Martin on May 31, 1884.

The next two conveyance records involving Pierre's acquisitions were dated January 29, 1885, when he bought from W.H. Buford 140 acres, 14 arpents on the left descending bank of Bayou Salé and on October 28, 1886, from the same W.H. Buford, nine arpents on Bayou Salé.

For an immigrant who arrived in America with very little in 1860, Pierre was becoming a man of considerable personal assets.

Three years later, Pierre made another purchase of property in Houma city proper when he bought from Andre Gaubert *et al.* on April 2, 1889, two lots on Grinage Street and one on Lafayette Street.

His Grand Caillou lands expanded even more when Pierre acquired public auction parcels previously separately owned by Joseph Ozio and Drausin Toups, both on October 4, 1890. Two years later, Pierre acquired acreage of three arpents, more or less, on both sides of Bayou Grassy, from F. Claiborne Lauret on March 5, 1892. Only a few months later, on July 26, Pierre bought 40 acres from Laurent Pellegrin on Bayou Four Points at Dulac.

When possibilities presented themselves for land acquisition where he wanted it, Pierre obviously was not a man to pass up the opportunity. Perhaps the seed of this drive to own ever more land had its origin in his home country—where his family had access only to tiny parcels.

Almost as important as the lands the Cenac family acquired were the boats that became agents of the family's success in the seafood and shipping industry. One prized possession began its life north of Lake Pontchartrain in 1881 when its builder, Peter Casano, gave the vessel his own name. Sometime at the end of the 1880s, the double-masted sailboat ran aground near Isle de Jean Charles in lower Terrebonne. Albert and his brothers salvaged

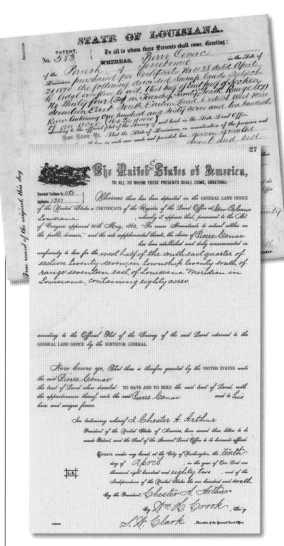

Above top, Pierre's patent number 583 purchase dated April 22, 1870, and patent number 1180 purchase dated April 10, 1882

Armand St. Martin

Below, the photo boat Success *on Bayou Lafourche c. 1885*

A page from Merchants, Tradesmen and Manufacturers Financial Conditions for 1902, Lafourche Parish and Terrebonne Parish, Louisiana, *information compiled by R.G. Dun, later Dun & Bradstreet*

Fire House and the fire truck "Effie Hellier" on Main Street, Houma c. 1918; the building housed governmental offices on the second floor

Below, Main Street looking east from Lafayette street in 1905, Courthouse oaks in the distance

the sailboat, and Albert bought the vessel for 800 silver dollars in 1892.[5] It was the largest and the most distinctive of the early sailing luggers the Cenacs owned and used.

Sailboats were among a vast number of vessel types that plied Terrebonne's bayous. Local historian Helen Wurzlow wrote, "Through the years you could see sail boats and mail boats, flat boats and school boats, moving van boats and freight boats, even funeral boats passing up and down on Houma's water Main Street as bayou traffic went from pirogue to motor boat, not to mention the romantic age of the old bayou steamboats."

Amid all these acquisitions of various types, Pierre obtained bedding grounds and he was cultivating oysters, probably before his sons grew to adulthood and married. Family members have confirmed that Pierre held extensive oyster leases in widespread coastal waters, from the Mississippi Sound to Atchafalaya Bay. He also owned shucking plants on Little Caillou and on Delacroix Island.[6] This particular occupation of oyster cultivation, and subsequent expansion into oyster distribution and exportation, was to become a Cenac family hallmark that would develop into the main foundation of Terrebonne's seafood-based economy in later years.

Pierre's personal healthy financial status is reflected in the fact that in 1902, his credit rating was among the highest that could be awarded by Dun, precursor to Dun and Bradstreet.[1]

The Cenacs' business interests grew at the same rate that Houma expanded in population and in amenities, as well as in the latest necessities. The town's 1890 population was 1,280, and its 1900 population grew to 3,212. Parishwide, the population went from 20,167 in 1890 to 24,464 by 1900. This shows that about three-fourths of the population growth in this decade occurred in the town proper rather than in outlying areas. Part of the reason for this had to be caused by families moving from

Main Street, Houma, La.

the coastal areas more northerly to escape the worst of flooding and other damages from frequent hurricanes. The main reason for the increase, however, was the influx of workers from other parts of the country—Bohemians (Czechoslovakians and [loosely] others of Eastern European origin, who had previously lived on America's East Coast) seeking employment in Houma's burgeoning seafood industry.[5]

The town of Houma suffered two major fires during the 1880s and 90s, which seriously damaged the city center and required significant rebuilding. The first conflagration of this period occurred on the morning of December 29, 1887. The fire destroyed all the buildings on the south side of Main Street from the site of the current Le Petit Theatre building westward to Canal Street. In addition, the fire spread as far as School Street, seriously damaging property in the area between Main, Grinage, and School streets. There was additional heavy damage on the north half of the square bounded by School, Verret, Lafayette, and Canal streets.

One of the reasons for the extensive damage caused by the 1887 fire was that the only organized firefighting capability in Houma at the time, the Houma Volunteer Fire Company No. 1 founded in 1872, had only 36 volunteers manning a bucket brigade.

Probably in response to the catastrophic fire of the year before, the town rebounded with the construction of both utilitarian and cultural structures. Houma Hook and Ladder Company No. 1 was organized in 1888. One record documented that "This company owns a hall, truck and ladders, a Babcock [pumper] and other equipments, and is an efficient body of fire fighters."[7] The pumper was horse-drawn and steam-powered, and was named the "Lula Ruth Wright," currently on display in the Cabildo in New Orleans.

The second major fire occurred on the morning of April 4, 1892. It destroyed all buildings on the north side of Main Street from Church to Canal Street. After the fires of 1887 and 1892 had destroyed much of the town, new commercial buildings were constructed with fireproof materials (brick). The next major firefighting improvement came in 1916 with purchase of the first motor-driven fire truck by the Hook and Ladder Company. The fire truck was named the "Effie Hellier," for the daughter of Houma City Councilman Harry Hellier.[5]

In 1896 Main Street became the site of an "elegant" Opera House erected by Houma Fire Company No. 1, at a cost of $8,000. It was on the bayouside, across the street from the courthouse. Hugh Berger, in his small book *A Leisure Walk Down Main Street, Houma, Louisiana, 60 Odd Years Ago*, chronicled from memory the building and its many uses:

"This was a large three story wood building which would be recognized by its turn of the century construction. There was a wide stairway at the center of the building which led up to the theater on the second floor....The theater was quite large and had a main floor and a balcony which was held up by large round iron

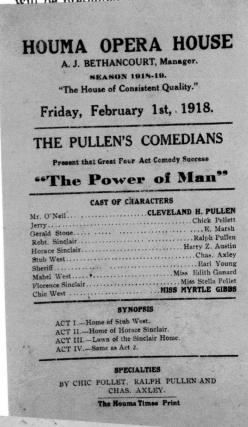

Houma Opera House.

Among the many offerings booked for appearance at the Houma Opera House, none is deserving of more favorable attention than the production of "Ishmael," a stage version of the well read and popular novel of the same name, a favorite with the readers of a by-gone day, and a standard work to-day. "Ishmael" will be presented here Wednesday

HOUMA OPERA HOUSE
A. J. BETHANCOURT, Manager.
SEASON 1918-19.
"The House of Consistent Quality."

Friday, February 1st, 1918.

THE PULLEN'S COMEDIANS

Present that Great Four Act Comedy Success

"The Power of Man"

CAST OF CHARACTERS

Mr. O'Neil..................CLEVELAND H. PULLEN
Jerry........................Chick Pellett
Gerald Stone..................E. Marsh
Robt. Sinclair................Ralph Pullen
Horace Sinclair..............Harry Z. Austin
Stub West...................Chas. Axley
Sheriff.....................Earl Young
Mabel West..................Miss Edith Ganard
Florence Sinclair............Miss Stella Pellet
Chic West...................MISS MYRTLE GIBBS

SYNOPSIS

ACT I.—Home of Stub West.
ACT II.—Home of Horace Sinclair.
ACT III.—Lawn of the Sinclair Home.
ACT IV.—Same as Act 2.

SPECIALTIES

BY CHIC POLLET, RALPH PULLEN AND
CHAS. AXLEY.

The Houma Times Print

Opera House, Houma, La.

"The Adventures of Kathlyn"
Third Number
"THE TEMPLE OF THE LION"
A Thrill in every Foot
OPERA HOUSE
Friday, May 1-1st.

From left, Gabriel Montegut, Alphonse Dupont, Louis Caranne, and Julius Blum in front of Peoples Bank c. 1896

posts...." Berger wrote that in 1914 "there were establishments on both sides of the stairs," including a tailor shop and the office of the city Clerk. The area "just below the main floor of the theater" was a storage place for "old outdated fire engines which still belonged to the city." The office of the Cumberland Telephone and Telegraph Company was also located in the Opera House building at one time.

Above, Bazet Hotel on Church Street, Houma c. 1900

Left, Bank of Houma at present day 7833 Main Street, c. 1892.

Another of Berger's fond memories was the "beautiful white tourist boat" *The Polly* which would come up Bayou Terrebonne, through Barrow's Canal, and on into Bayou Black. "On many occasions [the passengers] would throw us large sticks of peppermint candy."

Houma expanded its services to include the establishment of financial institutions and hospitality services to accommodate both locals and visitors. The two major financial institutions, the Spanish Renaissance style Bank of Houma (founded 1892) and the Beaux Arts style People's Bank (founded 1896, later becoming the City Hall and now Le Petit Theatre de Terrebonne), had a combined capital of $30,000 in 1897. In 1910, a new bank opened—Bank of Terrebonne, of which Theophile Cenac was a founding stockholder. The banks made available the credit required especially by sugar planters, as well as merchants and business people of the community.

The consolidation of the regional economy in Houma reflected a trend toward centralization and urbanization which was occurring all over the United States. Every city and town in the nation, large or small, developed its "Main Street" central business district.[8] The Terrebonne Building & Loan Association was established at the turn of the century and had $1 million in authorized capital, an indication of increased prosperity in the town. This growing prosperity gave families such as the Cenacs access to the capital necessary to take advantage of investment opportunities.

The hospitality industry catered to traveling salesmen called "drummers" who had the thriving parish seat on their circuits. Several hotels located downtown accommodated these men and other visitors to the town. These included the Bazet Hotel, Commercial Hotel, Sanders Hotel, Breaux's House (the Cosmopolitan Hotel), Wurzlow Hotel and the Durand Hotel.

One passage from Hugh Berger's book describes treading his way "between the ship type chairs which were on the side walk in front of the Commercial Hotel. Each evening and night these chairs were occupied by drummers, who were occupants of the hotel, and by many of the townspeople. Above the first floor were two covered galleries lined with chairs which could be occupied by visitors to the hotel...."

Wurzlow's Commercial Hotel, Main Street, Houma (burned April 4, 1892). Below, painting of the original Houma Methodist Church located on the corner of Goode and Belanger streets in Houma, 1845-1888

Above, St. Matthew's Episcopal Church's second building c. 1892. Below, First Presbyterian Church's 1895 second building on the corner of Barrow and Verret streets

Newspaper ads from Houma Courier *editions in 1892 (Professional Cards) and 1896 (Suthon, Bourg). Right bottom, J.M. Durand Restaurant and Oyster Saloon on Main Street c. 1890*

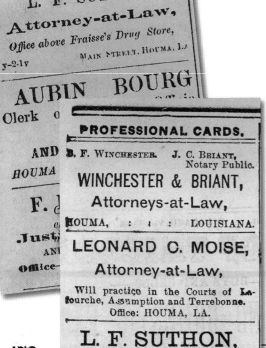

Churches of Houma were established earlier during the days of the civil parish. Methodists had the oldest recorded church congregation in Terrebonne Parish's boundaries, located in Gibson as early as 1825. That denomination in 1850 had one church in Terrebonne Parish, and an additional church which was built in 1870. St. Francis de Sales Catholic Church parish was founded in 1847 and completed its first church building in 1848. The Presbyterian Church in Houma dates from 1848. St. Matthew's Episcopal Church was established in 1855. By 1870, four Baptist churches had combined "sittings" of 500.

Cultural and social opportunities, other than in the much-used Opera House, included the Knights of Pythias Castle Hall on Main

Street which served as a men's society. Other societies circa 1897 for whites were Knights of Honor, Ancient O.U. Workmen, Ladies of St. Ann, the Branch Catholic Knights of America at St. Francis de Sales Church, and Order of Red Men. For black men, societies included King Solomon No. 14 F.A. and M., which met at the Good Templars Hall on Canal Street. For black women, there was the Sprig of Myrtle No. 31 K. of M. which met at the Good Templars Hall as well.

More longstanding establishments for amusement included the many saloons along Main Street: Wright's Saloon, (William Wright, proprietor) A. Ridley, the Sazerac Bar, (J.H. Bower, proprietor), A. Zeringer, and the Bank Exchange, (V.J. Lirette, proprietor). Two restaurants were separately owned by John M.

Durand and Jurant Martin.

Near Houma's bustling Main Street, Colonel Gabriel Montegut, who was a cashier at Peoples Bank, had established the Montegut Insurance Agency in 1875.

During this period, more and more professionals made Houma their chosen place of livelihood. Among them were prominent attorneys at the firms of Hugh M. Wallis, Jr., Lucius F. Suthon, and Winchester and Briant.

The number of medical professionals grew exponentially with the population and with centralization of services in Houma. These included practicing physicians R.A. McBride, C.M. Menville, A.J. and A.P. Delcourt, Hugh M. Wallis, Sr., C.A. Duval, L.H. Jastremski, and R. Fleming Jones. Dr. R.L. Zelenka, Alphonse A. Verret, and Dr. C.A. Lovejoy were dentists. Adjunct to these medical men were the pharmacies of H.F. Belanger, L.J.

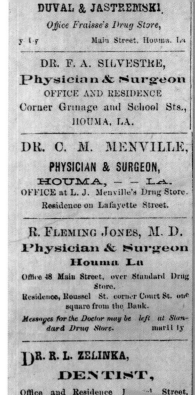

Above, the Order of the Red Men c. 1895. Below at right, E.C. Wurzlow, longtime Terrebonne Parish Clerk of Court, c. 1901. Top right ads from 1896 Houma Courier newspaper; bottom "leprosy" article from Terrebonne Times of September 25, 1897

May be Leprosy.

Alfred Jackson, a negro, residing on the Honduras plantation was sent to the Charity Hospital, this week. It is believed that Jackson has leprosy.

DO YOU INDULGE ?

The Zeringer Saloon On Goode Street Established In 1865 Is The Best House in Houma to Get Pure Liquors.

Mr. A. Zeringer proprietor of Zeringer's Saloon on Goode Street opposite the Court House is perhaps as widely and favorably known throughout the parish as any man in Houma having been in business here since 1865.

He handles the highest grades of wines and liquors, both foreign and domestic. By handling only a superior line of choice articles, and through his courteous and obliging manners, he has succeeded in building up a truly first-class trade, Here can always be obtained the purest grades of brandies, gin, whiskies, (Scotch, bourbon and rye,) Champagne and wines of all kinds bought direct from the manufacturers of this country and imported so that he has no hesitancy in guaranteeing his goods just as he represents them, first class in every particular. The commodious premises occupied by him are situated on Goode St. just across the street from the court-house.

The bar room is nicely fitted up and furnished. The mirror, cut-glass ware, and neatly polished bar attract the attention of all callers. In fact, his place is furnished with every convenience for the comfort and entertainment of patrons, and we commend such of our readers as delight in liquid and stimulating refreshments, to call at the 'Zeringer'. You will find Mr. Zeringer the proprietor, and son, George, his assistant, warm hearted, genial gentlemen.

Unknown saloon on Houma's Main Street at the turn of the 20th century.
Zeringer Saloon mentioned at left burned in 1900

Ads from Waterways Edition *of 1910*

Montegut mail boat, early 1900s

*William Wright Sr.'s stable c. 1910
Below,* Delatour *dredging Bayou
Terrebonne c. 1915*

Menville, Standard Drug Store, Fraisse Drug Store, and Francois Gouaux, a manufacturer of proprietary medicines. Gouaux was a graduate of the Bordeaux School of Pharmacy, and was a founding member of the Louisiana Pharmacy Association. No hospitals were located in Houma at the time; seriously ill people had to go to New Orleans' Charity Hospital for medical care. (The first Houma hospital was established by Dr. Prentis Parker, but was short-lived, 1924-1928.)

"Some of the most startling developments of the time were in the areas of communication and transportation. The Gray Telephone and Telegraph Line from Schriever was built in 1889. This was the town's first wire communication with the outside world. Nine years later, on July 3, 1898, the Ray Telephone System secured a franchise from the City Council and inaugurated the first local service. The directory disclosed that there were 40 patrons; the Houma Fish and Oyster Co. Ltd. phone number was 3. After the Cumberland Telephone and Telegraph Company was granted a franchise in 1899, the Ray Telephone System ceased business."[9] According to newspaper accounts, in 1913 Cumberland merged with what became Southern Bell Telephone and Telegraph Company; the total number of subscribers was 420. Ada Duthu, later Mrs. Harry Mey, Sr., was the first phone operator.

Local entrepreneur Emile Daigle owned a private telephone line to the Houma Fish and Oyster Co., Ltd. factory at Sea Breeze; it was the first private communication line in Terrebonne Parish, established because of the Daigle Barge Line that had an office at Sea Breeze.

Daily mail service in Houma did not begin until 1856. From 1834, when Houma's first post office was established, until 1856, mail had been brought by boat from Pattersonville to Thibodaux twice each week, on Tuesdays and Thursdays. In 1897, the postal service was housed in the Opera House building on Main Street.

Like communication, transportation was in a state of flux between the old and the new. Traditional modes of travel were represented in Houma by several busy livery stables. Those included Berger Brothers Livery Stable on Main near the Barataria Canal, Albert and Pierre Cenac's Livery Stable on Main Street, A.G. Cage on Main Street near the courthouse, John R. Grinage, and William Wright, Sr.'s Livery Stable on the corner of Main and Grinage. O.L. Crosier ran one in Schriever.

Water travel improvements, particularly for freight, included the advent of steamboats in the 1880s. The steamer *S.P. Archer,* owned by J.J. Shaffer, was one of the first steam-powered craft operated exclusively in the parish of Terrebonne. It carried freight from Bayou Black to the railroad at Tigerville (Gibson). The first steamboat to travel on Bayou Terrebonne, *The Naturalized,* belonged to Jean Baptiste Ploton (d. 1883), a native of the Haute Loire region in France. The name of the boat shows his great pride in becoming a U.S. Citizen. Ploton owned and operated a barge line near the railroad station. He later sold the barge line to Emile Daigle, who expanded the business to become The Daigle

RAY TELEPHONE EXCHANGE.

DIRECTIONS :—Ring up Central. Call for Number wanted, and wait for answer. When through talking ring off. In case of storm, cut off box, as I will not be responsible for damage done in case of lightning. **T. N. REED,** Manager.

"B."

Bazet, O. F. [Residence]	18
Bazet Hotel	4
Bank of Houma	5
Berger Bros., Livery Stable	15
Bisland, J. & Co., [Store]	20
Belanger, H. F. [Drug Store]	22
Bisland, J. [Residence]	37

"C."

Commercial Hotel	24
Celestin, C. A. [Residence]	28
Court House	25
Connelly, A. W. [Residence]	36
Comeaux, Albert (Rising Sun Bakery)	40

"D."

Depot, [3 rings]	2
Dupont, Alphonse [Store]	6
Durand Hotel	7
Dupont, A. M. & J. C. [Store]	10
Daspit, O. B. [Store]	11
Delcourt, Dr. [Residence]	19
Daspit, O. B. [Residence]	23
Davidson & Avery	27
Daigle, Emile Sr., [Office]	30
Daspit, Chas. M. [Residence]	34
Dupont, J. C. (Residence)	39

"G."

Gaidry, J. W. [Store, 2 rings]	32

"H."

Houma Courier	9
Houma Fish & Oyster Co.,	3
Honduras Plantation [2 rings]	2

"J."

Jastremski, L H. [Office and Drug Store]	16

"K."

Kock, T. H. [Residence]	29

"L."

Larrieu & Bourg, [3rd. Justice Court]	
Live and Let Live Livery Stable	

"M."

Menville, L. J. (Drug Store)	8
Menville, Dr. C. M. (Residence)	26
McBride, Dr. R. E. (Residence)	21

"P."

Peoples Bank	1

"R."

Robichaux, Jos. A. (Residence)	35

"S."

Suthon & Wallis, (Office)	17
Southdown Plantation, (Residence)	13
Standard Drug Store	14

"W."

Wallis, H. M. Jr., (Residence)	12
Wolf, G. & Co.,	38

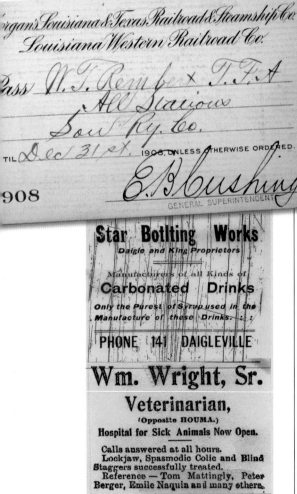
Ads from (descending) Houma Courier February 18, 1899; Waterways Edition 1910; 1908 railroad pass; ad for Star Bottling from Houma Courier of December 15, 1917; William Wright, Sr. ad from the Courier of April 13, 1901

Barge Line, Ltd. The company owned and operated the steamboats *Harry* and the *Laura*, and the gasoline launch *Moonlight*. Daigle also owned a large fleet of freight barges and two large freight warehouses. The company had a regular freight schedule on bayous Terrebonne, Little Caillou and Grand Caillou.

In the late 1800s and early 1900s, it became increasingly important to maintain navigability in Terrebonne and nearby waterways. Annual reports from the U.S. War Department show that from 1880 through 1893, several dredging projects in Bayou Terrebonne and Bayou Black kept the waterways cleared. Removal of trees, marsh grass, and hurricane debris and obstructions necessitated periodic dredging. By 1915, the reporting agent was the Chief of Engineers, U.S. Army. The U.S. dredge *Delatour* dredged "a channel 50 feet bottom width and 6 feet deep at mean low Gulf from mile 14.87 below the St. Louis Cypress Co.'s bridge in Houma, La., to Bush Canal, mile 24.11, the end of improvement." This work began on July 1, 1915, and ended December 10, 1915.

T.H. Kock

Near the turn of the twentieth century, Terrebonne Parish was home to three marine support companies, the Posecai Boat Ways (on Park at the present site of the Gabasse Street Bridge) and Evince Hebert's shipyard in Houma, and E.T. Morgan's Marine Ways in Gibson.

The major breakthrough in east-west rail service came after Charles Morgan reorganized the New Orleans, Opelousas, and Great Western Railroad into the Louisiana and Texas Railroad and Steamship Company in 1878. He bridged the Atchafalaya River in 1881 and completed the railroad line from Brashear (Morgan) City to Lafayette, which had been prevented by the Civil War. Simultaneous with this construction, the Louisiana Western Extension Railroad completed its rail line from Orange, Texas, across the Sabine River into Louisiana. One could now travel by rail, and ship freight, from New Orleans to Texas without interruption.

The Wells Fargo and Co. and the Western Union Telegraph Company were providing services in Houma in 1895 to their offices already established in Schriever at Terrebonne Station. T.H. Kock, a Wells Fargo superintendent at Brashear City, came to Houma in 1895, and became a pioneer in the transportation of oysters by rail.

Development of the gasoline engine brought about modernization in the transportation of seafood, through widespread conversion of the sailing lugger fleet to motor power. This conversion began slowly, but was complete by the mid-1930s.

The importance of access to local ice companies cannot be overstated. Availability of ice locally proved to be an enormous advantage to many local industries, including the seafood industry. The Houma Lighting & Ice Manufacturing Co., Ltd. was formed on December 17, 1898, by Dr. Leon H.

Jastremski, Harry L. Wilson, and Claiborne A. Duval, Jr. They manufactured ice from re-distilled water, and had a cold storage facility. They were also the agent for the famous Anheuser-Busch beer. The factory and office were located on the corner of Church and Park streets. This factory allowed Houma to join innumerable other communities that had profited from services as early as the 1870s. (Dr. Jastremski was so successful in this and other enterprises that he gave up his medical practice for these pursuits in 1906.)

The converging innovations in mechanization, refrigeration, communication, transportation, and electrification helped locals to exploit the vast natural coastal resources of Terrebonne: oysters, fish, shrimp, furs, sugar, and produce.

This convergence and the burgeoning population demanded support businesses and services of all kinds. Second- and third-generation Cenac boys who lived "in town" must have been fascinated by the many wares of hardware and general merchandise stores such as Daspit Hardware established in 1880 and Davidson and Kleiner General Merchandise established in 1888. Other general mercantile establishments were Alphonse Dupont, Stanwood Duval, A.M. & J.C. Dupont, Alex P. Haddad, Charles Abraham, Charles Porter, J. Bisland and Company, William Roddy, L. Gauthier, A. Hakel, L. Licota, D. Griffin, D. Palmieri, Joe Gannin, Abraham Blum, David Bach, Mrs. J. Kuhn, Mrs. M. P. Toujan, and Mrs. Mary L. Carrane. On Hugh Berger's *Leisure Walk*, he visited the store of Ignatius Lewald, Leon Heymann's Bargain Store, and Sam Elster's store, which dealt in dry goods and clothing.

Sam and Joseph Crispino owned a small delicatessen, a saloon, and a small grocery store next door to Elster's. Russell Strada's shoe repair shop was in the adjacent building.[10]

On a walk through the town on other errands, many a Cenac child saw these merchants' vast array of goods, from groceries to clothing to baby cribs to coffins. The girls of the family probably enjoyed visiting shops with more specialized products, including those of milliners and ladies' clothiers Miss M.C. McConnell, the Blahut sisters, Mrs. Julius Green Blum and Mrs. J.R. Grinage.

In the yard next to the A.M. and J.C. Dupont Department Store were "the bone remains of a large whale fish which had come ashore on the Gulf" during the period Hugh Berger's book describes. Many of the town's children must have reacted in the same way the young Hugh did: "I was always fascinated by the sight of these and would spend hours looking at them...."

Above, William Roddy Grocery Store near Main and Gabasse, Houma, 1895. Below, (descending) Francois Gouaux, pharmacien, John J. Kleiner, Jr. of Davidson and Kleiner, ad from Waterways Edition of 1910

A. F. DAVIDSON.   JOHN J. KLEINER, JR.

⊕ THE NEW FIRM ⊕

Davidson & Kleiner,

(SUCCESSORS TO DAVIDSON & AVERY,)

The Leaders in

⊃ General Merchandise, ⊂

PLANTATION SUPPLIES,

BUGGIES AND WAGONS.

The Fullest Assortment.   The Largest Stocks

HOUMA, LA.

Jean Marie Dupont

A.M. (left) and J.C. Dupont

A whale that washed up on Last Island in 1915

Below, a Houma Parade, Courthouse Square, 1895. Right, (from left) Professor Francis Fabregas, Sidney Fabregas, Frances Fabregas (Mrs. Clayton Doiron), Louis Fabregas, Martin Fabregas, Sr. c. 1902

J.H. Hellier

Above, Dupont's Store on Main Street c. 1886; tokens issued by A.M. and J.C. Dupont; Sidney Roddy barbershop on Verret Street between Gabasse and Barrow, 1911

Some of the Cenac girls, especially, no doubt watched the fine detail work of C.F. Monaco and P.E. Villeminot, who were jewelers and watch repairers during this period, since shopkeepers were generally more accommodating of childhood curiosity than those of later years. The children may also have posed for photographers Mrs. C.A. Lovejoy and P.A. Thibodaux.

Local musicians played a large role in the life of townspeople. Cenac adults and children probably sat through many band concerts in the courthouse square, where a round gazebo band stand held musicians many a Sunday afternoon. Often the town band was led by Professor F. Fabregas, teacher of vocal and instrumental music, who also owned a music store. The Helliers' Brass Band and Ridley's Brass Band also provided entertainment.

Family members could go to their grandfather Pierre's bakery across from A.M. and J. C. Dupont beginning January 1880. The smell of baking bread in the early morning also wafted from Morning Star Bakery and Excelsior Bakery [which survived from 1880 to 1980] also on Main Street, L. Duthu and Arthur F. Babin on Barrow Street near High Street, Fair Play Bakery at Main and Gabasse, Sam Achee's bakery (est. 1900) at Barrow and Verret, and Rising Sun Bakery and Grocery on Barrow Street near the Presbyterian Church.

Cenac children doubtless bought fruit from the dealers on Main Street: B. Grimaldi, P. Maranto, Joseph Picone, John Picone, Lawrence Hebert, and Mr. Gennello. Hugh Berger's book recalls that "On the southeast corner of Main and Barrow Streets stood the fruit store of Mr. Scurto. His display of fruits and vegetables was a sight to behold," a sight many Cenac children must have feasted their eyes upon.

For haircuts, the boys could go to barber shops owned by the Hebert Brothers on the corner of Main and Court, A. Adams and Sidney Roddy on Goode, and Acme on Main. They would have peeked into, but even then never have gone into, one of the barber shops for blacks—H.M. Riley on Canal, and J.A. Arceneaux on Main Street.

For young boys, the town's and outlying lumber mills had to have held great fascination. The lumber industry began to blossom during the final decades of the 1800s. Parish mills

Trade Tokens of Houma-Terrebonne

Theo Engeron Store 10 Cents

LeBlanc's Bakery Good For One Loaf

Pelican Bakery Good For One Loaf

Ladies Parlor 5 Cents

Haberdasher 5 Cents

Houma Elementary School 5 Cents

Excelsior Bakery 10 Cents

Claude P. Boudreaux Store 25 cents

C X Henry 5 Dollars

Achee Bakery Good For One Loaf

Tablette à Chaudière

Many south Louisiana homes of the 19th and early 20th centuries had a feature called a tablette à chaudière, *which was an extension of a window's sill to form a dishwashing shelf outside the window.* Tablette *in Cajun French translates as shelf in this instance. Since the French word* chaudière *translates as cooking pot, it was probably the container in which dishes were often washed.*

produced raw lumber, crossties, and shingles. The St. Louis Cypress Company, Ltd. was a longtime fixture at various locations in Terrebonne Parish. This company dug many canals in the parish to transport cypress logs to its mills. Minor's Canal was dug in 1909 by the estate of H.C. Minor, the Argyle Planting Company, and the estate of B. Marmande, from Bayou Black to Lake DeCade to float logs to Bayou Terrebonne for the mills located there.

In Dulac were two mills, the Caillou Manufacturing Co. at Live Oak Plantation, and the Dulac Sawmill on Dulac Plantation. Houma Cypress Company produced shutters and other cypress wood products. C.P. Smith and Mrs. Rosa Carrane formed a partnership, C.P. Smith & Co., in 1895, a saw and shingle mill. A.C. Daspit was about to erect another such facility in 1897 in the town. Dibert, Stark & Brown Cypress Co., Ltd. was the largest such company, located in Donner, along with F.E. Boudreaux's lumber company. The Gibson Cypress Lumber Company was in Gibson, and the L.S. Boudreaux Company was in Chacahoula. The lumber industry in Terrebonne and surrounding parishes was short-lived, reaching its zenith later, from 1900 through 1920.

A venture related to cypress lumbering, and later affected by increasing cypress scarcity, was Walter T. Kelly's business. He established Gulf Coast Bee Company in Houma in 1924, and fashioned cypress beehives, distributing them nationwide until the cypress shortage. The owner relocated his enterprise to Kentucky after leaving Houma, and his company is still providing beekeeping supplies.

A.A. Bonvillain brickworks was well-established, producing 12,000 bricks per day. One can only imagine young Cenacs and other schoolboys looking over the huge orderly mounds at the brickworks company as they walked home from school. Brickmasons in 1897 were Alphonse Bonvillain, Ernest Chauvin, Louis A. Chauvin, Clay Chauvin, H.C. Chauvin, and Lawson Bergeron, who doubled as a sugarmaker.

Coopers (barrelmakers) listed in Houma for 1897 were Milfred Mazureau, John Crochet, Elijah Miller, and John McCullough, who owned the cooper shop in which the former three were employed. McCullough was a "dealer in wood, hoop poles and molasses barrels" located on Main near Gabasse Street.[2] Another specialist tradesman was tinsmith Teles Babin, who invented and patented the Babin Pump.

When the Cenacs got water from cisterns either inside (as in Pierre and Victorine's house) or outside their homes, they were using the handiwork of three Houma families known for producing a necessity before the advent of piped water. Their products were the large, barrel-like cisterns that collected rainwater from roofs and supplied homes with drinking water and water for other home uses. Isidore Duthu, of Scottish descent, arrived in Houma around 1851. He began a family cistern-making business that continued for three generations and spanned many decades of local history. The same is true for the

Top, St. Louis Cypress Company log slip c. 1900. Above, Caillou Manufacturing Company at Dulac c. 1900

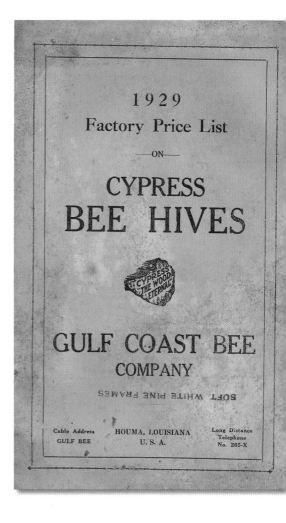

*Ads (in descending order) from
Houma Courier of February 26,
1897; Waterways Edition of 1910;
Terrebonne Times of July 17, 1887*

*A Hutchinson spring stopper bottle
made by Polmer Brothers Louisiana
Bottling Works, c. late 1800s*

*Right, blown glass bottles from 1890 to
1900, most embossed with "Houma":
Front row, unknown, Pico's Cure
for Consumption, H.F. Belanger,
Druggist, Dr. J.A. Pujos at Schriever
Drug Store, F. Gouaux Pharmacien
(small brown bottle); second row, H.F.
Belanger Druggist, Standard Drug
Store, Fraisse Standard Drug Store,
La Fraisse Apothecary, L.J. Menville
Pharmacist, F. Gouaux Pharmacien,
H.F. Belanger, E. Daigle Jr.
Apothecary; back row, H.F. Belanger,
La Fraisse/Houma Bottling Works
(embossed with both names)*

Klingman family, of German descent. Brothers Joseph, Henry, and Frank Klingman arrived in Terrebonne in the mid-1800s. Joseph and his son John made barrels, cisterns, and the wooden tools to build them with. Grandson Richard continued the craft until water purification, mass production, and loss of cypress forests made the occupation obsolete. Andrew Jackson Duet, son of cooper Eugene of Galliano, built cisterns when he arrived in Houma in 1923, many decades after the Duthus and Klingmans first began the same occupation in the century preceding his. Duet was probably the last of Terrebonne Parish's cistern makers.[5]

Blacksmiths in the town were still doing a robust business before the turn of the century. H.C. Porche , George Porche and Joseph Porche were blacksmiths and wheelwrights located near the railroad depot, as was Charles Dumoit, in the same vicinity and performing the same work. Crochet Brothers at No. 58 Main Street were blacksmiths and farriers. Willie Hamilton was a blacksmith on Bayou Terrebonne at Daigleville. Children who gathered outside their doors to watch burly men wielding heavy hammers to shape horseshoes probably included a Cenac or two in their midst. Machinists John and James Foolkes worked together in a shop that repaired machinery, and did pipe fitting as well as blacksmithing. O.J. Theriot sold cane carts, wheels, spokes and felloes along with flooring, ceiling materials, shingles, blinds, doors, moldings and mantels.

D.F. Gray, Ltd. of Houma, which had been established in 1885, was a wholesale shipper of Spanish moss, with a production capacity of 40 bales a day. Children had to have watched as moss pickers unloaded their boats into the shippers' facilities, the black cured heaps on their way to being cleaned for use as upholstery stuffing. V.J. Lirette & Bros. located on Bayou Cane, three miles from Houma, bought and sold moss from its steam factory. Pierre Cenac was also in the moss shipping business with his factory located on Park Avenue beginning in 1908.

A sure sign of transformation to a more modern era was that Houma taxpayers voted for a utilities proposition in January 1898 to construct waterworks and erect an electric lighting system. Lighting evolved from kerosene lanterns, to arc lights, and subsequently to incandescent lights by 1910.

One amenity that began during this period was the local

Left, Southern Pacific Railraod depot in Thibodaux c. 1900. Pictured, Ben Walthers and Paul Auslet (standing in cab); above, bottle from Lirette's Tropica Bottling Works, c. 1920s; budget below published in Houma Courier *of May 17, 1902*

manufacture of carbonated beverages by Houma Bottling Works on the bayouside on Church Street. The business was owned by the ever-enterprising Dr. Leon H. Jastremski. Proprietors Aubin Daigle, Ernest Daigle and Wilfred King owned Star Bottling Works begun in Daigleville in 1912. Frank F. Lirette and Volzie J. Lirette owned Lirette's Tropica Bottling Works which opened in 1920. He was the husband of Eugenie Bourgeois Lirette, oldest sister of William Jean Pierre Cenac's wife Marie and her sister Gertrude Bourgeois Cenac. A Houma newspaper reported in 1922 that the total annual production of local bottling works was "40,000 cases of pop and other soft drinks of all flavors."

Houma had more than doubled in size in relatively little time by the end of the 1800s. The town and parish had at long last recuperated from the repressive commercial and agricultural atmosphere of the post-war years, and citizens were becoming more invested in the parish's future professional, business, and cultural possibilities.

Since many of the Cenac clan had moved to Houma by this time, they were postured, along with the city itself, to reap the benefits of greatly expanded local services, facilities, infrastructure, and a general air of optimism about the future. Even through personal losses and environmental setbacks, Pierre Cenac's far-sighted, methodical assessment of opportunities and timing was serving him and his family well.

NOTES

1. In the Cenac Collection of the Nicholls State University Archives
2. E.C. Wurzlow. *A Directory of the Parish of Terrebonne, 1897.* This volume is a valuable resource for a brief historical sketch of the parish, as well as an updated state-of-the parish account to date. Mr. Wurzlow lists, community by community, categories of tradesmen, business owners and professionals, and participants in various occupations. His book is the source for many of the specific names and businesses enumerated in this chapter.
3. Marguerite Watkins thesis
4. Plaques in the Courthouse Square document the Cenac family's gifts.
5. Helen Wurzlow accounts
6. Herbert Wurzlow. Abstract of Pierre Cenac Properties: This document is a part of the Cenac Collection in the Nicholls State University Archives.
7. E.C. Wurzlow
8. Donald J. Millet, Sr. *The Economic Development of Southwest Louisiana, 1865-1900,* Ph.D. dissertation, 1964
9. Thomas Blum Cobb and Mara Currie. *Images of America: Houma,* Arcadia Publishing, 2004
10. Hugh W. Berger. *A Leisure Walk Down Main Street, Houma, Louisiana, 60 Odd Years Ago,* 1979

Budget For The Parish of Terrebonne.

Budget of Expenditures for next Fiscal Year.

For jurors and witnesses court	$2500.00
For Sheriffs salary, prisoners board, conveying prisoners to penitentiary and some to asylum and serving jury notices for District Court	$2,000.00
Coroner's jury fees	500.00
Parish Physician	50.00
Paris Treasurer	500.00
Clerk of the Police Jury	350.00
Parish Assessor	700.00
Justices of the Peace	2000.00
Constables	2000.00
District Attorney conviction fees	500.00
Parish printing	400.00
Police Jurors	450.00
Roads and Bridges	1,500.00
Road Inspector	500.00
Elections	900.00
Jail Constructions	1,500.00
Health Officer and Board of Health	1,000.00
For incidentals	1,800.00
Total	19,150,00

Alex McCollam, Pres.

Xavier Bourg, Clerk.

CHAPTER 19
May 30, 1899:
Expanding Visions

Fannie Gatewood Cenac stood on the kitchen steps of her in-laws' Dulac house. Her oldest daughter was pouting. "Maman, Adenise keeps telling me that I have to call her *Tante* Adenise. I'm 10 and she's just eight. Why should I call her that?" Fannie giggled at the long-standing argument.

"Edna, you don't have to call her *tante*, just so you agree that she *is* your aunt." Fannie adjusted the woven clover crown Edna had let slip over one ear. "Now go out and play with all the other children."

She walked back into the kitchen where the rest of the Cenac women were having mid-afternoon coffee around the big table. Victorine sat at the head, and told her daughters and daughters-in-law yet another time how *glorieuse* it was to have everyone together to celebrate her and Pierre's birthdays. "You won't hear it from Pierre, but he's so happy to have all of you here under this roof at one time. All your cakes were delicious. Marie, your *gateau de sirop* tastes just like mine. And there's not even one of the children's *oreilles de cochon* left! It was a *bon idée* to have a *fête de naissance* for both of us between our birthdays." As she spoke, she smoothed the apron in her lap, a long-time habit all the other women had come to recognize as a sign of her contentment. Then she folded her hands over her abdomen in the age-old manner of her ancestors.

Marie laughed, "Listen to the children! What a racket that bunch makes! I bet you don't miss that, Maman."

Marguerite gently handed over her three-week-old baby, Victorine Louise, to her sister Victorine, and walked over to the stove. Marguerite picked up the pot of freshly-brewed coffee and walked with it through the house to the *galerie* to see if the men wanted another cup. She first served *gouttes* to Pierre and Baptiste, who were sitting on the porch swing that hung from two knotted ropes. Then she poured a *demitasse* for Theophile, who had claimed the rocker. Albert and his brother Jean Pierre were leaning on opposite sides of a post, and held their cups up. Jean Charles and Paul sat on the first and second steps, resting back on their elbows. In-laws Eugene Carlos and Jean Pierre Carrere leaned against the front wall of the house, their legs stretched out before them.

The steamboat Mamie D. *on a pleasure excursion at Belle Isle, Louisiana c. 1909. Top deck, extreme left, John Dalton, Sr. and his second wife, Elizabeth Bourgeois. Priest is Rev. Andrew Souby, pastor of Sacred Heart Church in Morgan City. To left of him is Mamie Dalton, namesake of the boat. The seven nuns were from Sacred Heart convent. Standing to the rear of closer funnel is John Dalton, Jr. next to his wife Eugenie Terrebonne. In front of him is his oldest son John K. Dalton. Others in photo are other relatives, and crew members.*

Eugene pretended to trip up his wife Marguerite, which she answered with a soft kick to his foot. He gave her a stage wink, and the other men chuckled. William and Dennis, who were 15 and 12, rolled their eyes at their sister's and her husband's playfulness. They sat on the bottom step, their faces taking on what they thought to be grown-up seriousness. Both were proud to be allowed to join the other men in their after-lunch talk.

Pierre steered the conversation about where the redfish were biting to something that had been on his mind a long time. "*Mes fils...non, mes hommes*, we need to talk about what's coming up for us. All of us. Theophile, you just moved back. Theo, tell us what you're planning. I know you have something in that head of yours."

"Papa, I think anybody who wants to make a good living, beginning now, needs to think wider and bigger than hauling oysters to the cannery in Morgan City. While I was working there, I saw that the owners of the cannery are the ones making the real money, off the harder work of the men who harvest and haul. That's why I am buying into Houma Fish and Oyster. I want a bigger cut than I'm getting now."

"We have the boats, the bedding grounds, the ice factory in town, and the people. But we don't have a place," Albert answered. "Charles and I have made up our minds to stay in business in town. Paul, you're already at Papa's livery stable there, so that's three of us in Houma. We haven't said anything, but Tican Duplantis has agreed to sell Charles and me his butcher shop in the City Market soon. We don't know exactly when, but he has promised."

Charles nodded. "Word is that old man Ghirardi may want to sell his oyster packery on the other side of Bayou Terrebonne."

Theophile interrupted. "Papa, you always said that a real businessman can't rely on just one thing. We have to be willing to take chances in other things we're not even part of now. *Écoutez.* It takes a lot of money to start from scratch. I know that from experience. But if we don't risk, we don't gain anything."

His father didn't speak, but nodded approval.

Charles continued, "*C'est vrai.* If y'all want to get into packing and shipping, let me know and I'll go see Ghirardi. His place is already set up to shuck and pack. So we wouldn't have to build anything...maybe he'll lease."

Eugene piped in. "I'm not ready to change what I do. I like being a boat captain."

Baptiste shook his head, too. "I like it here, working the reefs. But I'll supply you in town, if you open a place." Baptiste looked at brother Jean Pierre, his eyebrows raised in a question. "What about you?"

Jean Pierre hesitated, then answered, "You work the reefs off Grand Caillou, and I'll work the ones off Dularge and Petit Caillou. I want to stay on the water."

Papa Pierre glanced at Pierre Carrere, knowing his son-in-law's satisfaction with being a farmer and fisherman, and his sense of responsibility to Victorine Aimée and their five children. Pierre was not surprised at the younger man's silence on the matter.

Maman Victorine opened the screen door a little. "Eugene, *votre bébé est malade. Elle a colique. C'est temps d'aller, Marguerite dit.*"

They all stood and hugged each other the Continental way Pierre had taught them when they were still youngsters. While the men walked away to gather their families, Theophile called out to the others, "Let's talk some more soon. *Le temps se passe.*"

John Dalton's Fish and Oyster Depot in Morgan City c. 1895. On the steps, John M. Dalton, Jr. and in the doorway, John Ratcliff. At corner, John Dalton, Sr., holding a portrait of his deceased wife Catherine Keane Dalton. Small child on wagon extreme right, Richard Dalton. Others pictured are employees.

CHAPTER 20
Houma's Golden Age

As the turn of the twentieth century approached, Pierre had already made plans for a momentous change in his and Victorine's day-to-day lives. In a number of purchases from January through the end of the year 1899, Pierre had amassed property opposite the town of Houma on the north side of Bayou Terrebonne. Most of Pierre's purchases were from former Houma mayor Felix Daspit's family and heirs. The Daspit house he acquired on September 5, 1904, was a comfortable *bousillage-entre-poteaux* (mud-moss walls between timbers) structure. On the south side of Houma's "water main street" were located its business district and its older residential areas extending southward off the town's major thoroughfare.

He and Victorine and four of their children still living at home did not move from Dulac immediately after the purchases. The household of Pierre, Victorine, Jean Pierre, Jr., William, Dennis, and Adenise was listed as residing in Dulac when the 1900 census was taken. Sometime in 1905 the Cenacs relocated to Houma to live on Park Avenue. The batture land, between the bayou and the public road—Park—measured one arpent (192 feet) wide, minus 12 feet. That land is adjacent to the current location of the Terrebonne Waterlife Museum. The Cenac home site across the public road (*chemin publique*) measured one arpent wide by one arpent deep, bounded by Park and extending northward. Pierre's homesite was adjacent to the property of L.F. Suthon upstream and to that of Mrs. J.P. Viguerie downstream.

The Cenacs had lived in Dulac nearly 40 years, so the move from the rural setting to a Houma that had expanded considerably since Pierre lived there as a young man had to be prompted by important considerations.

One enticement was the fact that many of the Cenac children were already residing in Houma and working there soon after 1900. Another was that Pierre already owned businesses (livery stable, bakery, moss and broom factories among them) in Houma. In 1899, he saw the opportunity to purchase further properties in the town: on May 23 on Barrow Street from Denis Bourgeois, on July 8 on Barrow Street from Francois Gouaux, and on September 6 three lots on Gouaux Avenue, also from Francois Gouaux.

Perhaps the fact that the City of Houma incorporated the expanding area across Bayou Terrebonne in 1898 gave impetus

Right, Pierre and Victorine Cenac home on Park, present-day 7905 Park Avenue, Houma. Below, Police Jury minutes published in the Houma Courier *of August 27, 1900*

The petition of Pierre Cenac requesting pay for the road to be traced along left descending bank of Bayou Grand Caillou, through his property, was received and read.

On motion of J. M. Breaux, seconded by Jas. S. Miller and carried, the Road Committee was instructed to lay out a public road along the left descending bank of Bayou Grand Caillou from Pierre Cenac's upper line to Belamour Canal, and report same at next regular meeting.

The President appointed the following gentlemen to assist said Road Committee in laying out said Road: F. Lottinger, Etienne LeBoeuf and Alfred Thibodeaux.

F. A. Aycock moved the following resolution seconded by F. E. Boudreaux and adopted; all members at roll call voting for:

"Be it resolved, That the sum of $900.00 or as much thereof, as may be necessary, be and the same, is hereby appropriated out of the General Fund not otherwise appropriated, to pay the Commissioners, Clerks, Deputy sheriffs, etc., said pay"

Originally built in the 1880s as a warehouse for Daigle Barge Line, the (renovated) building above is now the Terrebonne Waterlife Museum in downtown Houma. It was once owned by the Cenac family for use in their oyster packing business, and later was sold to the A. St. Martin family for use by Indian Ridge Canning Company, before its donation.

Above, the fire of November 8, 1900 at Court and Goode streets

to Pierre, who obviously enjoyed having elbow room between him and his neighbors. Open land was more expansive north of the bayou, and homes were not so closely situated as were those in the older section of town near Main Street. Age may also have been a factor in Pierre's decision to move closer to larger numbers of people and conveniences. He was 61 in 1899, at a time when the average life expectancy was in the forties. Although seemingly still mobile and robust in health—as well as ambitious in business—he no doubt was making arrangements for his and Victorine's declining years.

The purchase of land in Houma did not immediately sunder Pierre's involvement in the Dulac properties in which he had invested so many years. In the *Houma Courier* edition of August 27, 1900, a report of Terrebonne Parish Police Jury proceedings included "The petition of Pierre Cenac requesting pay for the road to be traced along left descending bank of Bayou Grand Caillou, through his property, was received and read."

The police jury at that meeting approved instructions to the Road Committee "to lay out a public road along the left descending bank of Bayou Grand Caillou from Pierre Cenac's upper line to Belamour Canal, and report same at the next regular meeting." The road became the precursor to Highway 57 that loops from Dulac to Little Caillou.

Pierre was not the only Cenac making plans for a move during 1899. That year, Theophile sold properties he owned in Morgan City, probably preparatory to moving to Houma.

The first years of the 1900s brought significant strides toward modernization in Houma. However, after January 1, 1900, rang in a new century, the town fell victim to several tragedies. In 1901 an anthrax epidemic took its toll on animals of all kinds. In 1902, the third widespread Houma fire destroyed both sides of Main Street between Goode and Roussell streets. In 1905, a statewide yellow fever epidemic left many families bereft.

But local citizens were heartened in 1903 when the town's first water system began to provide non-potable water for washing clothes, for gardens, and for fighting fires, among other uses excluding personal consumption. A brick tower constructed at the corner of Wood and Roussell streets provided forced pressure for the small town.

Cenac family men began to assert their interest in community service. Jean Charles was already the clerk for the Third Precinct in the Fourth Ward for which his father's Dulac house served as a voting place. In 1904 he was a candidate for justice of the peace in the Third Ward (Houma area), and Paul ran for the position of parish road inspector the same year. William Jean Pierre celebrated a milestone that year by graduating, on December 8, from Soulé Commercial College and Literary Institute in New Orleans. Because of his son's long-ago injury, Pierre had seen to it that William had an education, since his ability to do manual labor was limited. In 1906, a Cenac brother was in service to the Houma community in two ways. Jean Charles had a butcher shop downstairs in the City Market building, and an office upstairs in the same building, where he served as City of Houma Alderman in the Town Hall above the market. He served with Mayor H.M. Bourg and aldermen E.P. Roberts, Felicien A. Theriot, Harry Hellier, Clifford P. Smith and Hugo Kuhn.

As the early years of the century progressed on a community basis, so also did the Cenac family celebrate personal milestones during that time. Only a year after the turn of the twentieth century, two Cenac brothers married within a four-month period. At the age of 25, Jean Charles became the husband of 18-year-old Gertrude Laurentine Bourgeois on April 10, 1901. Four months

Wedding photo of Jean Charles Cenac and Gertrude Laurentine Cenac on April 10, 1901. Below, Paul Cenac's notice of intention to run for the post of road inspector, Houma Courier c. 1904 William's sheep skin (vellum) diploma from Soulé Commercial College and Literary Institute dated December 8, 1904

FOR ROAD INSPECTOR.

We are authorized to announce
PAUL CENAC
as a candidate for the office of Road Inspector of Terrebonne Parish, subject to the action of the Democratic Primary.

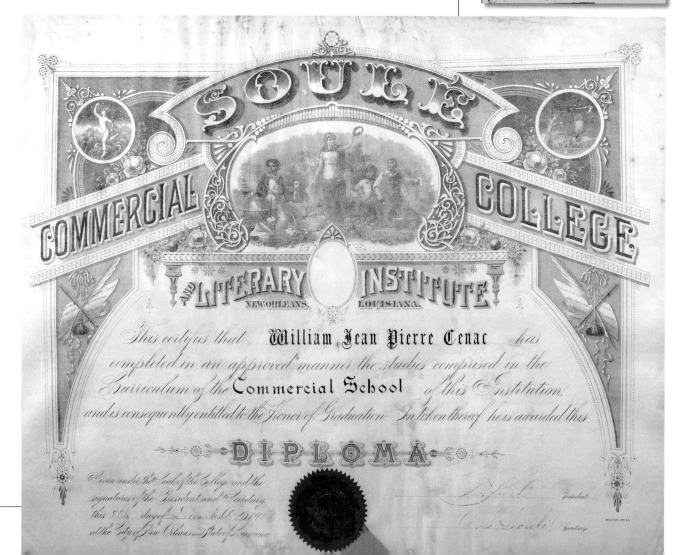

SOULÉ COMMERCIAL COLLEGE

AND LITERARY INSTITUTE

NEW ORLEANS, LOUISIANA.

This certifies that **William Jean Pierre Cenac** has completed in an approved manner the studies comprised in the Curriculum of the **Commercial School** of this Institution. and is consequently entitled to the Honor of Graduation. In token thereof he is awarded this

DIPLOMA

Marie Madeleine Bourgeois c. 1905

Left to right, Louis Caliste, Eugenie Octavie, Marie Madeleine, Gertrude Laurentine, Calicia Eleanor, Louise Palmyre, and Eleanor Monthieu Bourgeois c. 1900

Eleanor Monthieu Bourgeois' trunk used on her transatlantic voyage in 1900

Below, ad from the Terrebonne Times *of October 8, 1910. Right, record of sugar mill purchase by Pierre Cenac from Filhucan Duplantis on July 3, 1908*

later, on July 2, 27-year-old Jean Pierre, Jr. married 22-year-old Eva Luke. The widow Marie Cenac, 36 years old, married Louis Collins on May 12, 1903. Paul's marriage bond to Clothilde Klingman (both 28 years old) is dated April 18, 1906.

William Jean Pierre, at 24 years old, wedded 23-year-old Marie Madeleine Bourgeois on December 7, 1908. This was the second circumstance of two Cenac siblings marrying into the same family. Charles' wife Gertrude and William's Marie were sisters who were granddaughters of Bertrande de Soupsole, a French noblewoman.[1] Gertrude and Marie's mother, Eleanor Monthieu, celebrated her thirteenth birthday on October 6, 1869, during the Atlantic crossing with her mother on their journey to join Eleanor's father in Brashear (Morgan) City. They later moved to Houma. Eleanor returned to France when she took her daughter Calicia to the 1900 *Exposition Universelle* (World's Fair) in Paris, and used the occasion to visit family members in Carbonne, Haute Garonne.

Dennis married Nora Porche on October 1, 1912. He was 25 and she was 19 years old. The last-born child of Pierre and Victorine, Adenise Marie, married George V. Williams on April 25, 1921. They were 30 and 31 years old, respectively. George was descended from two pioneer Terrebonne families—from Michel Eloi Theriot who was an early settler of Bayou Dularge in 1839, and Jean Pierre Viguerie, a native of the *Hautes Pyrénées* who had arrived in 1849. Adenise's marriage came a full 35 years after the marriage of her oldest brother, Jean Baptiste—on February 1, 1886.

Concurrent with his children's marrying and having children of their own, Pierre continued to exhibit his business acumen by expanding his holdings in Houma while retaining the Dulac plantation and businesses. Several of his transactions were obviously prompted by a desire to further the business interests of his sons, as well as his own. Beginning in 1901, he bought land on Main Street from John Grinage and two years later another Main Street lot at a sheriff's sale. On East Park, Pierre bought property from Jean Charles in 1904. Pierre sold his Main Street livery stable and bakery property to Jean Charles in 1905, and by the next January, the Cenac and Blum Livery Stable opened for business. In October of 1910, the business was expanded to include undertaking.

Houma La July 3rd 1908
This is to certify that I, F. Duplantis have sold and delivered to Pierre Cenac one sugar mill complete with everything pertaining to said mill, which is now located in Mr Emile Caillouets yard at present, for the sum of $100 One Hundred Dollars Cash

F. Duplantis

Left, Bayou Terrebonne in Houma 1893, the wooden Church Street bridge visible in background. Above, the first steel bridge over Bayou Terrebonne at Church Street, 1906

The year 1908 was a particularly active one for Pierre in acquisitions. On June 23, he bought a machine shop from Emile Daigle on East Park, and on the same date he bought Daigle's moss ginning and shipping business, located on East Park as well. Less than two months later, with Emile Caillouet as partner, Pierre sold the machine shop equipment and rented the property on which it stood to Henry Daigle and Henry Bergeron. In July, Pierre bought a sugar mill from Filhucan "Tican" Duplantis,[2] who had sold his butcher shop to Charles and Albert six years earlier. The Cenac patriarch also bought land on Gouaux Avenue from Francois Gouaux, Marie Cenac Collins, and John O. Trahan.

Two years earlier than Pierre's aggressive 1908 purchasing period, businesses and residential areas across Bayou Terrebonne from Main Street had begun profiting from the 1906 opening of two bridges. One was the first bridge over Bayou Terrebonne at Barrow Street, built by Clifford P. Smith. The other was installation of an old iron railroad bridge crossing Bayou Terrebonne at Church Street. This bridge had once crossed Bayou Dularge. It was altered, moved to Houma, and replaced a wooden bridge that had been located at Church Street for years. The earliest bridge crossing the bayou at Church Street was recorded on the Sulakowski map of 1855. It had long before given way to other structures.

Lorton Preparatory School students of 1915 (seated, from left) May Sanders, J.C. Dupont, Jr., Herbert Gray, Ruth Wright, Fanny Bonvillain, Elsie Bonvillain; (standing) Judith Theriot, Isare Cenac, Dewey Watkins, Albert Aucoin, Lavinia Connelly, Mildred Smith, Hanson Dupont, Lottie Sanders, Marie Duhon, Francis Pullen (not shown)

Educational opportunities had also increased by the year 1907 when parish schools' accessibility was increased by the numbers of available school buildings and instructors. In 1906, the number of parish public schools was 43 for whites and 12 for blacks. The number of school attendees was 1,971 white children and 1,039 black children; they were taught by 54 teachers in the schools for whites, and by 14 in the schools for blacks.[3] Private-sector schools in Houma included the prestigious Lorton Preparatory School, which was founded by Winder sisters Sarah, Nina, and Louise in 1906; it closed in 1940. In the early part of the twentieth century Miss Ella Hooper founded what would become MacDonell Methodist Children's Services on East Main Street in Houma.

Below, the water tower built on the corner of Wood and Roussell streets in 1902

Another notable name in early Terrebonne education was Katie Quinan, whose family dates back to Houma of the 1850s. At the age of 15 she began four years as a governess. Her next job was teaching the Caliste Bourgeois children (including Gertrude

and Marie) and their neighbors in the Bourgeois home, for which she walked three miles to Bayou Cane and back each day. Beginning in 1888 she became a public school teacher, and after 23 years, she opened her own summer school, then a fulltime private school in a one-room schoolhouse in her back yard at the corner of Goode and Verret streets. Her career spanned an amazing 53 years, during which she taught countless children until she retired in 1936.

Entertainment opportunities during this period included the added attraction in the year 1907 of Wonderland, a movie theater for silent movies, in Block 300 of Main Street. It was owned by Mrs. Julius Green Behr Blum and operating partner Frank Wurzlow. The second movie theater was the Bijou in the 200 block of Main, owned by Dr. Clayton Breaux, Dr. Marcellin V. Marmande, and Harry Goode. The Dreamland was a movie theater on Lafayette Street owned by Joseph Celestin Cunningham. Opened in 1919 by Charles Delas, the Grand Theater was built on the site of the old Berger Hotel on Main Street; the price for tickets and refreshments was a nickel. The *Mayflower* showboat, which had begun its Terrebonne circuit of bayous in the 1880s, continued to bring diversion to the people where they lived by traveling the bayous to put on minstrel and other types of shows. The *Mayflower* continued its circuit until it sank in Bayou Little Caillou during the hurricane of 1926.

Around the turn of the 20th century, among the major leisure and sporting attractions were the boat races at Sea Breeze (at the mouth of Bayou Terrebonne) during the summer. Owners of pleasure boats from all over Terrebonne, most of them privileged families, participated in races with residents of the area from Morgan City to New Orleans. Many families made these events occasions for extended excursions. The Cenacs were part of those festivities; the family had a large "camp" at Sea Breeze.

Following Pierre's purchase of his Houma house and properties beginning in 1899, he and the remainder of his household moved to the parish seat around 1904-1905. It is recorded in a number of accounts that Pierre continued to run his Dulac businesses until 1909, which proved to be a sadly memorable year for many people in the coastal reaches of Terrebonne and neighboring parishes.

Top, Dreamland Theatre c. 1910. Above, Carnival scene in Houma c. 1916 (Bank of Houma at right, and Knights of Pythias at left in photo) Below, Houma Fish and Oyster Co., Ltd. factory at Sea Breeze c. 1905

Above, boat races at Sea Breeze c. 1913. Right, sailing oyster luggers at Sea Breeze c. 1909

Pierre and his son Albert were both in Dulac in September when a hurricane devastated properties in southernmost Terrebonne, and during which many families' lives were in peril. The two Cenac men took refuge on the *Peter Casano*, and during the storm and its rising waters, they took on board many neighbors who would otherwise have succumbed to the wind and flood.

One such family was the Ernest Lodrigue family of Dulac near Bayou Salé. Cyril Lodrigue later recounted how his father had taken his family by boat during the storm to Pierre Cenac's empty house, over barbed wire fences and other obstacles between their own home and the former Cenac residence. When Lodrigue had all but lost hope of surviving the rising water, Albert was able to maneuver *La Casanne* to within reach of the family, and the Lodrigues rode out the hurricane with the Cenac men and a total of 40 or so people aboard the boat. Cyril Lodrigue gave the Cenacs credit for saving the lives of all those people who had nowhere else to go when the storm surge reached 15 feet. After the storm dissipated, Theophile Cenac sailed in on the *Rosalina* with food and provisions for the survivors.[4]

When the census of 1910 was taken, Pierre and Victorine, Dennis (age 22), Adenise (age 18), and grandchild J.P. Eloi "Edward" Carlos (age 12, son of Marguerite and her husband Eugene) were listed as residing in the house on Park Avenue in Houma. The name of the public road that fronted Pierre and Victorine's home is Park because of Lucius Fane Suthon, the property owner immediately upstream from the Cenacs. Suthon, who was of English ancestry and an Oxford University graduate, had extensive open lands on which he allowed the citizens of Houma to picnic and to hold various other events. He also provided the location for periodic chautauqua shows (consisting of traveling performers from lecturers to bands to acting groups) to set up. Since his property was referred to as a park, the street was named Park Avenue.

Ads (from top) from the Terrebonne Times *of October 8, 1910 and February 21, 1903. Below, Main Street fair c. 1902*

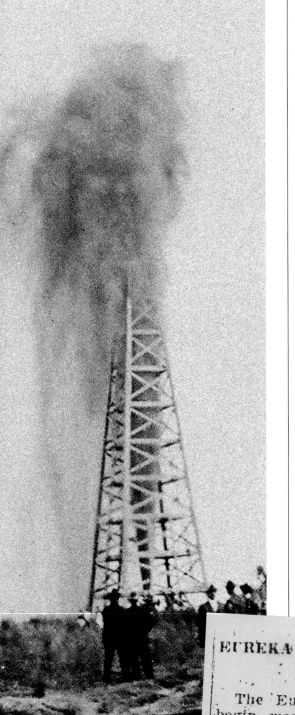

Blowout in Lirette Field at the Atlas Well in 1919. Eureka article from the Terrebonne Times *of October 19, 1912; McCormick article from the* Houma Courier *of November 22, 1913*

That census year of 1910 was a progressive one for Houma. Terrebonne Bank and Trust Company opened its doors, and paved sidewalks replaced wooden *banquettes* on Main Street. Cars began to make their appearance in the parish, and oyster shells covered streets beginning 1909-1910. A new organization in town was the Elks, of which Jean Charles and William Cenac became charter members.

While the Houma and Terrebonne oyster industry had for years begun to emerge as an important segment of the local economy, in 1912 its significance was publicly touted when the Krewe of Bivalve Mardi Gras organization was reigned over by King Bivalve, Joseph A. Robichaux and his queen, Fannie Bisland. (While Mardi Gras tableaux and balls had been held since 1875, the first actual Mardi Gras parade organized by Filhucan "Tican" Duplantis did not take to the streets until 1914.) It was an outward acknowledgement of the dependence of Terrebonne Parish's well-being on this booming industry.

Agricultural crops which had been grown in Terrebonne Parish for decades began their decline, and so also did their importance to the parish's economy, in the years preceding 1910. By that year, cultivation of indigo for market had long been abandoned. Rice and cotton, which had long been raised as subsistence crops by local landowners, were for the most part phased out in southeast Louisiana in the early 1900s. Sugar cane then took up most of the acreage formerly used for those two earlier agricultural staples.

Testimony in a 1906 court case, in which Pierre Cenac was a principal, contains evidence given by a witness that he transported cotton from a nearby farmer to Pierre's homestead. This was no doubt for Pierre's family's use or for resale, and points to the fact that the most southerly coastal landscape of Terrebonne Parish at the time was suitable for cultivation of a more uplands-friendly crop.

A glimmer of a major industry which would eventually dominate the local economy showed its first promise in the initial decade of the twentieth century. Local exploration for gas began in 1904, when I.N. Knapp drilled a well to a depth of 1,080 feet on the Lirette Farm near Montegut. It was completed without satisfactory results. Later, in 1917, J. Hunter Thatcher brought in

EUREKA OIL COMPANY TO DRILL NEW WE[LL]

The Eureka Oil Compa[ny] begin work Monday morni[ng] well at Point Barre and [ex] pected that the results will [be] futil because this section aff[ords] greatest promises of oil b[ut] the immediate vicinity whe[re] new well is to be drilled.

This well will be drilled one mile and a half north [of] Lirette gas well which is l[ocated] on the bayou Terrebonne [__] miles from Houma.

MC CORMICK WELL BRINGS UP PURE COMMERCIAL GAS

the first big gas well in the Lirette Field at a depth of 5,000 feet. He formed the Terrebonne Gas Company with W.B. McCormick, J.B. Hutchinson, and J.Y. Snyder. This first commercial gas well began serving the City of Houma and five sugar refineries.

The Texas Oil Company began to drill its first well in Terrebonne Parish in Lake Barré on March 22, 1920, and the next day the company began drilling in Dog Lake. State Dog Lake Well No. 1 in 1929 became the company's first producer, and the first commercial oil producer developed in Terrebonne Parish, although many tests were drilled during the preceding 25 years.[5] Pierre's grandson A.P. "Tenner" Cenac was a roughneck on that first producing Dog Lake well.

Another Dog Lake well began to produce gas distillate in 1929. A later Dog Lake well struck oil in 1935. The year 1929 launched the "black gold" industry which was to dominate Terrebonne's economy into the 21st century.

These early discoveries of gas and oil in Terrebonne Parish occurred when the seafood business was the backbone of the local economy. The seafood industry was to peak economically in the 1940s, at which time the petroleum industry began its future rise to dominance. Some Cenac sons, and more importantly, grandsons Alphonse, Ovide, Arthur, Alfred, Ernest, Henry Pierre, Norman, and William would also successfully complete the transition to this fledgling industry. With foresight, they recognized the future opportunity in the marine business, and began to convert their sailboats (the *Generosity, Moran, Rambler,* and the *S.J.*) to motor boats, and built their first motorized vessels (*The Beacon Light, The Mickey Mouse, The Mermaid, The Kingfisher, The Friendship, The Phillip C., The Donald C., The Joy Ann, The Robin Hood, The Washington C., The Cupid, The Elsie, The Cela and The Delphine*) for use in the oil industry.

Before then, however, the Cenacs were known for their extensive involvement in the Terrebonne oyster industry.

Cotton field at Leeville c. 1900.

The Cela, *built in 1932, in Bayou Terrebonne; owner Arthur R. "Tutty" Cenac*

Left, Captain Maurice Eddie Trahan aboard the Generosity *at Grand Pass c. 1935. The converted sailboat was owned by Albert Cenac.*

NOTES
1. Bourgeois family genealogical accounts

2. In the Cenac Collection of the Nicholls State University Archives

3. *Houma Courier Magazine Edition,* 1906

4. Helen Wurzlow accounts

5. *The Texaco Star,* January and February, 1930

Above, J.H. Thatcher, center. From left, Mr. Leach, driller J.P. Miller, W.H. Sedberry

The Algiers Ferry, Thomas Pickle, crossing the Mississippi River to New Orleans c. 1905-1910

CHAPTER 21
September 1913:
Looking Back

"Of course I'm not comfortable. I feel terrible. How can I feel comfortable?" Pierre snapped at Jean Charles. The younger man turned to look out of the train window and gripped the seat divider a little more firmly. He took a deep breath.

His father softened his voice a bit and brushed Charles' shoulder with his own. "I always enjoyed going back to *la Nouvelle Orleans*, but not this time. Not to go to the hospital, because I feel so *misérable.*"

Jean Charles nodded. *"Je comprends, Papa.* Maybe we'll get good news."

Pierre shook his head after his son turned to look at the Raceland refinery a distance from the tracks. *I don't think so. Not unless* Monsieur le Docteur *has a miracle up his sleeve.*

The old man closed his eyes and tried to forget the discomfort. Then he stirred, opened his eyes, and said, "Charles, it's four years ago that the hurricane destroyed our home. What made me think of that? Have you forgotten? Did you remember?"

"No, but you're right. My God, what a horrible time that was for you. And everybody else who was still living down the bayou *à Dulac.*"

Pierre was silent for a while, remembering.

"If it wasn't for the *Peter Casano* and other boats, we would have all drowned, the water came in so fast and so high. *Merci le bon Dieu* we had enough sense to board *La Casanne* before it got too bad. We had maybe 40...so many neighbors with the family aboard that boat, I thought we'd sink every time the wind gusted harder.*" Just like the* Texas *in the ocean storm. But this time, my family was in danger, too.*

"I know the Lodrigue family can't do enough for us, even now," Charles said. "They brought me a load of fresh produce when they came to town last week, even though I wasn't with you and Albert during the storm."

"Pauvre Lodrigue. He was sure the house would be underwater before your brother could pole the boat into position for them to jump to the deck. Lodrigue was pale as a ghost when they came aboard. I thought his heart would give out."

Pierre's voice got a little muffled. "The women all held tight to their rosaries, and I could hear them praying even over the howling wind."

The French Market in
New Orleans, 1900

King Rex's Royal Chariot at the Canal
Street Ferry at Mardi Gras, 1890s.

Milk cart, New Orleans c. 1900

French Market 1910

Morgan's Louisiana & Texas Railroad and Steamship Company freight depot, Algiers, c. 1900

The steamer Terrebonne *docked in New Orleans c. 1925*

The train lurched with the tracks' slight curve, and Pierre looked out at *la prairie tremblante* as they approached Des Allemands. *A lot may have changed since I first rode this train in the opposite direction, but this landscape is still as I remember it when I saw it more than 50 years ago. Étrange. For some reason, that satisfies me. Maybe it's because so much else has changed. The changes have been good ones, but it's nice to see things as my young eyes saw them all those years ago.* He caught his reflection in the window, and focused on the gray in his eyebrows and the squint lines around his eyes. *The young eyes are long gone, too.*

"Papa?" Pierre realized Jean Charles had been trying to get his attention. "I was saying what a good thing it was that you had bought the Daspit property in town before the '09 hurricane hit."

"Ah, *oui*. I was relieved that Victorine and the younger children were safe in Houma when I was tending the store that day in Dulac when the storm hit. I never minded going back and forth after we moved. I still had the sugar mill, cane lands, and store to keep me busy on the bayou. Near the oyster beds, too. Your Maman is so close to all of you and *les petits enfants*. She was even willing to move away from her brothers and sisters on Grand Caillou to be near all of you in town."

Pauvre Victorine. That day we went back to Bayou Salé after the water receded to see the damage to our house and land....She bit her lip when she found a little child-sized hoe, the tip of its handle poking out of the soggy dirt that had been the children's vegetable garden. How many of the younger children had chopped away at the soil among rows of pole beans through the years? When she spied the numbers scratched into what had been the fourth board up from the floor in a corner of the kitchen wall, she looked at me with sad eyes under the folds of her garde-soleil *and whispered, "Look, Pierre. Remember how we fussed at Dennis for writing his times tables on the wall?" Now the board lay in a haphazard heap where most of the kitchen had come to rest in the field behind the spot the house had stood. Victorine was* triste, *the way she wiped that board off on her apron. Watching the grown boys load other mud-soaked bits and pieces on the wagon, I felt relieved, but sad, too. It was hard to leave that land for good. But the store was gone, and I'm too old to deal with the storms anymore. When the horses started to pull the wagon toward town, Victorine kept wiping her eyes with the hem of her apron. This was the real end of us and Dulac. When I looked back, I swore I could see all my children, young again, running after the wagons, even Celestine and Josephine.*

Jean Charles nodded. "Anyway, you already had settled into the new house. Imagine how awful it would have been if all the furniture had still been in the Dulac house, along with the things you had left in storage at the old place. That was good timing...." Jean Charles went on, but Pierre didn't hear him.

He was thinking that timing did have something to do with it. *But I knew years ago that Houma was the place for us now. The town has grown so much, and so much is happening there. I wanted to be in the middle of it. I wanted to see my boys run their businesses, visit with them and old town friends more.*

The train pulled in to Algiers Station, and Pierre was brought even further back.

"Jean Charles, this is the exact spot where I boarded the ferry to take me to the city after I arrived on the *Texas*. It's where I boarded the train to go to Houma in 1861, too. Look at that city. The river, the cathedral, the opera house, the busy streets. I walked those streets as a young man. Hard to believe, eh?"

His son nodded offhandedly like one who had heard this many times before, and stood to get their bags.

No parades and bands and fireworks like that first year, though. Now it's just talk and newspaper headlines about another war coming, this time on the Continent. Pauvre la France. I wonder if I will have any great-nephews in this one, like my brothers in Napoleon's war when I left to come here. If America gets involved, will my own children and grandchildren end up fighting there, too?

When Pierre tried to stand, his stomach pain made him sit down hard again. He let Jean Charles help him straighten himself to get off at the station. But then he walked without help toward the ferry that would take him all the way to the city across the river.

St. Louis Cathedral and Jackson Square in 1902

No Claims for Deduction allowed unless made within one Day after receipt of Goods.

ESTABLISHED 1850.

PAID UP CAPITAL STOCK $ 1,000,000.

HIGHEST MEDALS & AWARDS IN ENGLAND FRANCE, GERMANY & THE UNITED STATES.

A. BOOTH PACKING CO.

OVAL BRAND

Formerly
A. BOOTH & SON

Oysters, Fish and Canned Goods.

BRANCH HOUSES:
CHICAGO, BALTIMORE, ST. PAUL, KANSAS CITY,
ST. LOUIS, LOUISVILLE, OMAHA, DULUTH, INDIANAPOLIS,
MINNEAPOLIS, BAYFIELD, ESCANABA, ASTORIA, OREGON,
MANISTIQUE, PORT ARTHUR, CANADA.

TERMS CASH.

Duluth, Minn.   3/16   1888

Ft. Atkinson Wis.

35	Whitefish,		9	2 85
25	Small Trout,		9	2 25
	Large Trout,	50 Market Cod	5	2 50
	Pike,	19 Smelts	7	1 33
	Pickerel.	15 Wally Pike	8	1 20
	Herring.	Total	35	9 78

Box.

Charges for Return of Money.

We do not allow for Boxes returned.

AND TROUT

PACKERS

327 & 329 McElderry's
502 & 504 Mil

PRODUCE

DELIGHT BRAND

PACKERS OF THE CELEBRATED

PAY NO MONEY TO SALESMEN. MAKE ALL REMITTANCES DIRECT TO THE HOUSE.

Baltimore   7   189

M. U. S. Hospital

BOUGHT OF

LOUIS GREBB,

OYSTER & FRUIT

PACKER.

ALL GOODS SHIPPED C.O.D.
UNLESS SATISFACTORY
REFERENCE IS GIVEN.
DRAFTS WEEKLY.
PURCHASERS ARE REQUIRED
TO HONOR THE SAME, OR
SHIPMENT WILL BE STOPPED.

BURKE STREET WHARF

E POINTS.

N SHAPE OF AN OYSTER
LTED OR BUTTER

PATENTED

ent, Jan. 16th, 1883. May 20th,
r 4th, 1887.

k—"Blue Points," Crackers in
ster. Registered Oct. 9th, 1883.

ESTABLISHED 1826.

Philadelphia,   189

M. J. Garity

To JOHN HARTMAN, Dr.

EAST END STEAM BISCUIT WORKS,

No. 412 SOUTH WHARVES AND 413 PENN STREET.

PLAIN AND FANCY BISCUITS AND CRACKER

J. WARREN GILL,
Dealer in
FRESH AND SALT FISH,
Oysters, Clams, Lobsters &c.,
54 & 56 Green St., cor. Stanford,
BOSTON.

74 lbs   Pilot Bread   5

CHAPTER 22
The Oyster is King

Oyster harvesting, packing, and shipping in Terrebonne Parish had its early origins in oystermen's working the natural reefs in coastal waters. The industry in later years accounted for a full 50 percent employment of the population in Houma. However, no local packing (canning) and little to no shipping was performed in Houma until the advent of the availability of ice in the final decade of the 1800s.

After the Civil War, Baltimore, Maryland, became the pivotal city to oyster shipping. It was the first city to can oysters on a large scale (and the first to can corn). The number of manufacturing establishments doubled there from 1880 to 1900.

Opposite, both photos are Pratt Street Wharf, Baltimore, Maryland: top c. 1880, left c. 1905. Industry invoices of the era

Top, The Union Oyster House in Boston, the oldest restaurant in continuous service (since 1826) in the United States: building more than 250 years old; Chesapeake Bay oyster cans

Bottom photo, ship repair yard at Crisfield, Maryland c. 1920s

Photos right and below, oyster schooners unloading at canning factories in Biloxi, Mississippi c. 1900; bottom right, Pass Packing Co., Pass Christian, Mississipi. Bottom, oyster transfer bucket used to unload oysters from boat to dock c. 1900

Unloading Oysters. BILOXI, Miss.

9654 OYSTER SCHOONERS UNLOADING AT CANNING FACTORY BILOXI, MISS.

This tremendous growth without regulation led to the beginning of the decline of the industry on Chesapeake Bay.[1] By 1880, oyster canneries began migrating to the Gulf Coast of the southern states, specifically Biloxi, Mississippi; Appalachicola, Florida; Bayou LaBatre, Alabama; and southeast Louisiana.

On a national scale, the oyster industry had been centralized on the East Coast and Chesapeake Bay since 1850.[2] The industry grew with the combination of development of the tin can, the artificial production of ice, the development of the canning process, and the use of the railroad which had been expanded dramatically after the Civil War. Improvements in sailing vessels also occurred at this time.

The "bugeye" made its appearance on Chesapeake Bay in 1860 by adding a sail to the canoe-like dugout used by Native Americans. The "skipjack" became familiar in the bay in the early 1900s; most watermen called them "bateaux." A Maryland law restricting oyster dredging to sailing vessels promoted the construction of larger boats. The "bay schooner" (shoal draft, broad beam, clear deck, graceful longhead) was designed and placed into service.[3]

These vessels remained the workhorses of the Bay well into the twentieth century. Early on, Baltimore became the seafood and canning capital of the world. During the late 1800s, use of the eastern oyster grew phenomenally. For a time, it outranked beef as a source of protein in some parts of the nation. Social events grew up around it, as it became an important aspect of culture and myth. Oyster saloons became popular hangouts.[3] Oyster bars, oyster parlors, oyster restaurants, and other such establishments became the craze in cities and towns across the U.S.

Oyster schooner on Mississippi Gulf Coast c. 1900

Right, Oyster Saloon list from New Orleans City Directory c. 1860

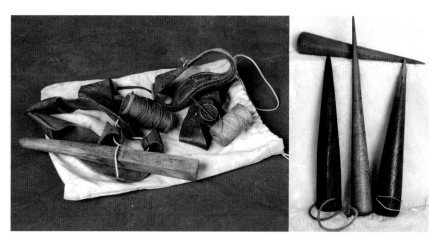

Sail repair kit and fids used for knot making and rope repair.

The oyster sloop J.T. Leonard of St. Michaels, Maryland, built 1882.

Oyster Saloons.

Alfred Luther P 135 Royal
Bertucci Dominick 1730 St Charles
Bertucci Frank J 322 Magazine
Bertucci Frank J 1628 S Franklin
Bertucci Peter 1500 Magazine
Betterwolf William L 601 Carondelet
Bruno Jacob 548 S Rampart .
Catanzaro Ignatius 1310 Dryades
Cazzetta Charles 1839 Canal
Ciriminna Joseph 1430 Royal
Commander Charles J 2743 Amelia
Compagno Anthony 900 Washington a
Compagno C & F 1601 Magazine
Credo Alexander R 3965 Magazine
Debelo John Mrs 2301 Carondelet
Deris John 1030 N Rocheblave
DiCorte Charles 1301 Marengo
Diosini Michel 1613 Milan
Disimone Joseph 2509 Carondelet
DiTrapani George 704 N Claiborne
Dominguez Joaquin 2605 Tchoupitoula
Fallo Angelo 610 Common
Favaloro John 3341 Tulane av
Favaloro J 1839 Canal
Ferrari Charles 813 Bienville
Figallo Joseph 1517 Orleans
Fiol Theodore 924 Common
Gambino J 1916 Valence
Gem Restaurant 129 Royal
Giuffria Salvador 1736 Washington av
Graffagnino F 6102 Laurel
Greco Joseph 3501 Baronne
Greco Pascal 1500 Baronne
Groetsch Julius 137 St Charles
Ilich Vincent 510 Madison
LaRosa S 4139 Canal
Licciardi Bartholomew 5431 Magazin
Mancuso Bartholomew 3632 Prytania
Mancuso Philip 1100 Jena
Masera Antoine 809 St Louis
Milazzo V 700 Constantinople
Mumfrey Anthony 736 Canal
Nesanovich Anthony 2001 Royal
Palma Santa 8321 Oak
Palmisano Felix 6316 Hurst
Palmisano Frank 3236 Magazine
Palmisano John 3700 Magazine
Perez Peter 8237 Oak
Perino S 4539 Freret
Petrosi Samuel 133 St Charles
Pflueger John G 1548 N Claiborne
Picolo Samuel 133 Exchange pl
Polizzi Lawrence 2600 Ursuline av
Profumo Anthony 1824 St Charles av
Rando Anton 1239 Josephine
Rando Murphy 742 Jackson av
Rando P 733 Cherokee
Rapp Frederick 5601 Magazine
Rordiguez Felix A 1306 Upper Line
Rozes Peter Mrs 4540 S Liberty
Russo James A 1939 Lapeyrouse
Saltalamachia Felix 740 Iberville
Scuttari Nicholas 508 Bourbon
Springer George W 130 Royal
Sunseri Lucian 514 Ursuline
Swindler G J 1500 N Broad
Tortorich D J Liquor Co 118 Baronne
Tranchina Anthony 3927 Magazine
Tranchina Dominick 5534 Perrier
Tranchina Dominick J 1001 Carondelet
Tranchina Frank 1601 St Charles av
Tranchina Peter 6131 Hurst

By 1900, however, as a result of increasing population along the East Coast, pollution, over-harvesting, and with a well-publicized case of a death from typhoid fever following consumption of a raw oyster,[2] the decline of the industry in that area accelerated.

In response to these events, and in order to prevent further outbreaks of typhoid fever and other illnesses, the U.S. Congress passed the Pure Food Laws in 1906 with several specific regulations aimed at the oyster industry. These new laws regulated oyster beds, packing houses, shell fish sources, shipping methods, and labeling. To restore public confidence, the oyster industry publicized the sanitary conditions under which oysters were handled and the high standard used in packing fresh oyster meat. (One gallon yielded 120-144 oysters.) Oyster tins were stamped with packers' certification numbers and advertised the oysters inside as fresh, pure, healthful, and, of course, delicious. Thus was born the age of colorful advertising on the oyster can to promote the industry.

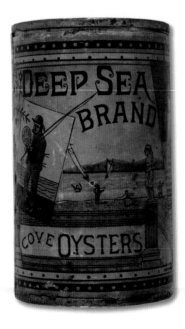

Representative cans of
the Oyster Era c. 1900

Saint Clement French Majolica
c.1880

19ᵗʰ Century Oyster Plate

Coiffe; Limoges, France
c. 1891-1915

Theodore Haviland; Limoges France
c. 1900

Theodore Haviland; Limoges France
c. 1900

Hand painted Porcelain in Opalescent
c. 1900

French Gilt Porcelain; Mono McFadden
c. 1880

French Majolica; Viellard, Bordeaux
c. 1880

Theodore Haviland Porcelain; Limoges France
c. 1881

Victoria and Schmidt Co.; Austria
c. 1904

"Bertha" c. 1912; Top right, children workers at Alabama Canning Company, Bayou LaBatre, AL c. 1910

"Rosie" at Bluffton, SC c. 1915

Child laborer, Biloxi, MS c. 1911

Right, Dunbar & Dukate workers, New Orleans, Louisiana c. 1911

Another concern in the canning industry was the use of child labor. Children were a common sight in the canneries in the late 1800s and early 1900s until child labor began to become a major concern. A major reason for the decline of child labor in the canning industry was the passage of increasingly restrictive child labor laws. Further, child labor was found to be unreliable and inconsistent, particularly with the advent of mechanization in the canning industry. Adult laborers were usually more skilled, better trained, and more reliable in the working environment. Between 1880 to 1920, the percentage of children under the age of 16 working in U. S. manufacturing declined from 7% to 1%. In addition to restrictive child labor laws and mechanization that demanded adult laborers, another factor that limited the use of children in the canning industry was the passage of mandatory school attendance laws.[1]

One local instance of the ease with which child labor laws were circumvented was recounted by Hattie Blanchard, who was 92 in 2009 when interviewed about her experiences. Born in 1917, she was only a child when she worked in a shrimp factory on Little Caillou in Terrebonne Parish. She remembered being ordered to run outside the factory and hide whenever inspectors came to the plant. This scenario was undoubtedly replicated in many locations in the U.S. at the time, regardless of laws to the contrary.

Baltimore's oyster industry never regained its former prominence after the health concerns that had been made so public and so widespread. Through a series of events, that area's former status gave way to Louisiana's new dominance of the industry.

One requisite component of shipping oysters, the availability of ice, had its local origins in the first successful commercial manufacturing of ice in the U.S., which took place in Louisiana as early as Reconstruction years. In 1867 the first plant to make ice on a regular basis opened in New Orleans at the Louisiana Ice Works. Before this date, ice was brought to New Orleans by ship from northern suppliers, the largest of whom was Frederic Tudor of Boston, Massachusetts. His firm harvested ice from the Great Lakes.

Under natural conditions, oysters grew abundantly in the estuarine areas of the Mississippi Delta. Louisiana oysters matured in 20 months; northern oysters took up to five years to mature. In a five-year period Louisiana oyster beds yielded three crops, compared to only one in northern waters.[4] New Orleans, which was located near the oyster reefs in St. Bernard and Plaquemines parishes, constituted a large and growing market demand which encouraged expansion of the industry.

Not far away from Terrebonne, Croatians and Slovaks made their homes in Plaquemines Parish as early as the 1820s. The early immigrant Slavonians, who had a coastal past in their homeland, adapted their old techniques to new environmental conditions in the business of oyster cultivation. "Their boats were called luggers because of their Mediterranean style of rigging or lug sail."[3] Later, "Those built by the Croatian oystermen living around Olga, Empire and Buras were similar to the *Leuti* which was used in the Old Country Dalmatian sardine fishing industry. In a slightly modified version, they were low-decked, shallow draught, one masted, latteen-rigged sailboats from 30 to 40 feet long."[3] They were also outfitted with "a centerboard, or hinged keel that allowed the boat to operate in shallow waters."[5] These sailing oyster transport vessels continued in use in Louisiana until the 1930s, when they were replaced by engine-powered boats. The word *lugger* continues to describe boats on the waters of South Louisiana.[6] Another contribution to the industry from these immigrants was the introduction of the rake-like tool for harvesting oysters, called *tongs*. They continue using tongs to this day, as fishermen and "farmers of the sea."[3]

Oyster luggers in lower Terrebonne c. 1900

Oyster Bayou, lower Terrebonne, c. 1920

Oyster camps at Bayou Bruleau (paddlewheeler in background, Barataria Bay) c. 1906

Tonging for oysters lower Terrebonne, c. 1920

R.B. Butler

A.J. Bonvillain

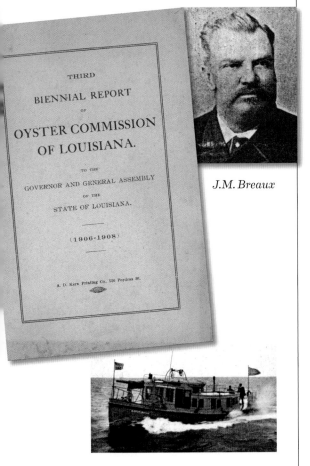

J.M. Breaux

Report of the Conservation Commission of Louisiana, above. The Oyster Commission launch Baton Rouge *with gun on bow c. 1920. Below, "Pirates Dredging at Night" from* Harper's Weekly *of March 1, 1884*

This combination of demand, ice, knowledgeable oystermen, vast abundant resources and absence of regulation, led to unwise harvesting practices. The natural reefs were depleted in St. Bernard and Plaquemines parishes by 1880. This accelerated confrontations among citizens of different parishes as they crossed parish boundaries seeking marketable oysters and seed for bedding purposes. This combination of events resulted in legislation to protect the natural renewable (self-perpetuating reefs) resource, as well as the private property rights of those with cultivated holdings.[7]

After a series of unsatisfactory laws, a comprehensive oyster law was passed, Act of 1902 by the Louisiana Legislature. Senator John Dymond Jr. was the chairman of the Oyster Committee in Baton Rouge which convened on April 6, 1902. The Act of 1902 established the Oyster Commission. In addition, this legislation removed the old system of parish supervision and established state regulation of the industry. The Oyster Commission was a committee of five persons appointed by the state legislature, three representatives and two senators. Representative A.J. Bonvillain of Terrebonne was an original member. The act was further amended in June of 1904 to promote the right of private enterprise through recognition of private oyster grounds, either owned or leased. J. M. Breaux of Houma became president of the Oyster Commission in 1906, replacing Representative Bonvillian.[8] Houma resident R.B. Butler was also a member of the Oyster Commission.

Confrontations among oystermen were not unusual in Louisiana; however, they never reached the level of discord that had occurred in Chesapeake Bay before the turn of the century. The Oyster War, as it was called, consisted of violent skirmishes between tongers and dredgers, Maryland versus Virginia watermen, and oyster "pirates" against the "Oyster Navy" of the state of Maryland's marine patrol.

The Louisiana Legislature at this period made a special appropriation for the purchase of patrol boats and equipment by the Commission for the purpose of keeping order. Four new vessels were acquired, including the *Louisiana*, *Baton Rouge*, *New Orleans*, and *Nita*, all armed with cannon. Furthermore, the United States Supreme Court rendered a decision on March 5, 1906, in which the State of Louisiana was given title to the valuable oyster beds in the Mississippi Sound and adjacent waters. This greatly expanded oyster production acreage.

Further legislation occurred with Act 265 of 1910. The Oyster Commission of Louisiana was consolidated with the Board of Commissioners for the Protection of Birds, Game and Fish. In 1912, Act 127 consolidated all activities under the name "Conservation Commission of Louisiana." The act was further amended by Act 105 of 1916 which stated that the "Department of Conservation is hereby created." The Department of Conservation began extensive planting of shell for rehabilitation purposes. One of the first areas to be set aside for planting was

Caillou Lake (Sister Lake) in Terrebonne Parish.

By 1900, cultivation was a well established component of the Louisiana oyster industry. Because of the abundant natural resources in the Terrebonne and Barataria estuaries, the local industry in Houma was primed to expand. Louisiana, with Terrebonne Parish leading the way, became an industry leader in the United States in the early twentieth century, ranking fourth in the nation in oyster production at the time.

The State of Louisiana possessed approximately 500,000 acres of producing oyster water bottoms. This represented more than the sum total acreage of all other states in the Union. By the time state leasing began, most of the natural reefs east of the Mississippi River had been depleted. Extensive reefs remained in the Terrebonne and Barataria estuaries.[7] The most productive area was along the northwestern shores of Terrebonne Bay east of Bayou Little Caillou and north of Lake Pelto to the western edge of Lake Barré. The greatest concentration of reefs was in Caillou Lake, stretching from Bayou Grand Caillou to Bay Castagnet. Mud Hole Bay and Jack Stout Bay also had extensive resources. Caillou Lake, along with Jack Stout Bayou to Bay Provincial southwest of Caillou Lake, were also described as the best oyster planting grounds in the parish.[7]

The Cenac brothers, Jean Baptiste, Albert, Theophile, and Jean Pierre, Jr., and their brothers-in-law Salvador and Eugene

REPORT ON THE OYSTER-BEDS OF LOUISIANA.

BY

H. F. MOORE,

ASSISTANT, U. S. FISH COMMISSION.

"Terrebonne Parish contains the most important oyster-grounds of the State, and there are 600 boats of all kinds licensed to fish within its borders. The oyster-producing waters extend from the eastern part of Timbalier Bay almost to Atchafalaya Bay, where the influx of fresh water places a limit upon the growth of the oyster-beds."

So reported Dr. Hugh F. Moore of the United States Fish Commission, who investigated the Louisiana oyster industry in 1898, at the request of the Louisiana Legislature.

"The object ... was to obtain information on which to base a revision of the oyster laws, with a view to place the oyster industry on a more substantial basis."

Below, Oyster bed map printed 1896.
Inset below, Ovide Filhucan Bazet, Sr.
in his college cadet uniform

Map Showing The Oyster Beds Of Terrebonne For Which The Courier Is Indebted To Mr. O. F. Bazet, Superintendent Of The Houma Fish & Oyster Co.

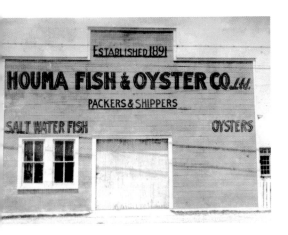

Houma Fish & Oyster Co., Ltd. c. 1930
(present-day 8061 Main Street, Houma)

Berwick Bay Fish Co. Morgan City c. 1900

Carlos, had acquired extensive leases by 1900. These leased water bottoms, combined with the water bottoms owned and leased by patriarch Pierre Cenac, firmly established their foothold in the fledgling industry.

Houma Fish & Oyster Company was founded in 1891, but 1893 was dubbed the Year of the Oyster in Houma-Terrebonne years later, by virtue of the incorporation of Houma Fish & Oyster Co. Ltd., on May 23 that year. Sixteen farsighted, prominent business leaders at that time provided an influx of capital the enterprise required. The Articles of Incorporation stated that the nature of the business was to "buy, sell, and *ship* fish and oysters, and to put up suitable buildings and structures for that purpose." The Company bought the batture on the right descending bank of Bayou Terrebonne from Houma Magnolia Cemetery (established 1884) on June 22, 1893. They started enthusiastically. However, the business floundered due to lack of expertise.

Jacques Lehmann, who had arrived in Brashear (Morgan) City from France in 1870, had begun buying and selling shucked oysters to the Morgan and Pharr steamships in 1886.[9] The Berwick Bay Fish and Oyster Co. started doing business there also, in 1887. Theophile Cenac and his brothers had been hauling oysters to the cannery for several years.

Theophile was an aggressive individual who put his experience to work by purchasing half of Houma Fish & Oyster Co. Ltd. in 1899, when he assumed management of the firm. The business prospered. He sold his property in Morgan City in 1899 and 1900. His action constituted the first of the Cenac brothers' involvement in the business end of the oyster industry.

The first of many non-family members who were longtime, loyal employees joined Theophile at the time. He hired Ovide Bazet, Sr., son of "Lafayette" Bernard Filhucan de Bazet, the man who had planted and tended the Courthouse Square Oaks donated by Pierre years before, to help manage the affairs of his new business.

A Houma resident, Etienne Ghiradi, was also a pioneer of the local oyster industry. He acquired a lease of 84 feet on the batture of the left descending bank of Bayou Terrebonne from Lafayette Fanguy on November 14, 1896. This property was adjacent to the present Gabasse Street Bridge. The lease granted him the right to "construct upon said property a shop or building 20x30 feet for the *reception* of oysters, shrimp, and other articles of merchandise and trade." This is the second official recording of a commercial seafood business in Terrebonne Parish.

Ghirardi sold an undivided one half interest in the lease to Jacob Burgonovich on December 23, 1896, thereby officially forming the firm of Ghiradi and Burgonovich. On May 29, 1897, Ghirardi sold the other half of the lease to Jean Marie Durand, a local hotel owner. On that same day, Durand transferred his interest in the lease and improvements to G. Wolf and Co. The business was local consumption; there was no organized shipping because of a lack of ice locally at the time. The future of the industry changed

Houma Fish & Oyster Co., Ltd. shucking room c. 1900. Identified men are, second from left, "Bee" Eschete, fourth from left, "Coal Oil" Eschete, eigth from left, "Coon" Eschete, and owner Theophile Cenac (standing in front). Note electric light bulbs overhead.

Houma Fish & Oyster Co., Ltd. tokens; below, Houma Fish and Oyster Co., Ltd. (owner Theophile Cenac in suit) c. 1900

People's Fish & Oyster Company c. 1906, Felicien A. Theriot

R. J. YOUNGER

PACKERS AND SHIPPERS OF THE

Celebrated Houma Oysters

THE STANDARD OF EXCELLENCE

HOUMA. :: :: :: LOUISIANA.

R.J. Younger & Company c. 1906

C.C. Miller & Co. c. 1905, C. C. Miller

Bottom, Eschete Oyster Shop on Barrow Street, early 1900s, (left to right) Sidney Eschete, Harry Bonvillain, and Francois Bergeron; At right, oyster shipping container, early 1900s

dramatically, however, after the opening of the Houma Lighting & Ice Manufacturing Co. Ltd. on December 17, 1898.

Other businessmen entered the packing and shipping arena after ice became available in Houma. On June 10, 1901, Felicien A. Theriot, Ernest Chauvin, Adam R. LeBlanc and Americus J. Roddy incorporated Peoples Fish and Oyster Co. Ltd. The Articles of Incorporation stated that the nature of the business was to "buy, sell, and *ship* fish, oysters, and shrimp and any other marine product."

Several individuals from Baltimore became aware of the abundance of oysters locally, and they began to arrive at the turn of the century. Robert J. Younger came to Houma and with his local partner, Charles Amedee Celestin, Sr., bought 160 feet of batture on the left descending bank of Bayou Terrebonne from Augustus Crochet on July 12, 1901. This purchase was located at the site of the present day Intracoastal Canal intersection with Bayou Terrebonne. On April 2, 1902, Gottlieb Wolf sold his lease and building improvements to Younger. A second Cenac brother entered the packing business when Younger in turn sold the "lease for that certain lot of ground with the buildings and improvements used for an Oyster Packery" to Jean Charles Cenac on August 2, 1902.

Another individual, Charles C. Miller, started C.C. Miller & Company in the first decade of the twentieth century, next door to the present-day Blum & Bergeron plant on Main Street. Miller was an original stockholder in the "SealShipt Oyster System" of South Norwalk, Connecticut, before his move to Louisiana.

Cade Eschete opened a seafood stall in the rear of the Old City Market in 1902. His business moved several times over the next few years but remained small. F. Gouaux Oyster Company was another early venture in the industry: the company closed in 1905.

On April 13, 1904, Charles Amedee Celestin sold his half interest in their batture purchased in 1901 to his partner Robert Younger. Allen Munson became the manager of R. J. Younger & Co.

An adjunct business became available to the Cenac oyster businesses on January 12, 1906, when Albert Cenac, Jean Charles Cenac, and Julius Blum incorporated Cenac & Blum Livery Stable for the purpose of "carrying on the business of Feed, Livery, and Sales." The new corporation then purchased Pierre Cenac's livery stable business and expanded its operations. They also had a large general store located with the post office in Chauvin.

Also at this time, William J. P. Cenac

returned from New Orleans with his degree from Soulé Commercial College. He opened his oyster shop on property owned by his mother-in-law, Mrs. Caliste Bourgeois, adjacent to the Bank of Houma on Main Street.

Now, with the purchase of the oyster packery, the livery stable, ice, and their business college-trained brother William, the Cenac family was firmly established in the trade. They had their own outlet to sell the oysters obtained from their extensive reef resources, both leased and private. Over the next four years they built the businesses with the assistance of their father Pierre and their brother Theophile at Houma Fish & Oyster Co., Ltd.

Jean Charles Cenac formed a partnership with Julius Blum on August 2, 1906 "for the purpose of carrying on the business of buying, opening, canning, shipping, selling and disposing of oysters and other fish." This partnership, C. Cenac & Co., was the first recorded business established to can seafood in Terrebonne Parish. Jean Charles and Blum took on two new partners when Felicien Theriot, part-owner and manager of People's Fish & Oyster Co. Ltd., joined the business on August 20, 1907; Albert Cenac, Jean Charles' older brother, became a new partner.

Above, company logo from letterhead. Below, oyster shipping containers and packing room at C. Cenac & Co. c. 1927. From left, John Hubert Carlos, Eugene Ledet, and Ovide Julien "Jock" Cenac

Albert Cenac

John Hubert Carlos

George Lee Cenac

Paul Cenac

William Cenac

C. Cenac & Co. - Houma, LA

Jean Baptiste Cenac   Jean Charles Cenac

Ovide F. Bazet   Theophile Cenac

Bayou Terrebonne - 1905

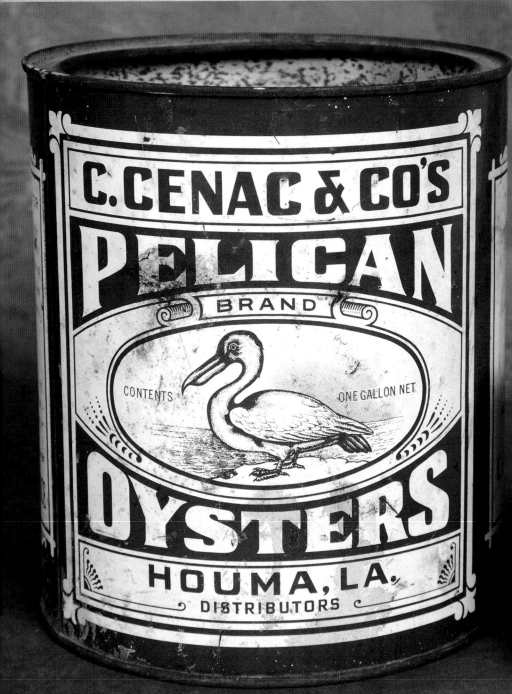

SPICED OYSTERS
(C. Cenac and Company)

1	quart oysters
½	cup (pure) tarragon (or malt) vinegar
1	teaspoon salt
8	cloves
8	peppercorns
2	blades mace
1	pod (red) pepper

Heat oysters in their own liquor until plump. Skim out the oysters and add other ingredients to the hot oyster liquor. Simmer 5 or 6 minutes, skim and pour over oysters. When cold, seal in glass jars. These may be kept in a cool place for 2 or 3 weeks.

In front of C. Cenac & Co., c. 1920, from left, William Jean Pierre Cenac, Russell Strada, Jean Baptiste Cenac, Jean Pierre Carrere

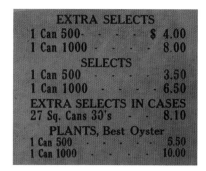

Lithograph calling card c. 1905.

C. Cenac & Co. shucking room, 1927, Left to right: Wilson Rhodes, Joe Bergeron, Wycliff Ledet, Nat Callahan, Joe Eschete, Kaiser, August Hebert, unknonwn, standing at end William Jean Pierre Cenac, bending over "Nonc" Bergeron.

Oyster crock early 1900s

C. Cenac & Co., present-day 8046 Park Avenue William Jean Pierre Cenac atop shell pile, 1927

Oyster pail early 1900s

William J.P. Cenac (far right) at his oyster shop c. 1910, adjacent to Bank of Houma, Main Street

R. J. YOUNGER, President
M. D. McBRIDE, Vice-President
A. J. BONVILLAIN, Treasurer
H. L. WILSON, Secretary
H. S. CHAUVIN, Manager

Citizens Ice & Manufacturing Company, Limited

CAPITAL STOCK, $25,000
HOUMA, LOUISIANA

Ad from The Waterways Edition, Morgan City to New Orleans via Houma and Lockport, *1910*

Main Street, Houma, looking east from Barataria Canal c. 1906

Below, a Fairbanks-Morse 3 hp engine, c. 1918

Also at this time, Theophile Cenac and Julius Blum, along with M.D. McBride, A.J. Bonvillain, H.L. Wilson, R.J. Younger and H.S. Chauvin, formed Citizen's Ice & Manufacturing Company, Ltd. The ice plant had a Frick Ice-Machine with a daily capacity of 15 tons, and was located on Main Street. This ice plant was the second such establishment in Houma which helped supply the increasing demand created by the boom in oyster shipments.[8]

Ovide Bazet, Sr., a valuable Cenac employee who had been a manager at Houma Fish and Oyster with Theophile, joined Jean Charles Cenac as office manager during his initial startup in 1902. Ovide died on January 17, 1906, of typhoid fever. He was the father of longtime Terrebonne Parish Clerk of Court Randolph A. Bazet.

The family nature of the business is evident in the fact that John Hubert "Hubbet" Carlos, Pierre's grandson and son of his daughter Marie, began his employment at C. Cenac & Co. in 1908 at age 18. He retired in 1945 as the packing room foreman.

Pierre Cenac was instrumental in the process of forming a conglomerate of Houma companies in 1910. On October 6, Pierre bought from Gilbert Fanguy the 84-foot-wide batture property and buildings, with improvements, that had been leased by Etienne Ghirardi from Lafayette Fanguy in 1896. Pierre then leased it back to a new firm called Houma Oyster Distributing Company, which was chartered on October 18, 1910. The partnership was made up of C. Cenac & Co., C. C. Miller & Co., and Little Caillou Fish & Oyster Co. Through a series of transactions in 1912-1913, William J. P. Cenac acquired the interest of Felicien Theriot and Julius Blum. The C. Cenac & Co. "trade name" continued as the operating company of the parent firm.

Transportation was another facet of trade which one of the Cenac brothers entered in September 12, 1910, when William J.P. Cenac and Emile Levron bought the Berger Brothers livery stable business. The inventory consisted of four drummers' wagons, four carriages, eight buggies, 14 sets of single harness, nine sets of double harness, three pairs of shafts, one clipping machine, 20 halters, one set of lamps, 15 horses, and one bus. They leased the property and buildings, with improvements, from Henry P. Berger.

During this period from 1902 to 1914, the local oyster business became the backbone of the parish economy. Besides ice, electricity greatly enhanced the development of the industry. Furthermore, the acquisition of the Ford Motor Co. Agency by Theophile Cenac in 1906 foreshadowed a dramatic change to come in the fishing fleet, which would soon begin its transformation from sail to engine power.

Among the first motorized boats in Terrebonne Parish were Leanus Lapeyrouse's *Junius*, powered by an 18 horsepower Wolverine engine; Claudio Belanger's gasoline-powered boat, the *Truscott*; and the *Espoire*, owned by Ernest Rhodes.[10] Engines were very large but had little power. Common examples were the Stanley (7 hp), Palmer (7 hp), Scripp, (15 hp), Fairbanks (12 hp), Bridgeport (15 hp), Lathrop (16 hp), and

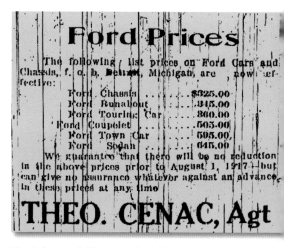

*Top left, a cordelle tow path c. 1895
Above, ad from* Houma Courier, *September 27, 1910*

The oyster industry of Houma has received a very black eye from the insane quarantine regulations of the Texas Board of Health.

Article from Terrebonne Times, *September 25, 1897*

International (20 hp). Arrival of engines marked the beginning of the end of cordelles.[11] The gasoline engine of choice was the four-cylinder 40 hp Model A followed by the 20 hp Model T.[5]

The industry was not without some setbacks. Raw oysters had been falsely accused of carrying yellow fever germs. But in 1904 a quarantine of oyster shipments from Louisiana to Texas was lifted. The industry became regulated and it prospered.[6]

A comparison from the year 1905 illustrates the dramatic impact of Houma and Terrebonne on the Louisiana oyster industry. In 1905, 60 million oysters were shipped from Baltimore, Maryland, to the cities of Chicago, Pittsburgh, Detroit, and Minneapolis. In that same year, 75 million oysters were shipped from Houma. Six hundred luggers (*canots*) were engaged in the local oyster fishing trade and 2,000 people were employed in the industry. An additional 250 people worked in the canning factory. In 1922, a Houma canning factory produced a daily capacity of 150,000 cans, and employed approximately 800. This employment number would increase to 2,500 after the Pelican Lake Oyster & Packing Co. Ltd. (est. 1906) expanded on West Park. This represented approximately 50 percent of the population of Houma at that time. Pelican Lake was capitalized

Messrs. W. J. Chapman, Chas. Daspit, Ovide Bazet, Hamilton and Norman Avery, Theodore Westphal and Mr. Tanner of Fort Worth, Tex., left for the sea-shore outing the first part of this week and are expected home to day. Mr. Tanner is a large dealer in oysters and a good customer of the oyster shippers of Houma. Barring the pleasure and novelty of a trip to our sea coast, the gentleman from Texas will have an excellent opportunity of studying the quiet ways, and manner of living of the luscious bivalve, that is destined to make Houma a familiar name in every city and hamlet of the great West. We will be greatly mistaken if Mr. Tanner does not return to Fort Worth firmly convinced that the Terrebonne coast abounds with the choicest oysters and the most affectionate mosquitoes of the world—not excepting the Baltimore bivalve or the Jersey skeeter.

Article from Terrebonne Times, *July 13, 1897*

Left, loaded oyster barges at Pelican Lake Oyster & Packing Co. in Bayou Terrebonne, downtown Houma c. 1927

Top right, interior of Pelican Lake Oyster & Packing Co.; Above, the company's logo, Below, barges loaded with pumpkins, 1927

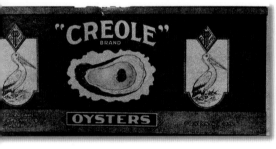

Can label from Pelican Lake Oyster & Packing Co., 1927

Pelican Lake Oyster & Packing Co. at what is now approximately 7491 Park Avenue in Houma c. 1927

with $100,000. The stockholders were leading businessmen of Louisiana, including locals Dr. Leon H. Jastremski, John D. Minor, Edmond McCollam, and Ringgold W. Cocke, as well as Frank E. Robertson of St. Mary Parish, and Charles Godchaux, Leon Cahn, and Sol Wexler of New Orleans.

In 1905, the raw oyster industry contributed $500,000 to the local economy. This resulted in a dramatic population increase and extensive development of the downtown City of Houma which occurred between 1890 and 1910.

In the State of Louisiana in 1908, only 16 firms were licensed by the Oyster Commission to buy oysters for *resale and shipment*. The majority of those firms were in New Orleans, St. Bernard, and Plaquemines. C. Cenac & Co. was the only licensed Houma firm. (C. Cenac & Co.'s Louisiana Health Permit Number was LA 4-RP.) The five local firms licensed in that year by the Commission to *buy* oysters were Houma Fish & Oyster Co. Ltd., Charles C. Miller & Co., People's Fish & Oyster Co. Ltd., Wallace Picou & Co., and R. J. Younger & Co.[7]

Some other attempts to establish oyster firms and related companies in the parish were short-lived. Enterprise Oyster Co. was incorporated on May 26, 1905, by Clifford P. Smith, J. Cyrille Dupont, Alcide J. Bonvillain, and Robert B. Butler with $15,000 in capital. The Articles of Incorporation stated the purpose was to "to fish, take, catch, bed and raise oysters and other shell fish; and other game, such as duck, geese, snipe, quail, doves, etc." This firm closed several years after its organization.

Robert J. Younger, Alcide J. Bonvillain, and Julius Blum established Independent Ice Co. on April 5, 1910, with $30,000 in capital. The Articles of Incorporation stated the purpose of the business was to "own and operate an Ice Manufacturing Plant, a cold-storage warehouse and an electric and gas light and power plant in the Town of Houma." The corporation was liquidated on September 16, 1913.

Even long-established and profitable companies were not always successful in sustaining their part in the seafood industry. "Around 1900, Edward Avery 'Ned' McIlhenny, of Tabasco fame, established a short-lived sister organization of the McIlhenny Company called McIlhenny Canning and Manufacturing Company at Avery Island near Lafayette, Louisiana. It existed primarily to process and can a number of non-pepper sauce items, including oysters, shrimp, okra, tomatoes, and figs. The company issued products under a variety of brand names, such as Cowboy, Neptune, and Little Cove brand oysters (the latter being an English translation of *Petite Anse*, the original name of Avery Island and still the name of a bayou that flows partly around the Island). Family lore blames the failure of these side products on storms that ravaged the Island's fruit and vegetable crops, and on a decline in canned seafood caused by the advent of refrigerated boxcars. Whatever the cause, the company was in trouble, and

Above, McIlhenny Canning and Manufacturing Company's oyster fleet c. 1905, near the current site of the Avery Island bridge and toll gate. Below, can label using the company's distinctive logos

in 1908, Ned refinanced the company's debt by appealing to his confidant, Avery in-law, attorney Joseph S. Clark of Philadelphia. He discontinued the unprofitable side products and refocused on the company's perennial success, the original red pepper sauce. Stung by this episode, McIlhenny Company would not experiment significantly with other side products for over a half-century (when in the early 1970s it would successfully introduce Tabasco Bloody Mary Mix)."[12]

The *Third Biennial Report of the Oyster Commission of Louisiana, 3/1/1906 to 4/1/1908*, stated that "the oyster industry of this State has during the past two years been enjoying a healthy and expansive growth. For a time this growth assumed the proportion of a 'boom' which, fortunately for the State and the industry itself, was very short-lived, many investors embarking in the business with but little knowledge, or insight, of the methods of oyster culture, and failing in brief time."

However, the renown of the Terrebonne Parish product was nationally secure. In 1907 the "Celebrated Houma Oyster" won the silver medal at the Jamestown Exposition in Virginia, and in 1910, it won the Grand Prix at the San Francisco World

A. St. Martin and Co.,
Boudreaux Canal c. 1911

Lake Oyster & Fish Co. office at present-
day 7900 Main Street, Houma, with
(left) Phillip Romaine and (middle)
owner Lee P. Lottinger (man in
doorway, right, unidentified), c. 1920

Lottinger Oyster Company,
Grand Caillou c. 1911

McIlhenny Canning & Mfg. Co.
oyster can label c. 1905

Ad from Houma Courier Magazine Edition 1906.

Exhibition.[8] "The Celebrated Houma Oyster" slogan was coined at the turn of the century by Frederick A. Daussat, who was the second general agent for the Wells Fargo Express in Houma, succeeding T.H. Kock.

In 1910, several individuals formed a general mercantile business in Houma to provide laborers (shuckers) and material to the companies they owned. Jean Charles Cenac, with Eugene LeCompte and Charles C. Miller, founded Houma Supply Co. for that purpose.

In keeping with the Cenacs' mindset of including other family members in their businesses, Dennis, the youngest of the Cenac brothers, joined Theophile at the Houma Fish & Oyster Co., Ltd. in 1910. In 1912, Jean Charles Cenac and his two brothers, William and Albert, organized the Houma Fish Distributing Co.

In 1913, through a series of transactions, William, Albert and Jean Charles each acquired a third interest in C. Cenac & Co. They bought their former partners' interests and were now sole owners of American Oyster Depot, People's Fish & Oyster Co., C. C. Miller & Co., Houma Oyster Distributing Co., and Winchester Oyster Co. Houma oysters were shipped by C. Cenac & Co. to every state in the Union and to Old Mexico.

Other Terrebonne Parish establishments at this time were the St. Martin Oyster Company, Daigle Oyster Company, Little Caillou Fish and Oyster Co., Chauvin Bros., Daspit Oyster and Trading Co. Ltd., John Labat & Bros., and Wallace Picou & Co. By 1920, still others joined them—Lake Oyster and Fish Co., Pelican Oyster & Fish Co., and Engeran Bros. Fish and Oyster Depot.

Drained Wt. 4⅔ Oz.

LAKE-VIEW
BRAND

OYSTERS

Packed By

LAKE OYSTER AND FISH CO.
HOUMA, LA.

For Consumption in the
State of Louisiana

Oyster can label c. 1930s.

Right, oyster cans, c. 1930.

Purchase document c. 1930.

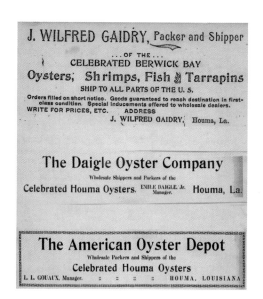

Ads from the Waterways *Edition of 1910*

Lottinger Oyster Co., Grand Caillou, c. 1911

Barataria Brand paper label shrimp can, c. 1920

Oyster was king of Terrebonne's economy at a vital point in the financial history of the parish. Oysters replaced sugar as the parish's premier commodity at a time when sugar cane was beginning to be decimated by the mosaic disease beginning at the turn of the century; the impact of the disease progressively became more severe and amounted to near-devastation by the year 1926.

By 1914 the Cenac brothers, with their associated interests in the oyster industry, had become prominent planters, packers and wholesale shippers of fish and raw oysters in the Louisiana seafood industry.

Opposite, Barataria Brand shrimp can, packers from New Orleans and Biloxi. At left and below, shipping containers from C. Cenac & Company c. early 1900s

NOTES

1. Stephanie A. Byanowski. *Exploring Maryland: Life in the Canneries at the Turn of the Century* Teacher Guide, edited by Jerome Bird

2. "On the Water—Fishing for a Living 1840-1920: Commercial Fishers: Chesapeake Oysters," americanhistory.si.edu

3. Karen M. Wicker. *The Development of the Louisiana Oyster Industry in the 19th Century*, a dissertation submitted to the graduate faculty of Louisiana State University, May, 1979

4. T.W. Campbell, Oysters. In *Biennial report of the Department of Conservation from September 1, 1912 to April 1, 1914*, Department of Conservation, 1914

5. Donald W. Davis, Ph.D., *Washed Away? The Invisible Peoples of Louisiana's Wetlands*, University of Louisiana at Lafayette Press, 2010

6. *Houma Courier Magazine Edition*, 1906

7. Third Biennial Report of the Oyster Commission of Louisiana (to the Governor and General Assembly of the State of Louisiana), 1905-1906

8. *Waterways Edition, A Sketch of the Louisiana Inter-Coastal Canal Route from Morgan City to New Orleans via Houma and Lockport*, 1910

9. The Morgan City Historical Society. *A History of Morgan City, Louisiana*, 1960

10. Helen Wurzlow accounts

11. Shallow-draft boats "had to be dragged with a tow rope (*haler à la cordelle*). '*La cordelle*' referred to the cord or rope used to pull the vessel along the channel. This halter was attached from the boat's bow mast to a horse, mule, or Cajun 'longshoreman' that pulled the vessel along a *cordelle* (path) worn in the bayou's bank....*La cordelle* paths—the forerunners of the region's highways—were used by local stores and others to haul groceries and merchandise to their customers." From Donald W. Davis book, number 5 note above.

12. Shane K. Bernard, Ph.D., *Tabasco, An Illustrated History*, August 2007

Barataria Canal Bridge, Main Street, 1914

CHAPTER 23
April 5, 1914:
Here to Stay

Pierre pulled aside the curtains and looked out a front window of his house, across Park Street toward Bayou Terrebonne. It was lined with sailboats, gasoline-powered oyster luggers, and towboats, in some places docked two deep.

He winced and let the curtains fall while he held his lower abdomen and breathed hard. Shuffling toward the screen door, he focused on the luggers. He inched open the screen door, stepped out onto the front porch, and straightened up. After a couple of halting steps, Pierre stopped to shield his eyes from the morning sun. He searched out the back of the Independent Ice Company where his livery stable and baker shop once stood, near the corner of Main and Barrow streets a little downstream. From his porch, Pierre could clearly see the ice factory, on the batture across from his house's side of the bayou. He made his eyes narrow slits, and the back of the ice company melted away into an image of his own former livery stable on that spot.

Just then a young man walked through the gate in the white picket fence, up the front path, and stopped when he reached the bottom of the steps. "*Monsieur* Cenac?" Pierre almost reeled with the flood of memories the young man's voice and face evoked.

"Yes, I am, and I can guess who you're related to. Come up and sit on the swing. You walk and look just like my old friend Jacques. I'm right, *oui*?"

The young man removed his hat and sat after Pierre did. "Yes, I'm his grandson Louis. My grandfather used to tell me about you and him together in the early days, not long after you both arrived here. I heard you were ill, and I've wanted to stop and introduce myself for a long time." The young man sounded as though he had practiced his little speech.

Pierre let out a long sigh. "I miss Jacques and Etienne. They were good friends in those young days. It was a comfort to speak with them in the Basque language we had all grown up with." After a brief silence, he turned to Louis. "Wouldn't he have been amazed at the town now? The three ice factories, and three banks?"

"Yes, and I'm sorry Grandpère didn't live to see the new high school and the grand opera house, too."

"I miss Jacques and so many of the others from that early time. Not many of us who spoke Gascon are still around, *vous connaissez*."

Louis hesitated a moment, then answered, "*Monsieur* Cenac,

Oyster lugger in Bayou Terrebonne c. 1900

Middle, Houma Fish and Oyster Co., Ltd., Theophile Cenac, owner, present-day 8061 Main Street, Houma, c. 1915. Foreground photo, Miss Agnes c. 1920, owned by Jean Pierre Cenac, Jr.

my grandfather had great affection for you. Even though the two of you were not close after your families came, he still kept up with what was going on in your life."

Pierre muttered, "Jacques was a good man," and looked at his feet.

Louis rose. "Yes, he was. Well, I don't want to be late for work." He extended his hand.

Louis walked down the steps and front path. Pierre called after him. "Thank you for stopping, *jeune homme*."

As he watched Louis striding down the road, his attention turned to the early-day bustle at his sons' oyster shops. He knew, more than saw, that Theophile's schooner *Woodman* and Albert's two-masted schooner *Peter Casano* were docked there, as well as William's *Terrebonne* and the other boys' *Angelica*, *Two Twin*, and *Dog Lake*. Pierre did see Theophile's other boat, the *Rosalina*, atop Louis Posecai's boatways. Reflected sunlight flickered from the tip of the oyster-shell mound farther down the road, visible all this way above the boys' shops and other buildings. *It's getting higher by the day. Closest thing to a mountain I've seen since I left Barbazan-Debat.*

His attention was caught by workmen's shouts from the direction of C. Cenac & Co. and Houma Fish and Oyster. Pierre looked back toward the Cenac boys' shops that stood on the fringe of Main Street's commercial district. They were across the bayou from the courthouse, banks, and other long-familiar businesses now being crowded onto Main Street by the building boom in town. More than one friend who had come to pay their respects during his illness had filled him in on the news that the town was expected to be twice the size it had been before the oyster became king of the parish's economy.

Pierre squinted, and was sure it was William he saw crossing Park toward the bayouside shops. *My sons. Albert, Theophile, Jean Charles, William, Dennis. All grand gens in the oyster business. We were right to buy up all those waterbottoms when we did after the War Between the States. Jean Baptiste still enjoys harvesting oysters in the beds near Dulac...but it would be good to have his family next door to us here, like in the early days down the bayou.*

In the clear early-morning air, Pierre again heard the workers from the direction of his sons' business places, and knew they were busy converting sailboats to be run by gasoline engines.

Pierre could hear, too, the sounds of herded cattle and knew it was from the holding pens behind Paul's dairy up the bayou on the edge of town. *Ready for slaughter. Paul and mon petit-fils George will have no trouble selling that beef in their butcher shops, with all the new people in town. I wonder whose brand those cattle bear. That brand of mine was one of the first things I applied for when I came here. P—C. My very own mark.*

Scanning the nearest bayou bank, he was not surprised to see his grandson Eloi out so early, fishing pole in hand. *Ever since that garçon and his frère Ruffin came to live with us, we can't keep them away from the water. I know how he feels. This minute I'd like to be*

down Little Caillou on Jean Pierre, Jr.'s boat St. Agnes *with him and Aurelie Eschete. Or maybe with Baptiste and Marguerite down Bayou Grand Caillou, so I could see the old place again...maybe even visit Josephine's and Celestine's graves one last time.*

Pierre ran his hand over his white beard and raised his face to the April breeze. For a minute he was reminded of the salt-air gusts that swept across the deck of the *Texas* on his crossing. He snickered a little when he remembered the fat German professor who stood at the rail next to him many days. Each time the professor retched over the side into the rough Atlantic waters, he uttered long formal apologies while wiping his corpulent face, until he gagged and leaned over again. He thought of the robust children whose parents had traveled with them to Bordeaux all the way from near the Belgian border. The constant mischief, the never-ending cajoling.

How did we all survive that trip? Food rations too small, barely mangeable. *Not enough facilities, no privacy. The thin mattresses, the smell of unwashed bodies,* les maladies. *Oh, but I was young and had courage. I had to survive it, so I did.*

Pierre glanced toward the fruit trees that draped into the front yard beside the porch. His own peaches, plums, oranges, pecans, and pears, even muscadine vines, growing on his own land. This is what he had come for. For land that would feed him, sustain him, make him independent, maybe even wealthy. He thought of the 4,000 acres he had owned near the coast until just five years ago. Oh, he had had land. Still owned some of it. And it had been all he could hope for, for a long time.

A sailboat's slow progress downstream caught his eye. The water had been a surprise, a kind of *lagniappe* to his young-man plans. The waterbottoms, bought because he always liked a challenge, had given him

C. Cenac & Co., present-day 8046 Park Avenue, c. 1910: (from left) William Jean Pierre Cenac, Jean Charles Cenac in buggy, Julius Blum, George Toups, and Alex Bergeron

Aurelie Eschete's shrimp drying platform, Little Caillou c. 1925. In center, children, Maurice Eddie and Dorris Josephine Trahan with their mother Exzelina Authement Trahan. Below, Bayou Terrebonne, sailboat in distance c. 1905

Mr R R Barrow

Houma, La., Aug 28 191 6

In account with **D. F. GRAY**

Oysters, Fish and Produce

Fresh and Salt Water Fish

HOUMA, LA., Oct 1st 191 6

Mr. R. R. Barrow

To **S. P. ACHEE,** Dr.

THE BAKER

𝕱𝖆𝖓𝖈𝖞 𝕮𝖆𝖐𝖊𝖘, 𝕻𝖎𝖊𝖘, 𝕽𝖔𝖑𝖑𝖘 𝖆𝖓𝖉 𝕭𝖗𝖊𝖆𝖉.

PHONE 90.

M. F. BRADFORD. President.
FELIX GARCIE, Vice-Pres.
T. W. COOK, Secretary.
T. J. BRADFORD, Director.

STATEMENT

Dec 1 191

M R R Barrow

To Bradford Transportation Co.,
LIMITED
Str. HOUMA, Dr.

Positively no Claim for Shortage or Damages allowed unless made within 30 days.

Office: Head of Iberville Street, = New Orleans
L. B. RIVET, Agent

STATEMENT

M R R

HOU

LOUISI

Aug 14
12

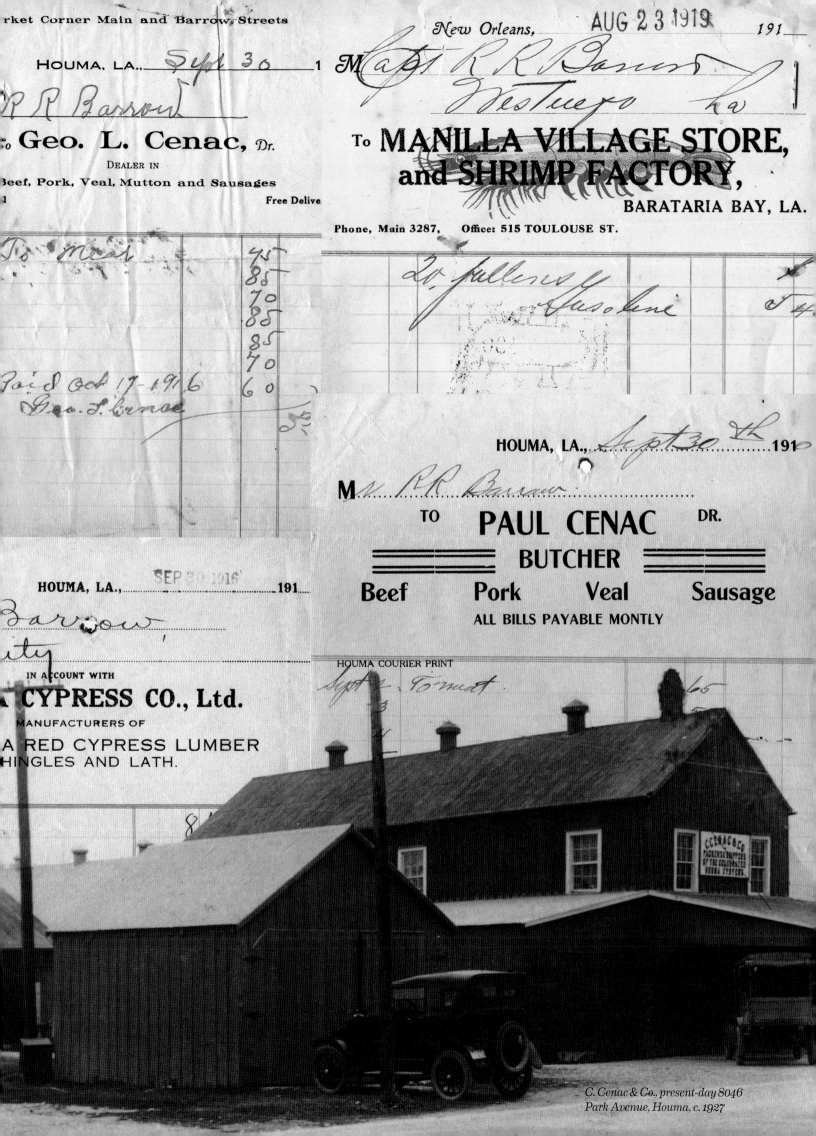

rket Corner Main and Barrow Streets

HOUMA, LA., _Sept 30_ 1

R R Barrow

to Geo. L. Cenac, Dr.

DEALER IN

Beef, Pork, Veal, Mutton and Sausages

Free Delive

To Meat		45
		85
		70
		80
		85
		70
Paid Oct 17-1916		60
Geo. L. Cenac		

New Orleans,   AUG 23 1919   191

M Capt R R Barrow

Westwego   La

To **MANILLA VILLAGE STORE,**
and **SHRIMP FACTORY,**

BARATARIA BAY, LA.

Phone, Main 3287,   Office: 515 TOULOUSE ST.

| 20 gallons of | | |
| Gasoline | | 4 |

HOUMA, LA., _Sept 30th_ 191

M R R Barrow

TO **PAUL CENAC** DR.

══ **BUTCHER** ══

Beef   Pork   Veal   Sausage

ALL BILLS PAYABLE MONTLY

HOUMA COURIER PRINT

Sept 1 To meat		65
3		
4		

HOUMA, LA.,   SEP 30 1916   191

Barrow

ity

IN ACCOUNT WITH

A CYPRESS CO., Ltd.

MANUFACTURERS OF

A RED CYPRESS LUMBER
HINGLES AND LATH.

8

*C. Cenac & Co., present-day 8046
Park Avenue, Houma, c. 1927*

William Jean Pierre Cenac, age 25, on white horse during Fourth of July Parade, Main Street, Houma, 1909. Others in foreground, from left, are Edgar Lirette, Henry Bourg, and Jules Lirette

something else to turn into *prospérité*. And that had started many of his sons on the way to their place in the world.

Marie touched his shoulder lightly as she walked out the front door. Pierre watched her as she walked across the porch and down the steps, maneuvered her carriage out of the yard, and waved as she drove past him on the street. *"Papa, prend un peu de repose."* This oldest of their daughters had come to have coffee with them before dawn, and he knew she was on her way to pick up Victorine Aimée. *How many babies have those two girls delivered since they started as midwives? Adelphine and her* bébé *will be in good hands this morning. Let's see, this will be...ah,* oui, *the twelfth for her and Albert.*

Les enfants. Victorine and I had our own good share of them. Fourteen babies, and twelve of them, merci le bon Dieu, *grown up. Eight boys. Good men. Four good women. When we got word Phine was showing first signs of labor late last night, Victorine counted again. Today's baby will be 55 grandchildren for us. Fifty-five.*

Frenchman Louis Bleriot's flight on July 25, 1909, above

Pierre smiled. *In Barbazan-Debat's old graveyard, I used to see headstones of Cenacs and other relatives all around. Maman and Papa: Jean Cenac 1803-1856 and Marguerite Duffourc Cenac 1805-1855. Grand-père Jean Cenac and Grand-mère Jeanne Lemoine Cenac. Grand-grand-père Dominique Cenac and Grande-grand-mère Domenge Descoula Cenac. When I was—what was it, 24?—and first walked into the cemetery here, how strange it was to realize there were no family, no friends' resting places. So alone. With all these children and their own children, I'm surely not alone now.*

While he shifted his weight from one foot onto the other, he let his sightline rise a bit. He marveled again that across the bayou, Main Street was flanked by telephone lines and electrical light poles. He listened for the train engine clanking and screeching into the depot at the western edge of town. At the same time, he watched high school students disembark from the transfer boats that had brought them up from rural areas to within a few blocks of Terrebonne High School in town. Just then, the still-unfamiliar sound of an automobile putt-putting down Main Street disoriented him for a second. *Ah, that'll be either Dr. Walton or young* avocat de la ville *Allen Ellender in one of their new Buicks.*

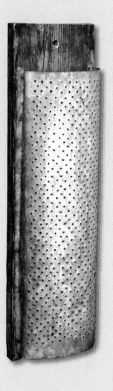

Victorine's rape à maïs (corn grater). Below, Locomotive 173 Houma Branch Railroad c. 1914. From left, Felicien Parr, James Bergeron, Pat Kerwin, Robert Spahr, Emile Ayo

Pierre shook his head and looked up at the blue skies of this clear spring day. *Incroyable.* Mon compatriote *Louis Blériot flew in that sky, over the English Channel, Calais to Dover, five years ago.* Quelle magique. *What is there left to see?*

Pierre's breaths became more shallow and he needed to lie down. He stole another glance at the Cenac oyster shops, and turned back toward the screen door. The smell of baking bread and frying bacon, usually so appealing, did not brace him today. He could see Adenise all the way down the main hall in the kitchen, busy with *la rape à maïs*, getting a head start preparing cornmeal to make bread for their *dîner*.

Pierre shuffled through the screen door toward the front bedroom and called, "Victorine."

IN LOVING
REMEMBRANCE OF

Pierre Cenac,
Died April 29, 1914.
Aged 76 Years.

Gone but not forgotten

A precious one from us has gone,
A voice we loved is stilled;
A place is vacant in our home,
Which never can be filled
God in His wisdom has recalled,
The boon his love had given,
And though the body slumbers here,
The soul is safe in Heaven.

CHAPTER 24
Passing the Torch

Pierre probably looked on with pride as his sons established themselves as industry leaders. But as the boys had been building and acquiring in the early years of the 1900s, their father had been divesting himself of some of his former properties and businesses. In January of 1912, 73-year-old Pierre sold 240 acres in Dulac to one of his brothers-in-law, William Fanguy. The next year, on November 21, 1913, he sold some of his sugar mill machinery and equipment from his plantation in Dulac to Fayport Planting Company. Only a month later, Pierre sold more than 1,000 acres of his Dulac holdings to Jewitt Allain & Son.

The French immigrant was aging and ailing. Only four months after his sale of those 1,000 acres, a personal family letter dated April 20, 1914, recounts the fact that Pierre had been staying in a New Orleans hotel while seeking medical attention, before moving to a boarding house.

Charles wrote that letter to Dennis about their father. The inside address is written simply, to "Mr. Dennis Cenac, Houma, La," with no street or number recorded.

Dear Brother,

We have moved to P. Breaux on Bourbon St. No. 416 which is a very nice and clean place. Mrs. Breaux made him a nice chicken broth this morning also coffee milk. He was perfectly satisfied, because he said they treat you like dogs at hotel, but still he is not well. He urinates pretty often. I suppose he will have to undergo an operation. We will see what the Doctor will say this morning. He is a little cross. I've got to stay with him all the time. Of course I am willing to do that but he is a little mean sometimes. Will telephone you this evening what the Doctor will say.

Your Brother
Charles Cenac[1]

Pierre died two months before his seventy-sixth birthday at his home nine days later, on April 29, 1914. Cause of death was chronic enlargement of the prostate that developed into chronic prostatitis and cystitis. Since Fr. August Vandebilt became pastor at Houma's St. Francis de Sales Church in March, Pierre's funeral was probably one of the first Fr. Vandebilt performed in Houma. Pierre was buried in the original St. Francis cemetery behind the church.[2] He left behind 12 children and 54 living grandchildren. Nineteen grandchildren were born between 1886

Ambulance in front of Charity Hospital New Orleans, 1907 or 1908

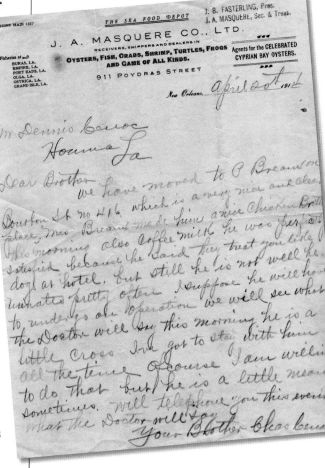

Jean Charles Cenac's letter to his brother Dennis from New Orleans April 20, 1914. Opposite, Pierre's death announcement circular

Above, Louise Violet Cenac at May Day Crowning, St. Francis de Sales Church, 1948. Below, Mary Ellen Cenac c. 1920. Both are daughters of Dennis J. Cenac

Extended family member Avery Carlos with William Jean Pierre's son Donald Joseph Cenac c. 1927 Opposite page, left column top to bottom: Ursule "Cela" Cenac c. 1910; Frances Annette Cenac c. 1916; Ovide Julien "Jock" Cenac 1906.; William Jean Pierre Cenac's children (c. 1921) group photo at left bottom, back row: William Jean Jr., Philip Louis, Ione Eleanor; front, Olga Louise, Rita Mae. Middle column, from top, Marie Cornelia Cenac and dolls c. 1910; Caliste Charles Cenac c. 1905; Marie Isare Cenac c. 1918; Lydia Cenac c. 1907. Right column Dennis J. Cenac's children c. 1935 (top photo, back row): Margaret, Mary Ellen, Jacques Augustin (front) John Abraham, Louise Violet; (middle photo) Philip Louis Cenac c. 1928; (bottom photo, from left) Alfred P. "Tenner" and Wilfred Francis "Boo" Cenac c. 1909

and 1898. Thirty-six additional grandchildren joined the family between 1898 and when Pierre died in 1914.

Jean Baptiste and Fannie had one additional child, Marie Cornelia Cenac.

Albert and Adelphine had Alphonse Joseph "Fonse," Arthur Robert "Tutty," Cecile Clair "Nan," Marie Louise "Weezie," Ovide Julien "Jock," Jules Henry "Jutte," twins Alfred Paul "Tenner" and Wilfred Francis "Boo," Odette Leonard "Dette," and Ernest Albert "Mannie" Cenac.

Marguerite and Eugene had Joseph Pierre Eloi "Edward," Victorine Louise, Joseph Ruffin, Jimmy Morris, Mary Viola, and Randolph Carlos.

Victorine and Jean Pierre Carrere had Jean Pierre, Jr., Leonie Victorine, Marie Inez, Frances, Blanche Marie, Cecile, and Adenise Adele Carrere.

Jean Pierre Cenac, Jr. and Eva had Henry Pierre, Josephine Marie, Martin Joseph, Esia Virginia, Helen Marie, and Norman Joseph Cenac.

Jean Charles and Gertrude had Caliste Charles Cenac.

Paul Michel (Michael) and Clothilde had Jeanne Eleanore, Delphine Helen, and Alice May Cenac.

William and Marie had Ione Eleanor Cenac and William Jean Cenac, Jr.

After Pierre's death, an additional 20 grandchildren were born. Albert and Adelphine added Annette Frances; Jean Pierre, Jr. and Eva added Beulah Agnes and Hilda Marie; William and Marie added Rita Mae, Olga Louise, Philip Louis, and Donald Joseph.

All the children of Dennis and Nora Cenac, and Adenise and George Williams, were born after the death of Pierre. Dennis and Nora's children were Dennis Laurence, Mary Ellen, Joseph Willard, Lucille Marie, Margaret Mary, Jacques Augustine, John Abraham, and Louise Violet.

Adenise Marie and George V. Williams' children were Marion Victorine, John Raymond, Emma Claire, Rosa Alice, and Margarette Rhea.

A total of 75 grandchildren were born to the offspring of Pierre and Victorine. The entire span of years over which the grandchildren were born was from 1886 through 1933, a period of 47 years.

Pierre lived well beyond the years of most of his siblings in France. Of the French family's seven children, five who had lived to adulthood were all deceased when Pierre died. Jacquette had passed away at an early age in 1862. One of the soldier brothers, Jean, died in 1870, and the other soldier, Dominique, died in 1873. Their brother Jean-Marie died that same year. The oldest son, Jean, was the longest-lived of all the Old Country Cenac children; he died at the age of 78 in 1911, only three years prior to Pierre's death.

Immigrants arriving from the *Hautes-Pyrénées* from time to time may have had word-of-mouth news about his French

LOUISIANA STATE BOARD OF HEALTH
BUREAU OF VITAL STATISTICS
CERTIFICATE OF DEATH

PLACE OF DEATH

Parish _Terrebonne_

Township
or ....
Village

Registration District No. ....

Primary Registration District No. ....

File No. ....

Registered No. _14104_

or
City _Houma_ (No. ....

St. .... Ward) [If death occurred in a hospital or institution, give its NAME instead of street and number.]

FULL NAME _Jean Pierre Cinac_

PERSONAL AND STATISTICAL PARTICULARS	MEDICAL CERTIFICATE OF DEATH

SEX _Male_ **COLOR or RACE** _White_ **Single Married Widowed or Divorced** (Write the word) _Married_

DATE OF DEATH _April 29th_ 1914
(Month) (Day) (Year)

DATE OF BIRTH _Unknown_ , 19
(Month) (Day) (Year)

I HEREBY CERTIFY, that I attended deceased from _April 14_, 1914, to _April 29_, 1914 that I last saw him alive on _April 29_, 1914 and that death occurred, on the date stated above, at _6 6._ m. The CAUSE OF DEATH* was as follows:

AGE _76_ yrs. _10_ mos. ds. **If LESS than 1 day** .... hrs. or .... min.

a Chronic enlargement of the prostate, developing a Chronic Prostate Cystitis

OCCUPATION
(a) Trade, profession, or particular kind of work _Butcher and Proprietor_
(b) General nature of industry, business, or establishment in which employed (or employer) _Planter_

(Duration) _many years_ mos.

Contributory (SECONDARY) _Arthritis Sclerosis_ duration _many years_ yrs. mos. ds.

BIRTHPLACE (City or Town State or foreign country) _Haute Garonne France_

(Signed) _A. R. Delcourt Jr._ M.D.
April 30. 1914 (Address) _Houma, La_

NAME OF FATHER _I don't Know_

BIRTHPLACE OF FATHER (City and State or foreign country) _France_

*State the Disease Causing Death, or, in deaths from Violent Causes, state (1) Means of Injury; (2) whether Accidental, Suicidal or Homicidal.

MAIDEN NAME OF MOTHER _I don't Know_

LENGTH OF RESIDENCE (for Hospitals, Institutions, Transients or Recent Residents)

BIRTHPLACE OF MOTHER (City and State or foreign country) _I don't Know_

At place of death _6_ yrs. mos. ds. In the State _58_ yrs. mos. ds.

Where was disease contracted if not at place of death?

THE ABOVE IS TRUE TO THE BEST OF MY KNOWLEDGE

Former or usual residence _Grand Caillou (Du Lac) La_

(Informant) _A. R. Delcourt Jr._

(Address) _Houma, La_

PLACE OF BURIAL OR REMOVAL _Houma, La_

DATE OF BURIAL _April 30_ 1914

Filed _May 21_ 191 _H. N. Wallis_ Registrar

UNDERTAKER _Ebenezer Church_

ADDRESS _Houma, La_

siblings for the American Cenac. However, Dennis discovered after Pierre's death a stash of old papers that Pierre had kept for 60 years. If Pierre had received direct correspondence from his siblings, he would in all probability have kept those letters, as well. No such letters were found with Pierre's papers, so he likely went to his grave without knowing his brothers' and sister's fate.

Two separate Terrebonne Parish newspapers' obituaries went beyond fact to enter the realm of tribute to a man who began his life in 1838 in French highlands, and whose life ended in Louisiana's low bayou country.

An obituary description in *The Houma Times*, by a writer who had known Pierre as a young man, indicated that the French immigrant arrived in Terrebonne Parish with what the reporter perceived as "...the most beautiful type of physical development we had ever seen; he stood straight as an arrow, tall, well proportioned, wavy hair, a bright and intelligent forehead and face, heavy eye brows and the eyes of an eagle. Behind this beautiful physique, you could see a thousand years of civilization and thrift."

That reporter described the manner in which Pierre was regarded when he stepped onto the land where he would father a bounteous family and where he would rise from being a baker, according to that same obituary, to becoming a successful entrepreneur on Terrebonne Parish lands and waters.

Eight generations of Pierre's progeny have since continued the mutually beneficial relationship with Terrebonne Parish that the French immigrant initiated when he arrived in Houma in 1861 with a strong desire to make his mark in his adopted homeland. In 1970, there were 218 great-grandchildren, 326 great-great grandchildren, and 40 great-great-great grandchildren. As of this writing, there are also an unknown number of great-great-great-great grandchildren.

A second obituary announcing Pierre's demise was printed in the *Houma Courier*: "Mr. Pierre Cenac died last Wednesday just before the shadows of night began to spread over the face of the earth," the *Houma Courier* article began, in the florid journalistic style of the day. "In his death this parish lost one of its oldest citizens, a man who believed in the rule of honesty and followed it to the letter. For there was never a man more honorable in everything he did than was he."

The Houma Courier, *which had been established in 1878, was the official journal of the city government around the turn of twentieth century. The* Houma Times *(masthead above) newspaper was also being circulated in 1914. Other newspapers had served as predecessors to these publications. Among the pre-Civil War papers were the* Houma Ceres *dating to at least 1855, the* Terrebonne Patriot, *and the* Civic Guard. *One pre-1900 newspaper was the* Terrebonne Republican, *and the* Gibson Times *of the early 1900s. Dating from 1845, the* Thibodaux Minerva *preceded all Terrebonne Parish newspapers, and was likely the first weekly in the state.*

Opposite, Pierre's death certificate. Below, tomb of Pierre Cenac and Victorine Fanguy Cenac in cemetery behind St. Francis de Sales Cathedral, Houma

NOTES

1. In the Cenac Collection of the Nicholls State University Archives

2. St. Francis de Sales Cemetery No. 1: Section 13, Plot 43

Michel's Grocery at Church and Main streets, bayouside, c. 1930

EPILOGUE

One indication of the extent of Pierre's holdings is that the Cenac estate sold 1,047 acres in Dulac on May 1, 1914, to Adriel S. McCord soon after Pierre died.[1]

Victorine continued to live in the family home on Park Avenue with her youngest daughter Adenise. Adenise married in 1921, and for a time she and her husband and first child Marion lived with her. Her oldest daughter, Marie, lived nearby on Carlos Street. Marie tended to her mother on a daily basis through Victorine's last years.

Her children remained in close touch. They took their own children to visit her often, some making it a ritual after attending Mass at St. Francis de Sales Church. The families sat close to each other in church on Sunday mornings, left of the main aisle: Charles' family rented Pew 20; William's, 21, and Dennis's, 22, from rental agreements conducted each Easter Sunday. William's children remember that after Mass, they would stop at LeBlanc's Candy Stand on the corner of Main and Church streets. They bought for Victorine the taffy she loved, and the peanut candy William's children enjoyed. Afterward, they crossed the street to Michel's Grocery on the bayouside, where they purchased fresh fruit and vegetables to take to Victorine. The family would then cross the old iron bridge over Bayou Terrebonne at Church Street to walk the few blocks to their grandmother Victorine's house. Many of Pierre and Victorine's children in Houma met at her house on Sunday mornings before returning to their own homes for *dîner*.

Above, notice from the Houma Courier *of February 8, 1899. Below, Marion Victorine Williams at Victorine Cenac's house on Park Avenue, Houma c. 1926. Bottom, pew rental receipts from 1869 and 1898*

Made On New Road via
Des Allemands and
Raceland

No longer is the motor trip from Houma to New Orleans one of more than 150 miles in length.

No longer is it necessary to drive from here to Donaldsonvile thence back to the Crescent City over a route forming a long sharp angle.

For the new hard-surfaced highway from Raceland to Des Allemands has been opened to traffic and this connecting with the Orleans-Des Allemands road gives quick access to New Orleans and brings the two cities less than 64 miles apart.

On Sunday a party of Houma men made the first trip over the highway and demonstrated to their own satisfaction, at least, the blessings that will accrue from the construction of good highways through the entire section. C. C. Krumbhaar, President Association of Commerce, T. Baker Smith, parish highway engineer, Calvin Wurzlow, attorney, and Arthur W. Van Pelt, secretary, of the Association of Commerce, started about nine o'clock Sunday to drive to Raceland, there expecting to meet Duncan Buie, State Highway Engineer, for a conference on the highway situation. The trip was made by way of Bonal Leyho and Bayou Blue road to Sarlos's store thence direct through the prairie to Raceland. With the exception of the incompleted portion of the Houma-Schriever road and a small portion of the Bayou Blue road, the entire route was in excellent condition. For the first three-quarters mile toward Raceland after leaving Bayou Blue the road is still rough but aside from this is very good.

Mr. Buie was not at Raceland when the party got there, so, desiring to try the new road, it was voted to continue. The new shell road paralleling the Southern Pacific is as yet somewhat rough in spots, the shells having not been settled in place, but in no place was the least trouble encountered.

A conference was held with Mr. Buie in the afternoon, he having been unable to leave the city as he expected that morning and plans were made to push the organization of further road districts in Terrebonne so as to connect up the Southern National Highway with all points east and west.

At 4:30 p. m. the party left on the return trip and Houma was reached once more about 8:30 p. m.

The trip was an epoch making one it being the first time that anyone had ever left Houma in the morning by motor car and returned the same day, after spending several hours in New Orleans. It was only the first, however. Many more will follow and within a short time, it is believed, cars from New Orleans will pass thru Houma and Terrebonne daily in large numbers, and the people of this parish will consider a motor trip to New Orleans and return the matter of only a few hours. Terrebonne products will be shipped to New Orleans by motor and return loads of goods from the city will be brought back the same way.

This is practicable at the present time. How much more so, then, will

---

This family closeness is reflected also in the fact that the sons arranged for grandson John Hubert "Hubbet" Carlos to take ice every morning to everyone in the family who lived in town—to his own mother Marie on Carlos Street, to his grandmother Victorine, and to all the other Cenac siblings.

This family togetherness was interrupted in 1914, when World War I began on July 28 that year. Many Cenac men joined the war effort both locally and overseas. Sons Jean Pierre, Jr., Jean Charles, Paul Michel, William Jean Pierre, and Dennis; son-in-law Eugene Carlos; grandsons Jean Pierre Carrere, Jr., Justilien Carrere, John Hubert Carlos; and grandsons-in-law Sidney Joseph Luke, Felix A. Delatte, Elie Bartholomew Belanger, Yancey Amedee Benoit, and Richard Clyde Allen were all registered for service.

Jean Baptiste's sons who served in the Army were Jean Albert, George Lee, and James William. Joseph Cyrille served in the Marine Corps and fought at St. Nazaire, France.

Albert's sons Alphonse J. and Arthur R. were in the Navy, as was his son-in-law Auguste William Wurzlow (husband of Odette Cenac). Alphonse served with his cousin Eloi "Edward" Carlos (Marguerite's son) on the battleship *South Carolina* off the coast of Norway in the North Sea. Marie's son Salvador Albert Carlos, Marguerite's son-in-law Rodney Roddy (husband of Eugenie), Theophile's son-in-law Armand Porchec (husband of Theo's only child Isare), Albert's son-in-law William P. Yancey, William's son-in-law Edward A. Rucker, and Adenise's husband George V. Williams were also in military service in "The Great War." Documentation is available for these Cenacs, but other grandchildren may have served, also. One family war fatality was Pierre Pujo, husband of Pierre's French niece Jeanne-Marie Cenac Pujo. She was the daughter of Pierre's older brother Jean Cenac.

Cenacs of Terrebonne around 1920 lived in a parish whose population had grown to 26,974. Houma was a thriving community of 5,160.

One important transportation advancement of the time allowed the Cenacs and other local businessmen to access the New Orleans market directly. The first one-day trip by motorcar from Houma to New Orleans and back on a hard-surface roadway occurred on Sunday, October 6, 1918, according to *The Houma Courier* edition of Saturday, October 12. The article lauded the historic record set by C.C. Krumbhaar, T. Baker Smith, Calvin Wurzlow, and Arthur W. Van Pelt, who completed that first round trip. It took the men from Houma to Raceland via Bayou Blue, on to Des Allemands, and then to Algiers on the West Bank of New Orleans—and back on the same route. Now, Terrebonne products could be shipped quickly to New Orleans by motor vehicles, which would then return with goods from the city for sale locally. By 1922, a local newspaper reported that the number of auto licenses issued for Terrebonne Parish was over 1,000.

Another transportation improvement came in 1923, when the Gulf Intracoastal Waterway connecting to Bayou Terrebonne was

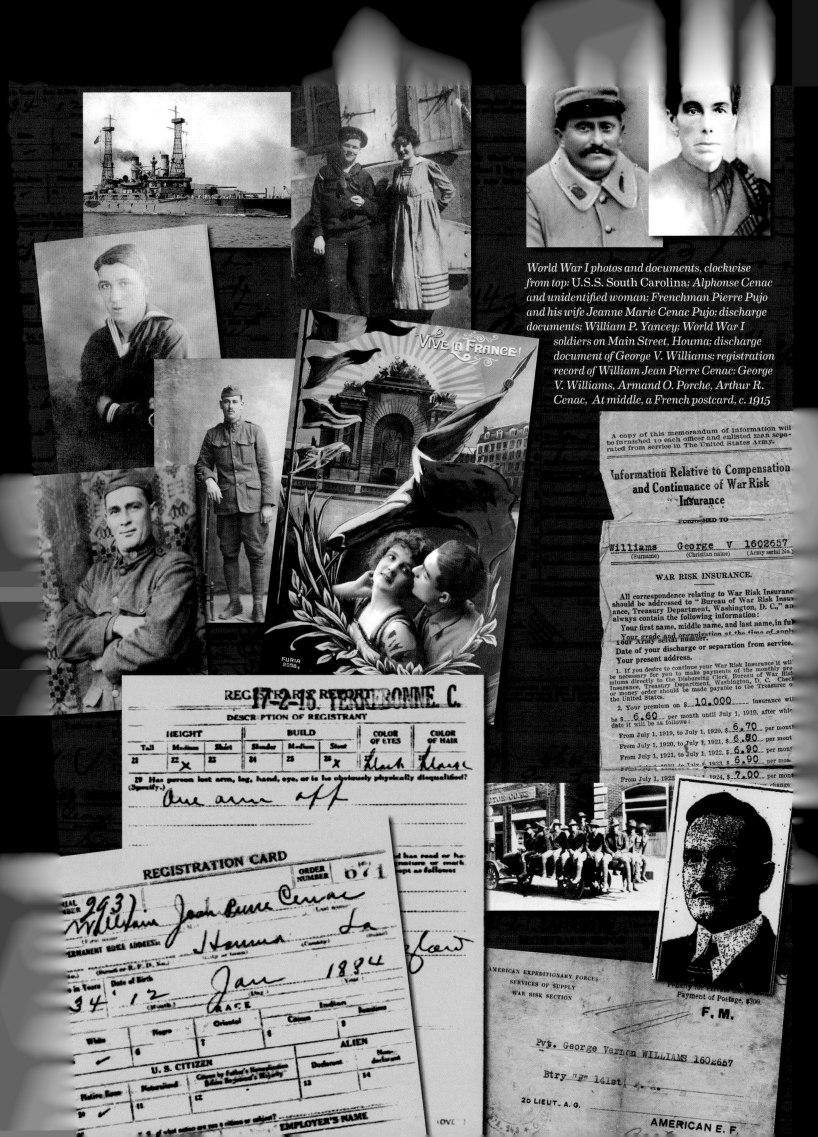

World War I photos and documents, clockwise from top: U.S.S. South Carolina; Alphonse Cenac and unidentified woman; Frenchman Pierre Pujo and his wife Jeanne Marie Cenac Pujo; discharge documents; William P. Yancey; World War I soldiers on Main Street, Houma; discharge document of George V. Williams; registration record of William Jean Pierre Cenac; George V. Williams, Armand O. Porche, Arthur R. Cenac, At middle, a French postcard, c. 1915

VIVE LA FRANCE!

FURIA 2098

A copy of this memorandum of information will be furnished to each officer and enlisted man separated from service in The United States Army.

Information Relative to Compensation and Continuance of War Risk Insurance

FURNISHED TO

Williams   George   V   1602657
(Surname)   (Christian name)   (Army serial No.)

WAR RISK INSURANCE.

All correspondence relating to War Risk Insurance should be addressed to "Bureau of War Risk Insurance, Treasury Department, Washington, D. C.," and always contain the following information:

Your first name, middle name, and last name, in full.
Your grade and organization at the time of apply.
Your Army serial number.
Date of your discharge or separation from service.
Your present address.

1. If you desire to continue your War Risk Insurance it will be necessary for you to make payments of the monthly premiums directly to the Disbursing Clerk, Bureau of War Risk Insurance, Treasury Department, Washington, D. C. Checks or money order should be made payable to the Treasurer of the United States.

2. Your premium on $ 10,000 insurance will be $ 6.60 per month until July 1, 1919, after which date it will be as follows:

From July 1, 1919, to July 1, 1920, $ 6.70 per month
From July 1, 1920, to July 1, 1921, $ 6.80 per mon
From July 1, 1921, to July 1, 1922, $ 6.90 per mon
From July 1, 1922, to July 1, 1923, $ 6.90 per mon
From July 1, 1923, to July 1, 1924, $ 7.00 per mont

REGISTRARS REPORT 17-2-18. TERREBONNE. C.
DESCRIPTION OF REGISTRANT

HEIGHT			BUILD			COLOR OF EYES	COLOR OF HAIR
Tall	Medium	Short	Slender	Medium	Stout		
21	22 X	23	24	25	28 X	Black	Brown

29 Has person lost arm, leg, hand, eye, or is he obviously physically disqualified? (Specify.)

One arm off

REGISTRATION CARD   ORDER NUMBER 071

293 William Jean Pierre Cenac

Houma La

34   12   Jan   1884

RACE

	White	Negro	Oriental	Indian		
	✓					

U. S. CITIZEN   ALIEN

AMERICAN EXPEDITIONARY FORCES
SERVICES OF SUPPLY
WAR RISK SECTION

F. M.

Pvt. George Vernon WILLIAMS 1602657

Btry "F" 141st

2D LIEUT. A. G.

AMERICAN E. F.

I Would Like the Person on the
Other Side to Vote For Me

WILLIAM "Bill" CENAC

— FOR —

SHERIFF

DEMOCRATIC CANDIDATE

January 1936

*William J.P. Cenac's campaign
handout appeared on the back side
of a mirror , 1936*

completed to the west of what was then the city. The Intracoastal was not extended from Bayou Terrebonne into Lafourche Parish until 1934.

Radio came to Houma in 1922 when Joe and Francis Pullen installed a transmitter and receiver in their home, using the nearby water tower to mount their antenna.

The status of Houma as a commercial center was affirmed in the year 1918 when the Houma-Terrebonne Association of Commerce was chartered. When the organization evolved into the Houma-Terrebonne Chamber of Commerce in 1929, William J.P. Cenac was elected to its first board of directors, and C. Cenac & Co. was a charter member. William entered public service earlier, in May of 1909 when he took on the job of clerk, later known as secretary, of the Terrebonne Parish Police Jury, at a salary of $29.15 a month. He continued in this position until July, 1912. For the City of Houma, he was elected alderman in 1930. He served until his death in 1945. His son William Jr. served the rest of his term, after which his nephew A.R. Cenac was elected to succeed him. William was also a founding member of the Houma chapter of Rotary International in 1921, and was active in the Knights of Columbus. He had diversified his business interests to include the Terrebonne Ice Company, serving as a member of its board of directors. With his partners Robert Younger, Theogene Engeron and James E. Chauvin, he purchased and incorporated a company that had been founded in 1919, the Louisiana Crushing Co., Inc. This business was an adjunct company to oyster packing and shipping. Processing the byproduct (shells) produced supplements for animal feed, road surfacing material, lime for fertilizer and material to use in making ornamental planters.

The Cenac sons continued to expand their businesses for many years after Pierre's death.

On August 21, 1923, Albert and William J. P. Cenac completed the purchase of the Sea Breeze Oyster Co., a subsidiary of C. C. Miller & Co.

The next year, on August 2, William and Albert purchased the interests of their brother Jean Charles in C. Cenac & Co. and became equal partners. On August 13, Dennis J. Cenac, Jean Charles Cenac, and Calvin Wurzlow formed Cenac Brothers Inc. The Articles of Incorporation stated the purpose of the business was to "buy, sell and market all varieties of seafood, fruit, vegetables or agricultural products, whether in prepared or raw intake; to lease, own, control or operate its own transportation system, either by water, rail or otherwise, its own communication facilities (telephone, telegraph, radio or otherwise), and all other enterprises and undertakings that may be necessary or helpful to the proper and profitable holdings, management, development and conduct of its business and the acquisition and disposal, of its goods, wares and merchandise, or the exercise and accomplishment of the objects and purposes herein declared or implied."

A May 1922 "Woman's Edition" of *The Houma Courier* listed companies in which women had positions of responsibility:

A planter made of oyster shells by Louisiana Crushing Co., Inc. c. 1920.

Ad from the Houma Courier, *October 27, 1917*

Terrebonne Ice Company near present-day 8029 Main Street, Houma c. 1920

Above, J. Alelard Drolet and Marie Ida Carlos Drolet's family of Montreal, Canada c. 1930.

Terrebonne Bank & Trust Co. office on Main Street c. 1910

"There are girl stenographers galore, among the firms employing them being...C. Cenac and Co,...Houma Fish and Oyster Co.,....."

In 1925, during the old age of Pierre's widow, she and her family suffered a loss it must have been difficult for her to bear—the death of her son Theophile. His death was a loss for the community as well, because Theophile had been one of the most proactive of Pierre and Victorine's children. Besides his involvement in the oyster business, his automobile agency, and the ice factory, Theophile's enterprising nature had taken him into the fields of banking and publishing. Theophile was a founder, stockholder in and on the board of directors for the Bank of Terrebonne when it was organized in 1910. For a short time he owned the printing and job office The Commercial Press, located in the Houma Opera House, when he bought the business from J. Alelard Drolet. Drolet was married to Theophile's cousin Marie Ida Carlos, and the native Canadian Drolet then moved his family to Montreal, Canada. Theophile sold that business on December 9, 1918, to the Houma Courier Publishing Company, Ltd., president Tristam B. Easton.

He and his family lived in New Orleans for a time, and were listed there in the census of 1920. While his daughter Isare

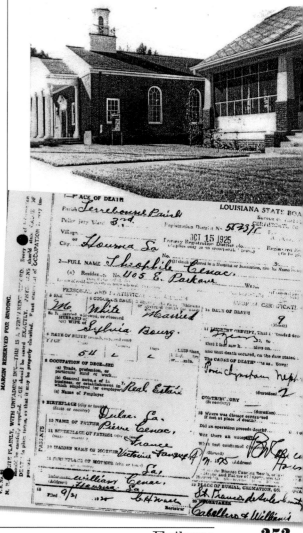

Houma City Council members 1936: (seated) J. Harry Hellier, Louis C. LeBlanc, Mayor Thomas Elward Wright, city clerk Dreux Angers; standing, chief of police C.A. Callahan, William J.P. Cenac, Leopold Blum, David J. Olivier

Theophile Cenac's house that was moved adjacent to the Presbyterian Church on Barrow Street; photo c. late 1920s. Below, Theophile Cenac's death certificate, September 20, 1925

attended Soulé Commercial College, Theophile worked in real estate in the Crescent City until he moved back to Houma. Theophile sold his ownership of the local Ford Agency to D.M. Kilpatrick, who incorporated that business as The Terrebonne Motor Co., Inc. in January 1920. Theophile retained ownership of the Overland auto agency, which sold the vehicle that was the forerunner of the Buick.

The home Theophile built on the batture across from the current Terrebonne General Medical Center was moved in 1921 to serve as the parsonage of the Presbyterian Church on Barrow Street. The house was rolled on logs pulled by mules up Main Street onto Barrow Street. After the mules gave out on Barrow, the Rev. J.N. Blackburn, who had recently been married and was to live in the house with his bride, hooked the structure to his own Ford automobile. He pulled it the rest of the way to its location fronting on Barrow Street immediately north of the church. Theo's house-turned-parsonage no longer stands.

At his demise four years later of renal failure on September 20, 1925, Theophile was only 54. The Cenac family had lost one of its most visionary and industrious members.

Dennis J. Cenac acquired Theophile's interest in the Houma Fish & Oyster Co., Ltd. upon the death of his brother. His partner was Abraham Blum, a founder and director of the Peoples Bank. Dennis ran the company until his 1945 retirement. The business closed, thus ending the legacy of Houma's oldest and first incorporated seafood establishment.

Dried Shrimp Industry c. 1920

Hauling cooked shrimp in wheelbarrows to platform, ready for spreading

Shrimp drying on the platform

Spreading the shrimp to dry

"Dancing the shrimp" to separate shrimp from shells

Indian Ridge Canning Co. label

Dried shrimp shelling machine invented by Shelly J. Bergeron and Fred Chauvin, patented in 1922

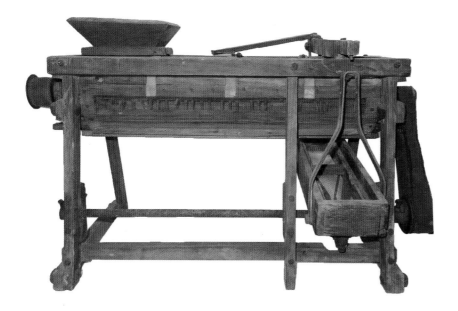

Blum and Bergeron
product label and token

Wooden shipping barrels at Blum and Bergeron pictured, from left, unidentified, Shelly Bergeron, Xavier St. Martin, Leopold Blum

Barrel stencils

Seining at Oyster Bayou Lower Terrebonne Coast, c. 1920

In numerical order, 1. shrimp camp; 2. sailing lugger setting the seine; 3. hauling the seine; 4. 24 barrels in this haul; 5. boat Bull Dog with 36 barrels of shrimp on board; 6. boiling the shrimp; 7. drying shrimp; 8. sifting the shrimp

When Pierre died in 1914, Terrebonne Parish was in a time of financial security and economic prosperity. By 1925-26, however, the community was being hard hit by the decline of the sugar industry caused by the mosaic disease which had appeared locally not long after the turn of the twentieth century. Plantations were failing from lower production caused by the effect of the disease on their crops, combined with plummeting sugar prices beginning in 1920. A total of 12 sugar refineries were working in Terrebonne Parish in 1920. By 1926, all but two of the refineries—Southdown and Lower Terrebonne Refinery—had shut down.

Local banks suffered from the devastation of the sugar industry. The Bank of Houma became over-extended in loans to the sugar industry, and closed in 1924. The Bank of Terrebonne took over that bank's deposit liability, so that depositors suffered no losses. Peoples Bank followed not long afterward, with closure in 1927. However, its liquidation process caused depositors to wait 20 years for full payment. Bourg State Bank, which had opened in that rural community in 1919, moved to Houma in 1924 as Citizen's Bank and Trust Company. George Lee Cenac, the third child of Jean Baptiste and Martha Frances Cenac, was a founding member and original stockholder in Bourg State Bank. Citizen's managed to weather the sugar industry's decline.[2]

While the sugar industry declined, fur trapping contributed $1 million to the local economy in 1925. Market hunting for waterfowl and other migratory birds ended with the passage of the Federal 1900 Lacey Act and the 1918 Migratory Bird Treaty Act. Seafood, however, became the economic kingpin of Terrebonne Parish in the mid-1920s. The dried shrimp industry peaked in 1929 with 5 million pounds sold. The shrimp industry as we know it today began its transition from the haul seine to the otter trawl and from inland waters to offshore fishing. Sailing luggers were converted to motorized vessels and production made a dramatic increase, peaking in the 1940s.

The commercial crab industry began in 1924 with

establishment of the first crabmeat plant in Morgan City. By 1930, there were eight processing facilities in the Morgan City-Berwick area. Fish and frogs still contributed to the area economy, as well as moss picking.

Bourg State Bank in Knights of Pythias building, Main Street, Houma 1920. Below, George Lee Cenac

Below, Lower Terrebonne Refinery on Bayou Terrebonne c. 1920s. At left, the Harry in Little Bayou Black at Southdown Refinery c. 1930

By 1929, seafood and furs continued to be the leading resources in Terrebonne Parish. The Chamber of Commerce, in its first year of organization, prepared a "Preliminary Survey of All Resources for Terrebonne Parish in 1929," which gave valuations of products as follows:

Seafoods (Canned) Shrimp	$1,012,630.00
Dried shrimp	254,336.16
Shrimp Meal	42,000.00
Oysters	487,500.00
Shells	20,000.00
Fish, Frogs and Crab Meat	300,000.00
Furs (misc.)	904,928.00
Minerals: Crude Oil	73,996.56
Moss	52,800.00

Most photos from 1930s. Top left, trapper's son age 5; middle, trapper's palmetto hut; setting traps in the marsh. Second row from left, man drying raccoon skins; Chamber of Commerce 1929 report, drying shrimp and fish at Manilla Village; third row left, Lady Eleanor pleasure boat owned by Dr. Leon H. Jastremski, third row right, duck hunters Dr. R.W. Collins, on left, and friend, c. 1920; bottom row, rowing moss home with a jourg, men cleaning bullfrogs, harvesting moss

By the late 1920s, the oyster industry was booming, with 125 million oysters being shipped annually from Houma by rail.

From that date to the present time, the town where the Cenac family helped to forge the oyster industry's development has led oyster production nationwide and maintained a leading position in the national seafood industry.

The family's matriarch, Victorine Fanguy Cenac, died on February 16, 1926, at the age of 78. Her cause of death was chronic nephritis and influenza. Victorine was buried in the tomb with her deceased husband in St. Francis de Sales Church cemetery.[3] Her obituary counted among her survivors 67 grandchildren and 66 great-grandchildren. Grandchildren reached an eventual total of 75; only one of the grandchildren preceded her in death—Marie's youngest child Helene, before the end of the nineteenth century. Victorine's obituary in the February 20 *Houma Courier* called her "one of Terrebonne's oldest and most esteemed ladies," and the mother of "pioneer builders of the great Houma oyster industry." Her sons now had a visible presence in the Terrebonne community. Pierre's enterprising spirit had not died with him.

NOTES

1. Pierre's succession is recorded in the Houma Courthouse as number 1268, filed in July 1914.

2. Madison Funderburk. "Banking Mirrors Parish History," *The Houma Daily Courier & The Terrebonne Press* issue of March 5, 1978

3. Victorine's funeral mass was at St. Francis de Sales Catholic Church. She was buried in the cemetery behind the church with Pierre (Section 13, Plot 43).

Mrs. Pierre Cenac Passes Away After Brief Illness

Was Mother Of Family Widely Known as Oyster Shippers

Mrs. Pierre Cenac, one of Terrebonne's oldest and most esteemed ladies, died Tuesday morning at 7:00 o'clock, her death being due to a general decline of health, culminating in an attack of influenza. She was 78 years old, and a native of the Grand Caillou section where she and her husband, the late Pierre Cenac, owned a small sugar plantation and resided there until twenty-five years ago, when they moved to Houma, residing in Park Avenue. Mrs. Cenac's maiden name was Miss Victorine Fanguy. She had twelve children, eleven of whom are living: Mrs. Salvidore Carlos, Mrs. Eugene Carlos, Mrs. Geo. Williams, Mrs. Pierre Carriere, Messrs. Batiste, Albert, Paul, Ulae, William, Pierre and Dennis Cenac, all of Houma. Another son, Theophile Cenac died last year. Mrs. Cenac had the distinction of being the grandmother of sixty-seven, and the great-grandmother of sixty-six. Nearly all of her sons have been engaged in the oyster business, being among the pioneer builders of the great Houma oyster industry.

The funeral took place Wednesday morning at 9:00 o'clock, services in the Houma Catholic Church, enterment in the Catholic Cemetery.

Top, article from the Houma Courier of February 20, 1926. Above, Victorine Cenac's death certificate. Left photo, Victorine Aimée Fanguy Cenac at right with her sister Eloise Anastasia "Tante Naz" Fanguy Luke c. 1925

Orange Grove, 1983

AFTERWORD

A longtime interest in the history of his family and south Louisiana in general prompted initial research by Christopher E. Cenac, Sr. for this book. His primary influence in honoring family ties came from his father Philip Louis Cenac, who had great respect and affection for his relatives. His father's attitude instilled in Chris, even as a child, an appreciation for the stories of older relatives, and encouraged his own frequent interaction with extended family members.

In his teens, he began collecting memorabilia and artifacts. As a younger adult, his interest in historic places resulted in restoration of Orange Grove plantation house in the late 1970s for his residence in his home parish of Terrebonne.

Around the year 2000, he made a conscious decision to begin active family research, with the ultimate goal of compiling it in some form. His first trip to the French village of his great-grandfather's birth was in 2003. He visited distant cousins, and collected more information. At the time of his transition to semi-retirement in the summer of 2007, he realized that he had the desire, the foundational documentation and artifacts, and the time to begin the actual writing phase.

Claire Domangue Joller took on the writing/compiling side of the project, and Chris redoubled his research and acquisitions efforts. During the course of the next four years, they sought assistance from multiple individuals in their respective fields of expertise while they wrote and revised many drafts of the book now in print.

This same interest in preserving historical information gave rise to a soon-to-be-published book, *The Firebrands of Terrebonne 1822-1940*. A pictorial history of Terrebonne is now being compiled for publication and outlines are being completed for a book about two Cenac families' transition from oysters to oil and medicine.

FAIR !   FAIR ! !

—WILL BE GIVEN—

At the Orange Grove Residence, SUNDAY, APRIL 28th, 1901.

For the purpose of raising funds to complete the interier of the Catholic Church on Lower Bayou Black. A cordial invitation is extended to all to attend and a good time is promised for those who do attend.

THIS PROPERTY
ORANGE GROVE
PLANTATION
HAS BEEN PLACED ON THE
NATIONAL REGISTER
OF HISTORIC PLACES
BY THE UNITED STATES
DEPARTMENT OF THE INTERIOR

Roberta Grove

APPENDIX I:
Named Terrebonne Parish Sugar Estates c. 1900

Plantation	Owner/s

UPPER BAYOU TERREBONNE

Evergreen	Joseph Ayo
Halfway	Lepine, Ferry
Hedgeford	Richard Lloyd
Myrtle Grove	R. R. Barrow, H.C. Duplantis
Pelie	Mastero, Miche and Co.
Roberta Grove	R. R. Barrow, H.C. Duplantis

LOWER BAYOU TERREBONNE

Angela	Eugene Fields
Aragon	J.L. LeBlanc, C.B. Maginnis
Front Lawn	Alfred Boudreaux
Hard Scrabble	John R. Bisland
Hope Farm *left bank of Bayou Terrebonne*	Ellender Bros.
Hope Farm *right bank of Bayou Terrebonne*	Ralph Bisland
Klondyke	Albert Champagne
Live Oak	Mrs. Monroe James Sanders
Magenta	Allen A. Sanders
Pointe Farm	A.R. Viguerie
Presque Isle	Gueno Bros.

Red Star	J.N. Robichaux
Residence	Volumnia Roberta Barrow Slatter
Rural Retreat	Joseph Bascle
Woodland	J.L. LeBlanc, C.B. Maginnis

LITTLE CAILLOU

Indian Ridge	E. Picou
Lacache (Little Caillou Plantation)	Mrs. Georgiana Greshem
Oak Farm	Henry G. Bush, Albert F. Tate
Ranch	H.C. Gage
Sarah	Henry G. Bush & Albert F. Tate

GRAND CAILLOU

Ashland	J.L. LeBlanc, Caillouet & Maginnis
Caillou Grove	Ernest Cantrelle
Cane Brake	Louis Waguespack
Cedar Grove	Blum & Cantrelle
Dulac	Mrs. F. Lottinger
Ellersley	Ashland Planting Co.
Grand Caillou	Combon Bros.
Good Hope	Ashland Planting Co.
Honduras	Shaffer & Morris
La Cordaire	Pierre Cenac
Live Oak	Joseph W. Martin
Woodlawn	Caillouet & Maginnis

Woodlawn second house, 1900

BAYOU DULARGE

Dularge	Traisimond Henry
High Ridge	Thomas W. Cook
Mulberry	Bonvillain Bros. Felix A., M.J., Senator A.J.
Ridgeland	Bonvillain Bros. Felix A., M.J., Senator A.J.
St. Eloi	Bernard Marmande; M. Rousseau, tutor
St. Michel (Michael)	P.N. Champagne, Mrs. A. Theriot
Sunrise	J.T. Theriot

BIG BAYOU BLACK

Argyle	Bonvillain Bros. Felix A., M.J., Senator A.J.
Belle Farm	C.W. Bocage
Boykin	Bonvillain Bros. Felix A., M.J., Senator A.J.
Concord	Estate of H.C. Minor
Eastonia	Dr. Claiborne Alexander Duval heirs
Flora	C.W. Bocage
Goat Field Farm	Estate of H.C. Minor
Greenwood	John A. Douglas, Thomas Casey, and Estate of H.C. Minor
Hollywood	John D. Minor
Laura Farm	John D. Minor
Mandalay	Estate of H.C. Minor
Oak Forest	John A. Douglas; Estate of H.C. Minor
Orange Grove	H.C. Gage
Ridgeland	Flavillus Sidney Goode heirs
Roseland	John D. Minor
Waterloo	Estate of H.C. Minor
Waterproof	John D. Minor

Left, McCollam family members of Ellendale are
(from left) Alexander McCollam, Edna McCollam, unidentified,
Mrs. William McCollam, Miss Eleanor Elizabeth McCollam,
unidentified, Edmond McCollam, William McCollam,
Andrew McCollam c. 1920

Right, four generations of Schaffer family members of Ardoyne
are (from left, adults) Etta Lee Shaffer, John Jackson Shaffer,
Julia Shaffer, John Dalton Shaffer, Minerva Shaffer, Captain
John J. Shaffer. Children are (from left) Milhado Lee Shaffer
and John Jackson Shaffer III c. 1916

LITTLE BAYOU BLACK

Ardoyne	John. D. Shaffer
Belle Grove	J.M. McBride
Crescent Farm	Estate of H.C. Minor
Ellendale	Edmund & William A. McCollam
Eureka	John D. Shaffer
Hollywood	Estate of H.C. Minor
Isle of Cuba	David Levy
Magnolia	J.J. Shaffer
Rebecca	R.W. Cocke & Prejean
Southdown	Estate of H.C. Minor

Belle Grove

Southdown Refinery c. 1930

SCHRIEVER

Ducros	R.S. and R.C.Wood
Julia	John T. Moore
Magnolia Grove	Mrs. Lemuel Tanner
St. Brigitte	Manuel Piedra
St. George	John T. Moore
Waubun	John T. Moore

CHACAHOULA

Bull Run	McCollam Bros., R.W. Cocke
Cedar Grove	McCollam Bros, R.W. Cocke
Forest Grove	Buford & Bernard
Poverty Flat	McCollam Bros., R.W. Cocke

Cedar Grove

Terrebonne Parish Canals

Barataria Canal: *financed by Robert Ruffin Barrow, dug c. 1840 to facilitate inland transportation from Bayou Terrebonne to Brashear City (Morgan City) via Bayou Black. It was filled in during the 1930s and is now the narrow strip of land between Barataria and Canal streets in Houma*

Bayou Guillaume: *dug prior to 1879 to connect Bayou Grand Caillou with Bayou Dularge*

Boudreaux Canal: *dug c. 1850s from Little Caillou to Lake Boudreaux to facilitate water access to Bayou Grand Caillou*

Brady Canal: *dug c. 1920 by Delaware Louisiana Fur Trapping Co. Inc. as a shortcut from Bayou Carencro to Bayou Penchant to access shells for mining and timber for logging*

Bush Canal: *dug c. 1912 from Bayou Little Caillou to Bayou Terrebonne to haul sugar to the Lower Terrebonne Sugar Refinery in Montegut*

Canal Belanger: *dug 1830s in Bourg from Bayou Terrebonne to Bayou Lafourche at Lockport; original canal adjacent to and parallel to the Company Canal; financed by Hubert Madison Belanger; partially filled, and now a drainage ditch*

Caro Canal: *dug 1910 from Bayou Terrebonne to Bayou Blue; beginning 1916, spoil surface became a dry road bed for wagons; then graveled for car traffic; canal filled 1929-1930; 1930s, road bed paved. Road became U.S. Highway 90; a portion in Houma proper is now New Orleans Boulevard; highway is now designated Highway 182 to Raceland along canal's former route*

Company Canal: *financed by Robert Ruffin Barrow, dug c. 1840 to facilitate inland water transportation to Brashear City via Bayou Terrebonne and Bayou Black from New Orleans*

Crochet Canal: *dug c. 1920 from Lost Lake to Bayou Carencro to access Crochet's Island in Lake Carencro to mine shells*

Falgout Canal: *dug before 1879, originally known as the Thibodeaux Canal. It connected Bayou Dularge to Lake Decade. By 1900 this canal was extended via Bayou Prevost to access Bayou Grand Caillou.*

Grand Pass: *originally a trapping traînasse to connect Sister Lake (Caillou Lake) and Lake Mechant (Lake Washa), c. 1900*

Huth Canal: *dug c. 1920 by Delaware Louisiana Fur*

Above, dredge at Caro Canal c. 1912. Below, an outing in the marsh c. 1920

...Trapping Co., Inc. from Bayou Copasaw to Lake Penchant for fur buying and cypress timber harvest. The shell pit at Lake Penchant was dug c. 1930 by three businessmen, Clarence A. Aycock, Nicholas G. Huth and Ruebin Laws. Clarence A. Aycock was the father of Lt. Gov. C.C. "Taddy" Aycock.

Houma Canal: dug 1923 to connect the partially completed Intracoastal Canal to Bayou Black

Lapeyrouse Canal: c. 1850s, traînasse from Bayou Terrebonne into the marsh for trapping; dug by Gustave Lapeyrouse

Liner's Canal: dug before 1879 from Lake Decade to access the Mauvais Bois Ridge Native American community. It was originally known as People's Canal. It was extended to Lake Penchant (Lake Allen) at a later date.

Madison Canal: dug c. 1870s, three miles long, from Bayou Terrebonne to Bay Madison by Hubert Madison Belanger for inland water transportation to New Orleans via Bayou Barataria and the Harvey Canal

Marmande Canal: dug c. 1912, from Bayou Dularge to Minor's Canal to provide water for the sugar mill on Bayou Dularge by B. Marmande

School boat - Bayou Black   La

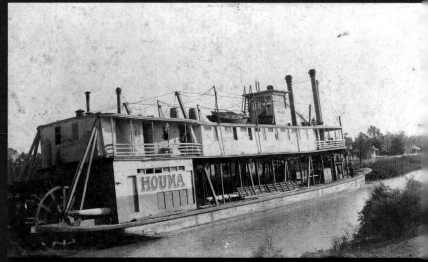

Top left, a steamboat with a load of bananas in the Barataria Canal c. 1910; top right, school boat in Bayou Black c. 1920; middle, steamboat Houma in the Barataria Canal c. 1910; bottom, swimmers at Dulac Beach c. 1920.

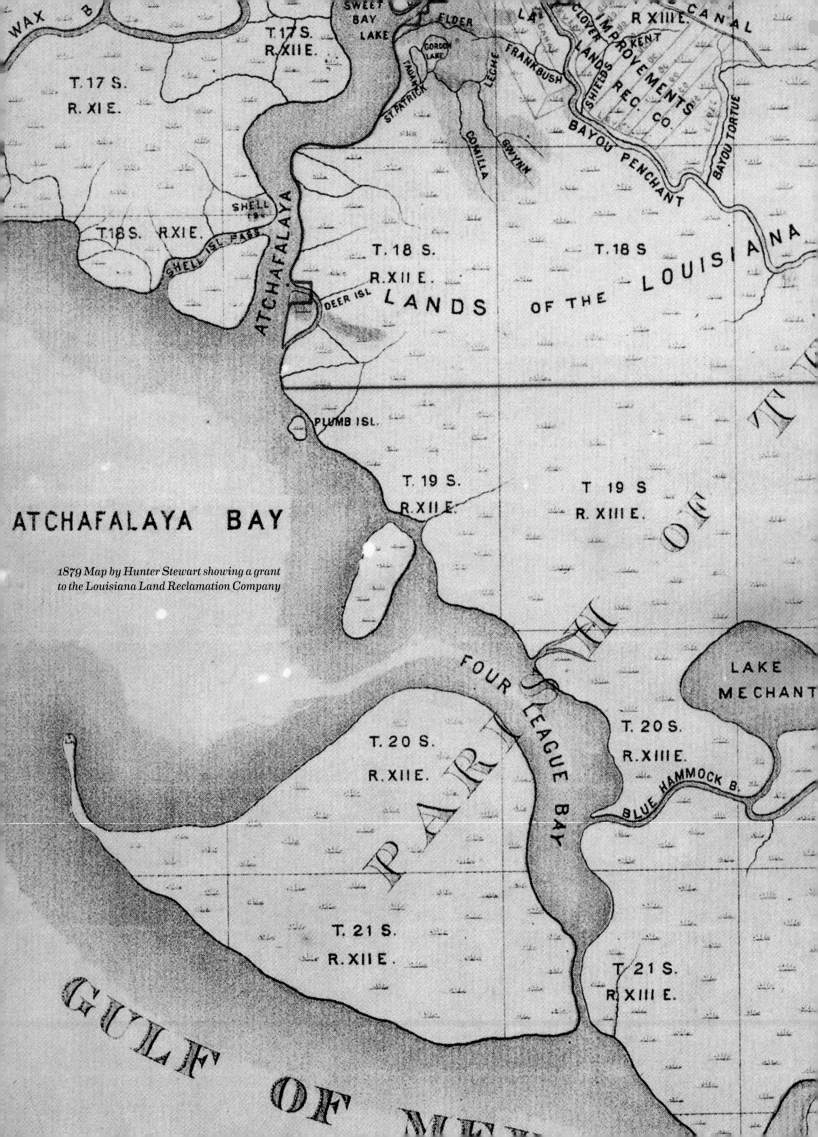

ATCHAFALAYA BAY

*1879 Map by Hunter Stewart showing a grant
to the Louisiana Land Reclamation Company*

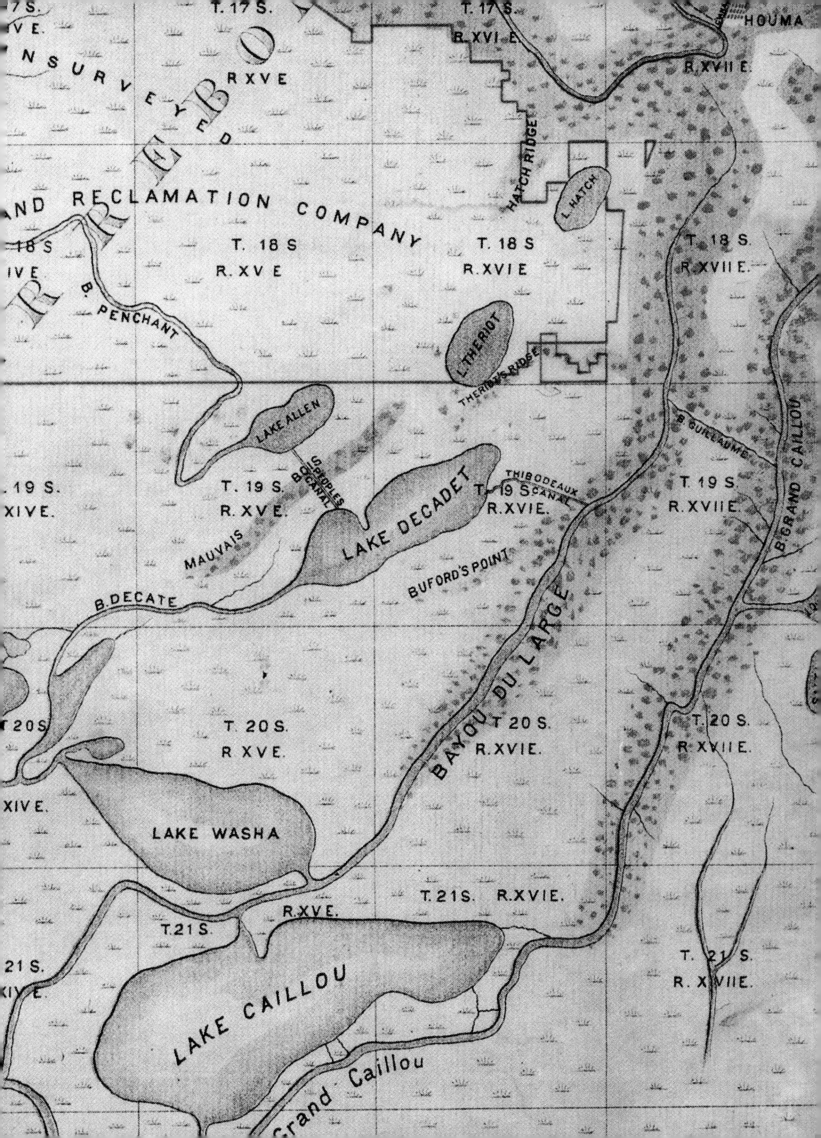

Minor's Canal: *dug 1909-1910, from Big Bayou Black to Lake Decade; two-fifths ownership by the estate of H.C. Minor, two-fifths by Argyle Planting Co. (Bonvillain estate), one-fifth by the* **estate** *of B. Marmande; for drainage, logging and sugar cane transportation*

Robinson Canal: *dug c. 1850s, from Little Caillou to Lake Quitman (Lake Robinson) for water transportation to Bayou Grand Caillou*

St. Louis Canals: *late 1800s, multiple canals throughout parish, by St. Louis Cypress Company for logging*

Seabreeze Canal: *dug c. 1870s by Yancey Sanders, from Bayou Terrebonne to Lake Barre (Lac Barré means enclosed lake), eliminating necessity of portage (carrying small boats) over the former land bridge*

Viguerie Canal: *dug c. 1870 from Pointe Farm to Bayou Terrebonne to haul lumber*

Voss Canal: *named for William Voss from Keil, Germany; dug c. 1920 from Bayou Decade to Bayou Little Carencro to access Lake Carencro from the north to mine shells. William Voss was associated with the early trapping industry*

Above, rowboats on Bayou Little Caillou at Cocodrie, c. 1911
Below, the agreement of April 17, 1909 to dig Minor's Canal

STATE OF LOUISIANA
PARISH OF TERREBONNE

The following agreement was this day entered into by and between the state H. C. Minor, herein represented by John D. Minor, The Argyle Planting and Manufacturing Co., herein represented by Felix A. Bonvillian, its resident and Estate B. Marmande, herein represented by Emile Marmande, towitt:

Whereas the said parties have agreed to cut a canal through Lake Hatch to Lake Decade, in the Parish of Terrebonne at the expense and cost of said parties, and

Whereas it has been agreed that the cost of same shall be prorated among the said parties,

Now, therefore, it is agreed and understood that said John D. Minor, shall cause said canal to be dug and cut out with the Dredge-Boat belonging to the Estate H.C.Minor, and the cost of operating the said Dredge-Boat as well as all repairs to same and all expenses whatever connected with the cutting of said canal shall be borne by said parties in the following proportion to wit:

The Estate of H. C. Minor, hereby binds itself to pay two fifths of said cost.

The Argyle Planting & Manufacturing Co., hereby binds itself to pay two fifths of said cost.

The Estate of B. Marmande, hereby binds itself to pay one fifth of said cost.

It is further agreed and understood that the Estate of H. C. Minor shall furnish a statement of the cost of dredging including all repairs to boat at the end of each month when settlement shall be made.

Their shall be no charge for the use of the boat, but all repairs to boat shall be charged and paid for in settlement at the end of each month.

In consideration of the amount above mentioned and paid, the Argyle Planting and manufacturing Company, Limited and the Estate of B.Marmande they will and shall have a perpetual ight of drainage and navigation and f parcipit ting in wh tever benifits that ray accrue in opening up the nare and have the privilege of cutting c nals or ditches into the above described canal or any enlargements or additions to same.

Witness our hands at Houma, Parish of Terrebonne, State of Louisiana, on this 17th day of April, 1909.

Witnesses:

Barbazan-Debat, in the Hautes-Pyrénées, France

Dominique Cenac *(d. 13 Feb. 1798)* m. **Domenge Descoula** *(d. 31 Jul. 1810)*

Children of Dominique Cenac and Domenge Descoula

1. Jean Cenac *(21 Jan 1764 - 7 Jun 1835)*
   m. Jeanne Lemoine *(20 Jan 1762 - 13 Mar 1836)*, *farmer*
2. Pierre Cenac *(10 May 1770 - 29 Sep 1774)*
3. Jean Cenac *(6 Jan 1773 - 28 Aug 1775)*

Children of Jean Cenac and Jeanne Lemoine

1.1. Jean Cenac *(8 Apr 1803 - 15 Nov 1856)*, *farmer*
   m. Marguerite Duffourc *(1805 - 17 May 1855)*, *pub, restaurant worker or owner*
1.2. Jean Cenac *(1807 - 25 Apr 1879)* m. Germaine Gassan *(d. 1879)*, *farmer*

Children of Jean Cenac and Marguerite Duffourc

1.1.1. Jean Cenac *(20 Aug 1833 - 1911)*
   m. Magdeleine Pomes *(b. 27 Jul 1840)*
1.1.2. Jean-Puis Jacques Cenac *(1 Dec 1835 - 24 Jan 1837)*
1.1.3. Jean-Pierre Cenac *(12 Jun 1838 - 29 Apr 1914)*, *baker when in France*
   m. Victorine Aimée Fanguy *(15 May 1844 - 16 Feb 1926)*
1.1.4. Dominique Cenac *(21 Nov 1840 - 1873)*, *soldier*
1.1.5. Jean Cenac *(20 Feb 1843 - 25 Nov1870)*, *soldier*
1.1.6. Jean-Marie Cenac *(twin, jumeau, 29 Feb 1846 - 1873)*
   m. Marie Barbe *(b. 1854)*, *servant, gardener*
1.1.7. Jacquette Cenac *(twin, jumeau, 29 Feb 1846 - 29 Nov 1862)*, *nun or novice, probably Carmelite at Lisieux*

Names highlighted in red are direct ancestors of Jean-Pierre Cenac

Terrebonne Parish, Louisiana

The Children Of
Jean-Pierre Cenac *(1838-1914)*

m.

Victorine Aimée Fanguy *(1844-1926)*

---

1. **Jean Baptiste** *(30 Aug 1865 - 10 May 1935)*
   m.
   Martha Frances "Fannie" Gatewood *(30 Apr 1866 - 23 Oct 1943)*
   Both buried in St. Francis de Sales Cemetery No. 1, Houma, LA

2. **Marie** *(24 Apr 1867 - 22 Aug 1942)*
   m.
   (1) Salvador Carlos, Jr. *(27 Jan 1865 - 20 Mar 1894)*
   (2) Louis Collins *on 12 May 1903*
   Salvador and Marie buried in St. Francis de Sales Cemetery No. 1, Houma, LA

3. **Albert** *(22 Jun 1868 - 17 Feb 1961)*
   m.
   Marie Adelphine Michel *(29 Apr 1877 - 26 Nov 1952)*
   Both buried in St. Francis de Sales Cemetery No. 1, Houma, LA

4. **Marguerite Laurentine** *(13 Jan 1870 - 3 Aug 1948)*
   m.
   Eugene Prosper Bertrand Carlos *(19 Oct 1873 - 1 Mar 1934)*
   Both buried in St. Francis de Sales Cemetery No. 1, Houma, LA

5. **Theophile** *(19 Mar 1871 - 20 Sep 1925)*
   m.
   Sylvia Bourque *(15 Oct 1876 - 12 Jan 1952)*
   Both buried in St. Francis de Sales Cemetery No. 1, Houma, LA

6. **Victorine Aimée** called "Tante Tile" *(11 Mar 1872 - 20 Apr 1966)*
   m.
   Jean Pierre Carrere *(18 Mar 1866 - 24 Dec 1952)*
   Both buried in St. Francis de Sales Cemetery No. 1, Houma, LA

7. **Jean Pierre, Jr.** *(27 Jan 1874 - 25 Feb 1948)*
   m.
   Eva Marie Luke *(16 Nov 1879 - 25 Aug 1963)*
   Both buried in Our Lady of the Most Holy Rosary Cemetery, Houma, LA

8. **Jean Charles** *(19 Feb 1876 - 19 Dec 1931)*
   m.
   Gertrude Laurentine Bourgeois *(28 Aug 1883 - 1 Feb 1976)*
   Both buried in St. Francis de Sales Cemetery No. 1, Houma, LA

9. **Paul Michel** *(12 Mar 1878 - 15 Jul 1947)*
   m.
   Marie Clothilde Klingman *(16 Apr 1878 - 26 Nov 1969)*
   Both buried in St. Francis de Sales Cemetery No. 2, Houma, LA

10. **Marie Anne Celestine** *(6 Mar 1879 - 1882)*
    Buried in Sacred Heart Cemetery, Montegut, LA

11. **Josephine** *(15 Dec 1880 - 3 May 1898)*
    [engaged to Charles Barthelemy "Bahya" Carlos (20 Jun 1877-
    13 Feb 1954)]
    Buried in Prevost Cemetery, Dulac, LA

12. **William Jean Pierre** *(12 Jan 1884 - 13 Nov 1945)*
    m.
    Marie Madeleine Bourgeois *(8 Aug 1885 - 12 Dec 1965)*
    Both buried in St. Francis de Sales Cemetery No. 1, Houma, LA

13. **Dennis Joseph** *(9 Jul 1887 - 8 Feb 1965)*
    m.
    Nora Marie Porche *(13 Mar 1893 - 17 Jul 1982)*
    Both buried in St. Francis de Sales Cemetery No. 1, Houma, LA

14. **Adenise Marie Cenac** *(10 Jan 1891 - 3 Jan 1968)*
    m.
    George Vernon Williams *(15 Jul 1888 - 10 May 1942)*
    (Adenise Marie legally changed name from Marie Azelie Ademise)
    Both buried in St. Francis de Sales Cemetery No. 1, Houma, LA

THE CHILDREN OF
1. Jean Baptiste and Martha Frances "Fannie" Gatewood Cenac

1.1 **Jean Albert Cenac** *(2 Dec 1886 - 1 Oct 1961)*
    m.
    Marie Fabiola Duplantis *(26 Sep 1889 - 4 Sep 1966)*

1.2 **Edna Marie Cenac** *(4 Oct 1889 - 14 Feb 1968)*
    m.
    Joseph Bass, M.D. *(1880 - 4 May 1932)*

1.3 **George Lee Cenac** *(12 Oct 1891 - 12 Oct 1955)*
    m.
    Irene Ceily Sterkens *(6 Oct 1893 - 9 Apr 1977)*

1.4 **Joseph Cyrille Cenac** *(20 Jul 1895 - 11 Jan 1971)*
    m.
    Alberta Chloe Theriot *(23 Dec 1901 - 3 Jul 1991)*

1.5 **James William Cenac** *(4 Aug 1898 - 7 May 1963)*
    m.
    Mary Helen Snell *(2 Oct 1899 - 31 Jan 1977)*

1.6 **Marie Cornelia Cenac** *(8 Dec 1905 - 28 Jan 1993)*
    m.
    Nolan Joseph Rogers *(31 Dec 1904 - 17 Feb 1976)*

THE CHILDREN OF
2. Marie and Salvador Carlos, Jr.
Marie and Louis Collins

2.1 **Salvador Albert Joseph Carlos** *(25 Jun 1887 - 15 Aug 1958)*
    m.
    Corinne Gonsoulin *(Dec. 1886 - 4 Feb 1972)*

2.2 **Elvire Victorine Carlos** *(28 Jun 1889 - 4 Jun 1985)*
    m.
    Norman Joseph Vice *(9 Apr 1899 - 24 Apr 1952)*

2.3 **John Hubert Carlos** *(2 Aug 1890 - 3 Jun 1975)*
    m.
    Bernadette Virginie Bergeron *(15 Dec 1890 - 3 Oct 1957)*

2.4 **Marie Ida Carlo**s *(6 May 1892 - 12 Aug 1963)*
    m.
    J. Alelard Drolet *(4 Jul 1880 - 6 Nov 1945)*

2.5 **Helene Carlos** *(18 Feb 1894 - 1895 or 1896)*

THE CHILDREN OF
3. Albert and Marie Adelphine Michel

3.1 **Lydia Cenac** *(8 Feb 1897 - 29 Jun 1997)*
    m.
    (1) William Paul Yancey, Ph.D. *(27 Mar 1892 - 11 Mar 1925)*
    (2) Dewey Luke Watkins *(19 May 1898 - 8 Jul 1987)*

(1)   (2)

3.2 **Ursule "Cela" Cenac** *(31 Jan 1898 - 21 Oct 1982)*

3.3 **Alphonse Joseph "Fonse" Cenac** *(3 Mar 1899 - 12 Aug 1947)*
    m.
    Leona Margaret Eschete *(4 Oct 1909 - 21 Jun 1996)*

3.4 **Arthur Robert "Tutty" Cenac** *(28 Jun 1900 - 9 Nov 1968)*
    m.
    (1) Ruby Mary Chauvin *(b 27 Jan 1901)*
    (2) Olympe Marie Labit *(13 Dec 1901 - 16 Feb 1986)*

(2)

  **3.5** **Cecile Clair "Nan" Cenac** *(8 Nov 1901 - 19 Feb 1999)*

m.

Guy Paul Guidry *(5 Jan 1902 - 15 May 1978)*

  3.6 **Marie Louise "Weezie" Cenac** *(5 Mar 1903 - 3 May 1990)*

m.

Felix Arthur Delatte *(17 May 1899 - 17 Nov 1972)*

  3.7 **Ovide Julien "Jock" Cenac** *(18 Oct 1904 - 22 May 1964)*

m.

Eugenie Aimée Hebert *(8 Apr 1907 - 7 Jan 1990)*

  3.8 **Jules Henry "Jutte" Cenac** *(12 May 1906 - 21 Aug 1937)*

m.

Eula Marie Acosta *(5 Jun 1909 - 10 Dec 1992)*

  3.9 **Alfred Paul "Tenner" Cenac** *(12 Jun 1908 - 27 Apr 1974)*

m.

Virgie Cecile Dugas *(20 Oct 1910 - 10 Nov 1969)*

 **3.10** **Wilfred Francis "Boo" Cenac** *(12 Jun 1908 - 26 Nov 1981)*

m.

(1) Verna King *(1 Aug 1908 - 4 Apr 1979)*

(2) Eunice Mary LeBlanc *(30 Aug 1924 - 1 May 1980)*

  3.11 **Odette Leonard "Dette" Cenac** *(18 Jan 1911 - 27 Jan 1972)*

m.

Auguste William Wurzlow *(18 Apr 1901 - 13 Mar 1949)*

  3.12 **Ernest Albert "Mannie" Cenac** *(5 Apr 1914 - 19 Oct 1984)*

m.

Marie Louise Clement *(31 Jan 1916 - 16 Feb 2009)*

 **3.13** **Frances Annette Cenac** *(12 Nov 1918 - 13 May 1995)*

m.

Cornealus "Neal" Anderson Brown *(29 Sep 1919 - 5 Dec 1995)*

The Children Of

4. Marguerite Laurentine and Eugene Prosper Bertrand Carlos

4.1 **Inez Carlos** *(2 Nov 1893 - 9 Apr 1983)*

m.

Richard Clyde Allen *(12 Jun 1900 - 22 Aug 1987)*

4.2 **Eugenie Celeste Carlos** *(11 Mar 1896 - 10 Apr 1973)*

m.

(1) William Joseph Callahan *(10 Jul 1891 - 22 Feb 1952)*
(2) Rodney Joseph Roddy *(8 Nov 1895 - 17 Oct 1949)*
(3) Raymond William Rowan *(22 Oct 1908 - Jul 1976)*

(2)

4.3 **Joseph Pierre Eloi "Edward" Carlos** *(8 Oct 1897 - 28 May 1973)*

m.

Olga Poirier *(22 Jun 1900 - 1 Oct 1983)*

4.4 **Victorine Louise Carlos** *(10 May 1899 - 22 Mar 1968)*

m.

Arthur Emile Chauvin, Jr. *(27 Oct 1900 - 24 Mar 1970)*

4.5 **Joseph Ruffin Carlos** *(18 Jan 1901 - 5 May 1991)*

m.

Lillian Herman *(30 Jul 1904 - 31 Aug 1994)*

4.6 **Jimmy Morris Carlos** *(26 Nov 1902 - 10 Oct 1983)*

m.

Lillian Eve Bergeron *(28 Feb 1907 - 18 Nov 2000)*

4.7 **Mary Viola Carlos** *(18 Oct 1909 - 19 May 1972)*

m.

Cecile James Martin *(20 Jan 1905 - 19 Nov 1999)*

4.8 **Randolph Joseph Carlos** *(12 Jan 1912 - 29 Oct 1974)*

m.

Felma Jean Bourg *(23 Jun 1911 - 4 Jan 2002)*

THE CHILDREN OF
5. Theophile and Sylvia Borque

5.1 **Marie Isare Cenac** *(5 Feb 1898 - 22 Jun 1978)*

m.

Armand Oliver Porche *(1 Apr 1896 - 9 Dec 1986)*

THE CHILDREN OF
6. Victorine Aimée Cenac and Jean Pierre Carrere

6.1 **Adam Enis Carrere** *(15 Jan 1891 - 30 Aug 1932)*

m.

Therese Angelique LeBlanc *(26 Jul 1886 - 24 Mar 1940)*

6.2 **Justilien Carrere** *(4 Feb 1893 - 4 Apr 1941)*

m.

Laura Julie Louviere *(20 Jul 1899 - 20 Aug 1961)*

6.3 **Lydie Carrere** *(6 Feb 1895 - 30 Apr 1960)*

m.

Sidney Paul Luke *(18 Nov 1893 - 9 Sep 1950)*

6.4 **Josephine Carrere** *(27 Feb 1897 - 16 Feb 1994)*

m.

Yancey Amedee Benoit *(21 Sep 1893 - 19 Jun 1956)*

6.5 **Jean Pierre Carrere, Jr.** *(12 Jul 1899 - 6 Jan 1971)*

m.

Effie Margaret Porche *(16 Nov 1904 - 1 Nov 1987)*

6.6 **Leonie Victorine Carrere** *(23 Aug 1901 - 4 Jan 1980)*

6.7   **Marie Inez Carrere** *(20 Nov 1903 - 23 Oct 1983)*

6.8   **Frances Carrere** *(9 Mar 1906 - 25 Oct 1986)*
> m.
> Floyd Urban Ashley *(25 May 1908 - 5 May 1991)*

6.9   **Blanche Marie Carrere** *(7 Apr 1908 - 26 Sep 2004)*
> m.
> (1) Albert Porche *(14 Jul 1905 - 5 Jun 1941)*
> (2) John Joseph Rome *(15 Jan 1910 - 7 Jun 1952)*

(2)

6.10   **Cecile Carrere** *(31 Jan 1910 - 24 Sep 2005)*
> m.
> Peter John Bergeron *(28 Mar 1909 - 28 Feb 1972)*

6.11   **Adenise Adele Carrere** *(17 Sep 1912 - 26 Sep 1995)*
> m.
> Sidney Joseph Aucoin *(9 Feb 1911 - 3 Aug 1951)*

THE CHILDREN OF
7. Jean Pierre, Jr. and Eva Marie Luke Cenac

7.1   **Henry Pierre Cenac** *(7 May 1902 - 4 Jan 1986)*
> m.
> Beatrice Bernadette Samanie *(1 Sep 1909 - 28 May 2003)*

7.2   **Josephine Marie Cenac** *(3 Mar 1904 - 15 Sep 1967)*
> m.
> Elie Bartholomew Belanger *(24 Apr 1889 - 9 Sep 1964)*

7.3   **Martin Joseph Cenac** *(19 Dec 1905 - 13 Jun 1978)*
> m.
> Walterine Marie "Sue" Blanchard *(16 Nov 1914 - 6 Nov 2002)*

7.4   **Esia Virginia Cenac** *(4 Nov 1907 - 3 Jan 1996)*

       m.

       (1) Elmer Peter Daigle *(15 Apr 1908 - 26 Sep 1968)*

       (2) Louis James Labat *(30 Apr 1910 - 22 Apr 1986)*

(2)

7.5   **Helen Marie Cenac** *(19 Jan 1910 - 13 Mar 1979)*

       m.

       (1) Randolph Paul LeBoeuf *(1910 - 19 Jan 1957)*

       (2) Lubey Bergeron *(2 Mar 1910 - 1 Jul 1982)*

       (3) Joseph Yancey Boudreaux *(25 Apr 1908 - 26 Nov 1992)*

(1)   (3)

7.6   **Norman Joseph "Noo" Cenac** *(20 Nov 1912 - 16 Aug 1981)*

       m.

       Melazie Marie "Mae" Klingman *(16 Nov 1916 - 11 Jun 2010)*

7.7   **Beulah Agnes Cenac** *(12 May 1915 - 1 Sep 2010)*

       m.

       Vila Paul Zeringue *(22 Apr 1912 - 21 Jun 1998)*

7.8   **Hilda Marie Cenac** *(22 Sep 1918 - 13 Apr 2010)*

       m.

       (1) Xavier Theriot *(20 Sep 1916 - 1 Dec 1964)*

       (2) Eulen Joseph Bergeron *(14 Jan 1923 - 3 Oct 1978)*

(2)

THE CHILDREN OF
8. Jean Charles Cenac and Gertrude Laurentine Bourgeois Cenac

8.1   **Caliste Charles Cenac** *(28 Mar 1902 - 14 Feb 1938)*

       m.

       Louise Ragas *(25 Aug 1908 - 8 Dec 1994)*

THE CHILDREN OF
9. Paul Michel and Marie Clothilde Klingman Cenac

9.1   **Jeanne Eleonore Cenac** *(11 Feb 1907 - 20 Dec 1994)*

9.2 **Delphine Helen Cenac** *(1 Mar 1909 - 17 Sep 1990)*

m.

Clarence Eugene Matherne *(14 May 1908 - 2 Sep 1995)*

9.3 **Alice May Cenac** *(28 Sep 1910 - 10 Apr 2007)*

m.

William Christian Steinkampf *(17 Apr 1909 - 22 Mar 1983)*

THE CHILDREN OF
12. William Jean Pierre Cenac and Marie Madeleine Bourgeois Cenac

12.1 **Ione Eleanor Cenac** *(1 Nov 1909 - 22 Mar 1991)*

m.

Edward Augustus Rucker, Jr. *(20 Sep 1894 - 11 Dec 1963)*

12.2 **William Jean Cenac, Jr.** *(23 Sep 1911 - 13 Oct 1967)*

m.

Catherine Orena Ber *(31 Mar 1913 - 15 Nov 1990)*

12.3 **Rita Mae Cenac** *(19 May 1915 -)*

m.
(1) Charles F. Landry *on 22 Dec 1934*
(2) George Washington Clark *(10 Nov 1913 - 2 Apr 1956)*
(3) Andrew Harold Hoffmann *(11 Jul 1890 - 23 Feb 1986)*

(2)

(3)

12.4 **Olga Louise Cenac** *(8 Oct 1916 -)*

m.

O'Neil Joseph Engeron *(23 Sep 1913 - 27 Feb 1983)*

12.5 **Philip Louis Cenac** *(27 Sep 1918 - 24 Jan 1990)*

m.

Dorothy Lee Stodghill *(2 Sep 1918 - 13 Nov 1993)*

12.6 **Donald Joseph Cenac** *(10 Aug 1922 -)*

m.

Eldies Marguerite Labbe *(20 Sep 1923 -)*

The Children Of
13. Dennis Joseph Cenac and Nora Marie Porche Cenac

  **13.1** **Dennis Lawrence "Mike" Cenac** *(10 Aug 1915 - 2 Jul 1950)*

m.

Emerite Marie Judice *(11 Oct 1919 - 24 Oct. 2004)*

 **13.2** **Mary Ellen Cenac** *(30 Dec 1917 - 12 Apr 1999)*

  **13.3** **Joseph Willard Cenac** *(17 Apr 1922 - 7 Jul 1981)*

m.

Maria Consuela Fernandez Mendia *(22 Apr 1922 - 2 Jun 2009)*

13.4 **Lucille Marie Cenac** *(4 Mar 1924 - 4 Feb 1928)*

 **13.5** **Margaret Mary Cenac** *(8 Sep 1925 -)*

  **13.6** **Jacques Augustin Cenac** *(28 May 1927 -)*

m.

Renee Bory Pelet *(11 Dec 1920 -)*

  **13.7** **John Abraham Cenac** *(5 May 1929 - 22 Jan 1994)*

m.

Lillias "Lee" Suire *(17 Jun 1931 - 10 June 2010)*

  **13.8** **Louise Violet Cenac** *(6 Aug 1930 -)*

m.

Joseph Bourg *(27 Oct 1932 - 15 Dec 1997)*

THE CHILDREN OF
14. Adenise Marie Cenac and George Vernon Williams

14.1 **Marion Victorine Williams** *(6 Jan 1924 - 1 May 2010)*
m.
Ernest Joseph Charpentier *(11 Feb 1929 - 15 Mar 1980)*

14.2 **John Raymond Williams** *(11 Feb 1925 - 15 Mar 1929)*

14.3 **Emma Claire Williams** *(21 Sep 1931 -)*
m.
H.J. Pelley *(3 Mar 1924 - 26 Dec 1992)*

14.4 **Rosa Alice Williams** *(1 Oct 1932 - 26 Mar 2005)*
m.
Leroy Adam Williamson *(22 Sep 1931 - 21 Nov 2005)*

14.5 **Margarette Rhea Williams** *(24 Jul 1933 -)*
m.
(1) Julien Curtis Smith
(2) Theo Murrah *(20 Oct 1906 - 1 Jul 1984)*
(1)

ABOUT THE AUTHORS

Christopher E. Cenac, Sr., M.D., F.A.C.S,

grew up in Houma, Louisiana, and graduated from the Louisiana State University system. He attended LSU undergraduate school on academic and athletic scholarships, and completed his residency in orthopedic surgery in 1976. He is a practicing orthopedic surgeon, and has served a term as Terrebonne Parish Coroner.

He is co-author of the Interprofessional Code approved by delegates of the Louisiana State Bar Association and the Louisiana State Medical Society in 1994. As a member of the Medical-Legal Interprofessional Committee, he was co-author of several published papers including "Subpoenas to Physicians: The Obligations and Consequences"; "Medical Review Panel Process"; and "The Physician as Witness." Professional affiliations are with the American Board of Orthopedic Surgery, as a Fellow in the American Academy of Orthopedic Surgeons, a Fellow in the American College of Surgeons, and a Fellow in the International College of Surgeons. He was appointed in 2003 by the Louisiana Supreme Court to the Judicial Campaign Oversight Committee and was reappointed in 2010. His current professional emphasis is expert testimony in the field of orthopedic surgery in medical-legal litigation at state and federal level judiciaries, and teaching professionalism and ethics to medical and law students, attorneys, and physicians.

One fond memory is the Mardi Gras season of 2003, when he was selected king of the Mystic Krewe of Louisianians in Washington, D.C. Today his greatest personal interests are history and international travel. He completed a five-year restoration of Orange Grove Plantation, his family's onetime home, and the house was named to the National Register of Historic Places in 1980. He and his wife Cindy reside at Winter Quarters on Bayou Black outside Houma. He has two sons and a daughter—two of whom are also physicians—eight grandchildren, and a widespread family both in and beyond Terrebonne Parish.

Claire Domangue Joller is a national and state award-winning writer. She received the first place award from the National Catholic Press Association in 2001 for her first year of Bayou Catholic newspaper columns in the Arts, Culture, and Leisure category. Her "Seeing Clairely" column also won a Louisiana Press Association award that year.

A native of Terrebonne Parish, she first received statewide recognition during Nicholls State collegiate days with a sweepstakes prize from the Louisiana College Writers Society.

After a short stint as English and journalism teacher, she variously worked as a newspaper section editor, public relations director for a children's home, technical writer for the environmental section of an engineering firm, development director for a Catholic high school, and editor of Terrebonne Magazine. Two entries she submitted were selected to be among the 120 nonfiction "minutes" included in Pelican Publishing Company's 2007 book Louisiana in Words.

She lives in Houma, Louisiana, with her husband Emil. She has a daughter, two grandchildren, and a large extended family. After beginning work on this book, she discovered that through her paternal grandmother, Elvire Fanguy Domangue, Victorine Fanguy Cenac was her great-great-aunt.

APPENDIX V:
Glossary of French Words and Terms

CHAPTER 1

tarte salée	a savory pie-like vegetable dish
boulanger	baker
boulangerie	bakery
Oui?	Yes?
Père	Father
Madame	Mrs.
Chiens de Montagne des Pyrénées	Great Pyrenees dogs, aka Pyrenean Mountain Dogs
département	a geographic governmental area

CHAPTER 2

boulangerie	bakery
rue	street
quai	embankment; levee

CHAPTER 3

fraulein	young woman (German)
baguette	French bread loaf
les Allemands	the Germans

CHAPTER 4

filée	dried, powdered sassafras leaves used to thicken gumbo

CHAPTER 5

les États-Unis	the United States
la Nouvelle Orleans	New Orleans
francs	French unit of currency
sérieux	serious

CHAPTER 6

raison d'être	reason for being
poules d'eau	literally "hens of the water"; American coot

CHAPTER 7

banquette	sidewalk
les femmes	women
beaucoup de l'eau	a lot of water

Comment ça va?	How are you? How's it going?
Bonjour	Good day; Hello
M.	abbreviation for *Monsieur*, Mr.
Mlle.	Miss
sous	copper coin; a penny
Un joli nom pour une jolie fille.	A pretty name for a pretty girl.
baguettes	loaves of French bread

CHAPTER 8

laissez-faire	noninterference in personal freedom

CHAPTER 9

furieuse	furious
Sapristi!	interjection expressing surprise, impatience, or hopelessness
Mon Dieu	My God
Bonjour, Pierre, mon frère.	Hello, Pierre, my brother.
puis je m'en vais	then I'm leaving
adieu	goodbye

CHAPTER 11

Mon Dieu!	My God!
Ils vont nous tuer ?	They're going to kill us?
les Acadiens	Acadians
la guerre	war

CHAPTER 13

moi	me
papa	daddy
un	a
garçon	boy
j'espère	I hope.

CHAPTER 14

fait accompli	a thing accomplished and presumably irreversible
patois	a dialect differing from the standard language of a country

CHAPTER 15

traiteur	folk "healer"
C'est étrange, non?	It's strange, isn't it?

CHAPTER 16

marraine	godmother
nainaine	colloquial title given to one's godmother
parrain	godfather
traînasse	a shallow, narrow waterway for pirogue travel

CHAPTER 17

La Tristesse	The Sadness
Joyeux Noel demain	Merry Christmas tomorrow
Tu est encore triste?	You are still sad?
Non, chère petite.	No, dear little one.

CHAPTER 19

Tante	aunt
glorieuse	glorious
gateau de sirop	cane syrup cake
oreilles de cochon	fried pastries, literally *pigs' ears*
bon idée	good idea
fête de naissance	birthday party
galerie	porch
goutte	a taste; a small amount
demitasse	a half-cup; a small cup
Mes fils...non, mes hommes.	My sons...no, my men.
Écoutez.	Listen.
C'est vrai.	It's true.
Votre bébé est malade.	Your baby is sick.
Elle a colique.	She has colic.
C'est temps d'aller, Marguerite dit.	Marguerite says it's time to leave.
Le temps se passe.	Time is passing.

CHAPTER 21

la Nouvelle Orleans	New Orleans
misérable	miserable
Je comprends.	I understand.
le Docteur	the doctor (colloquial)
miracle	miracle
à	at, to
pauvre	poor

la prairie tremblant	floating marsh (trembling prairie)
Étrange	strange
les petits enfants	grandchildren
garde-soleil	sunbonnet
triste	pitiful

CHAPTER 23

Monsieur	Mister
oui	yes
Gascon	An ancient dialect spoken by residents of the Spanish-French region of the High Pyrenees, with roots in Roman times
vous connaissez	you know
jeune homme	young man
grand gens	important people
mon petit-fils	my grandson
garçon	boy
frère	brother
mangeable	edible
les maladies	sicknesses
courage	fortitude, courage
lagniappe	extra; unexpected
prospérité	prosperity, success
Papa, prend un peu de repose	Dad, rest a little.
bébé	baby
les enfants	children
merci le bon Dieu	thank God
grand-père	grandfather
grand-mère	grandmother
grand-grand-père	great-grandfather
grand-grandmère	great-grandmother
avocat de la ville	city attorney
Incroyable	incredible
Mon compatriote	my (fellow) countryman
Quelle magique.	What magic.
Adieu	Goodbye
rape à maïs	dried corn grater
dîner	noon meal

MORE TO COME...

From left to right, Courthouse Square bandstand and Houma Indians baseball stadium, Legion Park, c. 1932; dedication of Lafayette Street draw bridge, 1937, (from left) Houma aldermen Leopold Blum, William J.P. Cenac, J. Harry Hellier, Louis C. LeBlanc, Mayor T. Elward Wright; Naval Air Station Houma (LTA) 1942-1949; Terrebonne General Medical Center, 1958; Church Street, 1938; Arab sheiks at the Texas Co. Caillou Island oilfield, c. 1945; U.S.D.A. Sugar Cane Research Station, Little Bayou Black, 1932; Terrebonne High School, 1938; Dr. Philip L. Cenac, Sr. standing under the Cenac Oaks during the 1986 centennial observance of their donation by his grandfather, Pierre Cenac; City Hall, the renovated Peoples Bank building, now Le Petit Theatre de Terrebonne, 1938; The Art Nouveau style Houma Elementary building, dedicated in May 1931; First Negro School Board of Terrebonne Parish, 1930, first row from left, Gus Anderson, Straight Matthews, V. Stevenson, J. Marshall; second row, Harry Stovall, Andrew Gauche, Abram Moor, Gus Hill, C. Brown; Houma Mardi Gras courts of 1926, 1927 and 1928; Main Street Bridge over the Gulf Intracoastal Waterway, 1938; U.S. Post Office, Main Street across from Courthouse Square, 1935 (replaced on a nearby site in the 1980s).

TERREBONE HIGH SCHOOL, HOUMA, LA.

INDEX

Grandchildren of Pierre and Victorine Cenac under the Cenac Oaks in the Courthouse Square in September, 2007. From left seated, Marion Williams Charpentier (since deceased), Louise Violet Cenac Bourg, Olga Cenac Engeron, Rita Mae Cenac Hoffman, Hilda Cenac Bergeron (since deceased), Beulah Cenac Zeringue (since deceased) and Jacques Augustin Cenac, standing with his wife Renee Pelet Cenac

Ad c. 1896 from The Story of Algiers *by William H. Seymour*

Philip Louis Cenac, age 5 years c. 1923

Home of Eleanor Monthieu Bourgeois c. 1930, on the corner of Grinage and Verret streets in Houma; future medical office of grandson Dr. Philip Louis Cenac

CREDITS

Unless otherwise noted, photos and maps are in the Cenac Collection at the Nicholls State University Archives, Thibodaux, Louisiana. Research of these materials may be arranged by contacting the Archives and Special Collections Department at Allen J. Ellender Memorial Library on the Nicholls campus in Thibodaux.

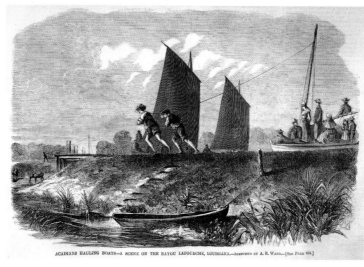

ACADIANS HAULING BOATS—A SCENE ON THE BAYOU LAFOURCHE, LOUISIANA.—Sketched by A. R. Waud.—[See Page 634.]

A cordelle on Bayou Lafourche, *sketch by A.R. Waud; October 13, 1856*

Cypress pirogue (c. 1890) owned by William Jean Pierre Cenac

Marie Madeleine Bourgeois Cenac with her children Ione Eleanor and William Jean Cenac, Jr. (in her lap), c. 1912

"Here is one of those rare books that invites you to peek through a keyhole, but then lets you see the whole wide world. The story of one special man becomes the story of a family, then a region, then an industry, then finally the story of America in a turbulent time when newcomers were flooding our shores with their ambition and innovation, when technology was outpacing tradition, and when the battle between old and new was reshaping where we lived, how we worked, and what we wanted."

Glen Pitre, movie director, **Belizaire the Cajun**

"More than a mere family history, Eyes of An Eagle provides about one hundred years of insights into the economy of the fishing, oil, and agricultural industries of the area, the environment, the culture of the people, and valuable sketches of the growth of the City of Houma. Readers will find themselves saying, 'I didn't know that," as they harvest many gems in this book. Louisiana history buffs and genealogists will want to add it to their collections."

Thomas A. Becnel, Ph.D., author, Distinguished Professor of History,
Fellow of the Louisiana Historical Association, book reviewer

---

"This is a sensational story and one that everyone who lives, cares about or has roots in South Louisiana should read. The resourcefulness, ingenuity and abilities of those who settled South Lousiana is shown clearly through the story of Pierre Cenac."

Mike Voisin, National Fisheries Institute executive committee member,
Louisiana Seafood Processors Council president, CEO Motivatit Seafoods

---

This "docu-novel showcases" the Cenac family patriarch who "carved a niche in south-central Louisiana in a landscape that was completely alien to his ancestral mountain home. Dr. Cenac has successfully recorded the family's legacy and documents the Cenacs' achievements through a liberal use of photos and memorabilia associated with the family and their Louisiana home place. A nimble text describes the historical events and the family's entrepreneurial success."

Donald W. Davis, Ph.D., author, **Washed Away;** *researcher;*
administrator of a Louisiana Sea Grant oral history project